IMAGES O
FV430 SERIES

RARE PHOTOGRAPHS FROM WARTIME ARCHIVES

Rob Griffin

Pen & Sword
MILITARY

First published in Great Britain in 2019 by
PEN & SWORD MILITARY
An imprint of
Pen & Sword Books Ltd
47 Church Street
Barnsley
South Yorkshire
S70 2AS

Copyright © Rob Griffin, 2019

ISBN 978-1-52674-289-6

The right of Rob Griffin to be identified as author of this work has been asserted by him in accordance with the Copyright, Designs and Patents Act 1988.

A CIP catalogue record for this book is available from the British Library.

All rights reserved. No part of this book may be reproduced or transmitted in any form or by any means, electronic or mechanical including photocopying, recording or by any information storage and retrieval system, without permission from the Publisher in writing.

Typeset by Concept, Huddersfield, West Yorkshire HD4 5JL
Printed and bound in China by Printworks Global Ltd.

Pen & Sword Books Limited incorporates the imprints of Atlas, Archaeology, Aviation, Discovery, Family History, Fiction, History, Maritime, Military, Military Classics, Politics, Select, Transport, True Crime, Air World, Frontline Publishing, Leo Cooper, Remember When, Seaforth Publishing, The Praetorian Press, Wharncliffe Local History, Wharncliffe Transport, Wharncliffe True Crime and White Owl.

For a complete list of Pen & Sword titles please contact
PEN & SWORD BOOKS LIMITED
47 Church Street, Barnsley, South Yorkshire S70 2AS, England
E-mail: enquiries@pen-and-sword.co.uk
Website: www.pen-and-sword.co.uk

Contents

Acknowledgements **4**

Chapter One
   Development **5**

Chapter Two
   Description **31**

Chapter Three
   Trials and Service **60**

Chapter Four
   Variants **108**

Chapter Five
   Growing Old Gracefully! **179**

Acknowledgements

There have been many people who have helped to contribute to this book and I would like to thank them all, the private owners who were subjected to questions on 'the vehicles registration' to the serving members of the army who took the time to show me around various locations, and to the Royal Engineers for allowing me to take part in the mine laying demonstration, many thanks to you all. In the following list I have endeavoured to include as many people as possible, if I have forgotten you then I apologise now: 2 Battalion Royal Green Jackets, ABRO Bovington, Accurate Armour, ACF Hospitality, Andreas Kirchhoff, Armour and Softskin, Ashchurch Vehicle Depot, BATUS QM Technical, Bombardier McKee, Bustard scrapyard Salisbury Plain, Carl Brown Cobbaton Vehicle Collection, Cromwell Models, David Norfolk, David Smale, Defence Logistics Chilwell, Dennis Lunn, East of England Tank Museum, Kevin Keefe (miniature mortars), Major (Retd) Chalkie White, Major (Retd) Mick Burgess RAC Gunnery School Lulworth, Major (Retd) Paul Evenson, Marcus Glenn, Merlin Robinson, Mike Veral, Patrick Moir, Peter Brincker, Phillip Hastings, Plain Military, Tank Museum Bovington, Tim Babb, Withams Specialist Vehicle Sales, WO2 Forrest.

Chapter One

Development

The deployment of large numbers of troops on the ground was restricted by the current technology of the day. Things would not get any better until technology advanced and a suitable vehicle that was powered by something other than animals became available. This became possible with the invention of the petrol engine in 1885 by Karl Benz followed a year later by a petrol driven car designed by Gottlieb Daimler.

A new type of weapon was needed to break the impasse of trench warfare and to try to reduce the slaughter. This was the moment that the tank came onto the scene. The first tanks were unwieldy, slow, noisy contraptions, but at last here was the means of advancing men across open ground in comparative safety with the marrying of armour plate to a power source capable of moving it along without tiring. However it was never envisaged to be used for the transportation of troops but purely as a means of defeating the machine guns and barbed wire of the Germans.

Towards the end of the First World War, trials were conducted using an Mk 1X stores tank. These were a development of the original tank but were designed for the transportation of stores to the front line. Into one of these vehicles were loaded thirty infantrymen in good health; by the time they reached the point at which they were meant to leap out of the vehicle, bayonets fixed and attack the enemy, they were in no fit state to fight. Complaints about nausea, likened to seasickness, noise, smells and a sense of being totally disorientated were plentiful. An Mk 1X exists today at the Tank Museum at Bovington and it gives a good idea of the space and claustrophobia those early armoured infantry must have felt.

This now leads us to the interwar period were most governments including the British reduced the defence budget time and time again till it was as low as possible. This was brought on by the fact that we had just fought and won the War to end Wars and the likes of that would never happen again. This meant that there was little need to provide up-to-date equipment, especially for new-fangled armoured vehicles. Thus at the outbreak of the Second World War Britain was nowhere near as well prepared as its enemies, and suffered for it; but thankfully lessons were learnt, though sometimes at a snail's pace. In the end the sheer weight of Allied numbers made up for the deficiencies in their vehicle design and allowed them to defeat Germany.

During the interwar years the War Office had dallied with many designs, with the main criteria being cheapness. In 1925 Major Gifford Le Q. Martel, a famous name from the early days of the Tank Corps in France, built a one-man tank at his home and Captain Carden also built one at the garage he managed for Captain Lloyd. These names were soon to become famous and still are remembered today. In 1925 the little Martel machine was tested in front of the War Office and they ordered four machines on the strength of the demonstration with the first two being delivered in 1926. The only change was they had become two-man machines as it was realised that one man had too much work to do. Eight of the improved two-man versions were supplied to the Experimental Mechanised force that was in existence for two years. Carden and Lloyd had by now joined forces and become Carden-Lloyd, a name that was to become associated with light tanks and carriers for many years. These little machines, known as tankettes, were tactically useless. The government of the day toyed with a similar idea during the talks to find Centurion's replacement.

During the trials the Martel machines proved more reliable than the Carden-Lloyd. Martel had become too busy at the War Office and could not develop the vehicle further. Also Morris cars, who had built the vehicles for him, were too busy building cars so the development of Carriers fell to the firm of Carden-Lloyd. They eventually produced the Mk VI and some 400 of these were built and employed in a variety of roles including tankettes, light and medium machine-gun carriers, mortar vehicles and smoke projector carriers.

The next stage was the involvement of Vickers who produced a vehicle called the VA D50 and this had the first shape of what would become known as the Bren gun carrier although there were still many changes to be made to it. On 1 February 1935 the War Office decided to purchase these vehicles as replacements for current in-service vehicles, one model to be used as a machine-gun carrier with room for the crew as well. The other version was to be a Dragon, this was the generic title given to a track-laying vehicle that was used for moving men or weapons around.

After Vickers had built forty-three No. 2 Mk 1 carriers they left the field of light carrier and moved on to other vehicle designs. The responsibility for producing carriers now fell to several firms, including Thornycroft. They carried out rework on a No. 2 Mk 1 carrier and produced the most famous carrier of them all, the Bren Gun Carrier. This was designed, as its name states, to carry the Bren Gun and its crew; also carried at times in the early days of the war was a Boys anti-tank rifle. These carriers were now known as Carriers Bren No. 2 Mk 1 and Mk 2. All carriers produced after this were known as Bren Gun carriers even if they were not.

For most of the first part of the war the infantry were carried in trucks until they were near where they were needed and then dropped off to go and fight. This sad state of affairs lasted until the Canadian General Guy Simmonds proposed in 1944 using battle-weary tank hulls as basic APCs. The idea was a concept that succeeded beyond anyone's wildest dreams and from 1944 onwards the Kangaroos, as they became known, did sterling service in transporting infantrymen around the battlefield in relative safety and also for the first time giving the infantry a means of carrying more equipment and ammunition forward with them so that they could, on return to the Kangaroo, replace used ammo ready for the next battle, instead of waiting till replenishment at night.

The basic idea was simple, take one tank that was past its fighting days, remove the turret, provide it with a fixed crew, usually a commander and driver, and then use the space where the fighting compartment had been to fit in a section of infantrymen. The first regiment formed to carry out this role was the 1st Canadian Armoured Carrier Regiment, and although their lifespan as a regiment was short, they were the world's first dedicated APC regiment, a tradition of which they are rightly proud even to this day. The Germans may dispute this as they had formed Panzer grenadiers to follow the tanks closely and they were often moved in the half-tracks, but the Canadians do seem to have the honour of forming the first dedicated APC regiment.

While providing a partial solution, the Kangaroos were by no means the ultimate APC. There was no overhead cover against air bursts and inclement weather; also it was impossible, given the base vehicle design, to incorporate access doors in the hull, thus leaving the troops forced to dismount from the top of the vehicle leaving them exposed to enemy machine-gun fire. The conditions inside the vehicle were not perfect either by any stretch of the imagination as no concession to crew comfort had been given. The original vehicles converted were seventy-two de-frocked Priest SPGs (de-frocked meaning that they had reached the end of their useful life as SPGs and the weapons had been removed). These vehicles proved the concept was absolutely correct but something much better was needed. The vehicle chosen was the Canadian Ram tank, a close relative of the Sherman; it had been built by the Canadians due to their misgivings with the American M3 and the general shortage of tanks. In the event the Sherman was mass produced and the Ram was withdrawn from front-line units.

One of these vehicles is preserved in the Tank Museum at Bovington. The museum does not allow access inside the vehicle, but it is possible to see inside, as it is open-topped, and get an idea of the configuration. As we have mentioned, no luxuries were fitted and it is still argued today that due to the vehicle layout no benches, even rudimentary ones, were officially fitted. I think that it was down to individual crews to how they equipped the vehicle, very much as it is today on modern AFVs.

The use of vehicles such as Kangaroos and to a certain extent American half-tracks gave the infantry a certain small degree of protection and definitely improved their mobility, but it was not the total answer, with the major criticism being the need to exit over the top. Nonetheless they did serve an important role in the war. The salient points in having infantry that were highly mobile on the battlefield, could move with a fair measure of protection, and also carry more equipment and have better communications, was taken in by the War Office and thought was given to designing a purpose-built carrier for the infantry.

Once the war was over, thoughts turned to trying to return to normality and new weapons were very much low down on the list of equipment required. The first post-war carrier was the FV3904 Churchill APC and was based on the Churchill Mk VII. It was not much of an improvement on the earlier Ram Kangaroo: seating may have been provided but no overhead cover or protection was fitted thus still leaving the troops vulnerable to air bursts. The section also still had to exit the vehicle via the top leaving them at risk from enemy fire. So really no improvement had been achieved; however things started to look up.

The last vehicle to be developed from the early Lloyd carriers was produced by the MG motor company at Abingdon. This vehicle was known as the CT20, or Oxford carrier. Due to the reluctance of the United States to release the Cadillac engines that were to power the Oxford, only about 400 were ever built. Although too late to see action in the war they did see active service in Korea where they were used in a variety of roles, including mortar carrier and towing the 6 and 17-pounder anti-tank guns. The Oxford carrier, although bigger than its predecessors, still retained many of the features of them, including the Horstman-type suspension (also used later on Centurion and Conqueror), the open top and limited crew space. The driver and commander were provided with overhead cover and a periscope each though. A few survive today with one located at the Tank Museum Bovington.

The shortfall of the Oxford carrier led the War Office to look for a new carrier or similar vehicle to fill the gap. It was to be designed to use all British components thus removing production problems associated with obtaining major components from abroad. The answer was the CT25 FV401 Cambridge. The FV400 series of vehicles was proposed, all using a similar chassis (a policy that has continued to this day). The FV400 series was designed to comply as nearly as possible with War Office policy statement No. 26 which had called for high performance from the new family of vehicles. The range of vehicles envisaged for the FV400 series was introduced in November 1946 and originally consisted of:

FV401 infantry carrier
FV402 observation post carrier
FV403 artillery tractor
FV404 charging vehicle

Like all WO programmes, changes, cancellations and reinstatement were to take place during the programme. FV400 had a major design break with the previous carriers in that the Horstman suspension had now been replaced with torsion bars, and the vehicle had four double road wheels each side with two top rollers and a front sprocket. In 1948 the WO decided that the carrier version would not be required and a new light carrier would be produced instead. Five more vehicles were added to the family list. In 1949 FV401 was actually ordered and by now the shape of the vehicle was taking place but due to the time-lag of decision on FV401 the FV402 was ready first. It looked like the Oxford carrier but due to a requirement for protection from air bursts the upper superstructure now formed an armoured roof containing four hatches. Eventually when the prototype FV401 finally appeared it resembled the FV402 except for the fighting compartment: this was open topped but had four armoured blast shields, one front, one rear and one either side; when these were raised and locked together it resembled the Second World War German half-track's rear configuration. When locked in the upright position they still did not give any overhead protection, and when lowered left an open-topped crew compartment, so the design had not really progressed since the early carrier had been built.

Near the end of the '50s the whole FV400 project was coming to a close, as various problems and operational changes took place. Also came the announcement of the FV420 which would prove to be the precursor to the FV432. In retrospect it was probably the best thing to let the FV400 project die. The infantry were not even sure if they wanted the vehicle and its inherent defects meant it would be at a disadvantage on a modern battlefield. For a very expensive vehicle designed as an infantry carrier it could only carry eight men and that was including the driver. The rear-mounted engine took up too much space that could have been used for crew area. The Saracen wheeled APC that entered service in 1952 could carry a twelve-man section. There was still no rear exit for the troops to dismount from the vehicle and if the shields were used it was even harder for them to exit from the top. Around 1945 the Americans had already established a principle in APC design that has not changed to this day: the mounting of the engine and transmission in the forward section of the APC. This allowed more space at the rear of the vehicle to house the section and to allow a rear door so that troops no longer would have to egress through the roof. Various trials had proved that vehicles embodying this design would be more suitable for nuclear conflict than the current vehicles.

The Americans produced the first vehicle embodying this principle and, true to USA form, it was big. The M44 was based around the powertrain of the 76mm gun motor carriage M18. It had the engine compartment at the front, between the driver and the bow gunner. The commander's station was just behind the engine compartment. The commander, driver and hull gunner each had their own vision cupolas and in the rear troop compartment were pistol ports to enable the section to fight from within the vehicle. This requirement, although used by many countries, cannot allow accurate fire to be laid down especially if the vehicle is moving. A .50 heavy machine gun was located to the rear of the vehicle next to the hatch over the troop compartment.

The M44 was built by the Cadillac motor car division of General Motors. It weighed in at 23,000kg (51,000lbs), it had a length of 651cm (96ft) and was 303.8cm (119.6ft) wide. It was powered by a Continental R-975-D4 9-cylinder radial petrol engine connected to a 900AD-torqmatic gearbox giving three forward gears and one reverse. This gave it a road speed of 51kph (32mph). Besides the three crew-members it could carry a twenty-four man section that could enter and exit the vehicle by two doors at the rear.

The war ended before the vehicle saw any active service and it was soon realised that big is not always beautiful and a replacement vehicle followed. This was the M75, which entered service in 1953 and saw combat in Korea. Constructed from welded steel, it was powered by an air cooled, six cylinder, horizontally opposed AO-500-4 continental petrol (gasoline) engine with CD-500-4 cross drive transmission. The M75 was one of the first of its type of carriers developed during the post-war years. The M75 could carry twelve men: ten fully loaded infantrymen plus the commander and driver. Combat weight was 41,500lbs. The M75 was originally developed and manufactured by the International Harvester Corporation. The Food Machinery and Chemical Corporation (FMC) were brought into the production programme, and a total of 1,729 vehicles were built. Production ceased in February 1954, due mostly to its high cost of $100,000 per vehicle. Further development led to the M113, which in its turn heavily influenced the British when the design for the FV432 was formulated.

Thus we now move on to the next vehicle in the evolutionary path to the FV432 and that is the FV420 series. This was developed in the late 1950s by the Fighting Vehicle Development division of what was then GKN. They were awarded the contract to build four prototypes and ten trial vehicles, all of which had to be delivered to the user by 1958. The Royal Ordnance also was awarded a contract to build an additional seven vehicles under licence from and under the control of GKN. Towards the end of 1962 all of these vehicles had been delivered and were ready for evaluation.

As with the FV400 series a whole family of vehicles was planned on the FV420 chassis including:

FV421 load carrier
FV422 APC
FV423 command post
FV424 Royal Engineers section vehicle
FV425 REME section vehicle
FV426 Orange William anti-tank guided missile

It was designed to carry the Fairey aerospace anti-tank missile, which weighed in at 102kg. The missile was to be guided by means of a radio command link but the whole project was cancelled in 1958 due to the specification being too demanding.

The shape of the FV420 series is beginning to take on the familiar looks that we have associated with the FV430 series but it is not quite there yet. The first major change was the decision to replace the well tried and tested Horstman suspension with torsion bars, which had proved a viable means of suspension when in use on the FV400 series. This would incur a height penalty as in all torsion bar suspensions: the torsion bars run through the hull from side to side and then have a floor over them, in effect giving any vehicle with torsion bars a double hull; this also provides better mine protection.

The first vehicle produced was the FV421, which was designated a tracked load carrier. This was a good idea as at that time all logistic back-up to the troops in the field was by trucks which sometimes struggled to keep up with the tanks and infantry. Although a step forward had been made with the provision of the torsion bar suspension, sad to say not so much thought had been given to the layout of the vehicle. The engine was still situated in the centre so everything had to be built around it. One change was that the engine, gearbox, radiator and engine air cooler could all be lifted from the vehicle in one unit.

The basic vehicle was box-like in shape with a long sloping glacis plate with two windows at the top for the commander and driver; no armoured shields were provided for these. Entry to the vehicle was via a door situated over the left track guard or one of two hatches above the commander's and driver's locations. The sides of the vehicle were slab side and vertical. At the rear was an exhaust duct for the cooling air, and the exhaust pipes were also located at the rear of the vehicle. This arrangement effectively ruled out any form of rear door or ramp entry for a section, so if it had been employed in the carrier role one wonders how or where the section would have left the vehicle. This was made worse due to the extra height caused by the use of torsion bars.

The sides of the FV421 could be lowered for ease of loading stores and equipment. If required the load space could have ammo racks fitted either side thus making the carriage of ammunition easier. A similar system would eventually appear in the early 1980s for fitting to HMLC Stalwart or the Bedford Mk/J. Until this made its appearance, troops would have to unpack the ammunition at an ammunition point and then load it onto the vehicle that was transporting it making sure that it was kept dry and secured. With the new system the tank would pull up alongside the truck and the truck crew would simply pull out the required rounds and hand them to the tank crew for storing. The advantage of this system was that the echelon crews could unpack the ammunition in the rear area then reload the rounds into the containers so that the tank crews did not have to mess around removing the packaging around the ammunition – a boon when doing tactical replenishment. There were rubber seals around the edge of the load doors so that they would be watertight for flotation. In the water the vehicle could move at around 3 mph, propelled and steered by its own tracks.

A Rolls Royce B80 No. 1 Mk 5F petrol engine powered the FV420 series. According to the design specification the power from the engine was then taken to a Rolls Royce Hydramatic gearbox which gave the driver four automatically-selected gears with one reverse gear. The driver had some control of the gears through a gear lever that had five positions:

2nd which gave 1st and 2nd gears selectable only;
3rd which gave 1st, 2nd and 3rd gears selectable only;
4th which allowed all forward gears to be selectable;
Drive giving automatic selection of all forward gears;
Reverse was driver-selectable.

This was similar to the system that would be employed on the FV430 series later. The use of a heavy-duty automatic gearbox was to try to eliminate the actions of gear changing that a driver would carry out during a normal day's driving, thus hopefully tiring him less. Instead of a conventional clutch and its associated linkage to a foot pedal, a fluid coupling was used. One advantage of this type of system is that a gear or gear range can be pre-selected but until the engine revolutions are high enough then no movement will take place. This system was used in the Ferret scout car and the Alvis Saladin and Saracen. Automatic gearboxes were not popular at this time as it was felt that a driver could better predict the required gear and moment to change gear than the gearbox.

A Cletrac steering box system was fitted giving the vehicle a controlled differential steering mechanism. The steering arrangement also allowed skid steering when 1st gear was selected by the use of the main brakes normally used for stopping or parking the vehicle by using them to lock either track.

FV420 had two types of braking system fitted. Military vehicles sometimes do not conform to the normal. The main brakes operated on the final drives and on the Cletrac steering brakes within the differential unit. Application of the main brakes was either by a foot pedal or by pulling on the inner set of two sets of levers located in front of the driver and suspended from the hull roof; these could be applied independently. To apply the parking brake, which was located below the main brake levers, the driver first had to depress the main brake foot pedal then push a control knob downwards to engage a pawl. This would automatically be released on a further depression of the foot pedal thus releasing the parking brake. Steering was achieved by the driver pulling to the rear one of the outer levers: therefore pulling the left lever made the vehicle steer to the left and the right lever steered to the right. This is a complicated system and the poor driver must have sat there looking at four levers, foot pedal and knobs and must have wished he was somewhere else.

In June 1956 the user had accepted the basic design, and work proceeded with the construction of the prototype vehicles. By June 1957 there were three prototypes of FV420 running. Also the design for the FV423 command post variant had been accepted and work had started on the construction of a prototype. The trial reports from the three vehicles that were running were proving positive. The 15th of June 1958 saw four vehicles running in the UK, six in the British Army of the Rhine, and one in the UK that had been returned to workshops for modifications and a full strip inspection. By August 1958 the Rolls Royce gearbox fitted to FV420 P2 had completed 4,377 miles. That however seemed to be the high point, for in August 1960 it was being reported that the gear box was not living up to expected requirements, with the Bovington-based vehicle using five gear boxes to cover only 2,500 miles – a figure not acceptable.

This may not have been too great a worry, as it would appear that the vehicle on the whole was performing well. But it seems doubts were being raised as to its design compared to the American M75 and M59. It was decided that a new vehicle would be required to replace the FV420. So far vehicles P1, P2, P3, P4, 00 CA 23, 00 CA 24, 00 CA 25, 00 CA 26, 00 CA 27, 00 CA 28, 00 CA 29, 00 CA 30 and 00 CA 31 had been built and run. However they now were to be disposed of (although there is evidence that the hulls were used in several trials before ending up on the ranges as hard targets).

Two known vehicles survive today: one resided for a long time at the Tank Museum at Bovington awaiting tender care for restoration. Sadly, as with all museums, there is never enough time, staff or money to carry out restoration on all the exhibits that require it. The vehicle remained there until it was purchased by a private buyer who intends to fully restore it and one can only wish him luck.

The second vehicle has proved to be a mystery and has starred in several 'what is this vehicle' type questions. The FVRDE decided to try and pre-empt a forthcoming project that they believed was about to be issued for a light air portable weapon. FVRDE used the chassis of one of the FV420s, the entire superstructure was removed and a 105mm gun fitted to a mock-up rig for trial purposes. In the end there was no requirement at the time for such a weapon and the hull was abandoned on Salisbury Plain were it still resides today (2002). A full FVRDE report, No. 71054 raised in June 1971, tells the whole trial story.

Document MF/513/01 dated 1 April 1959, part of recently released information, states that an order was placed with GKN group to design and develop an APC to be known as the FV432. The cost was estimated to be £150,000. As more declassified documents show, in 1959 WO record 286/61 lays the foundation for a new APC to be known as FV432 to be designed. Later in 1959, under contract 4/KL/D/022/DC.11 (b) 2 signed on 29 April with Joseph Sankey, part of the GKN group, they were to investigate the design and development of a tracked APC and for this they were paid £144,644.

In April the following year the managing director of Sankey's accepted the contract to build four prototypes, and ten vehicles to be used for troop trials based on the FV432. It was understood that some of the work might well be placed with the Royal Ordnance Factory and the vehicles built to conform to WOPS 26. The ROF did build a further seven vehicles under the parentage of GKN Sankey's. It was planned to design, build and introduce the FV432 in two stages: stage one was for the first vehicles to be built using as many components from FV420 as possible, including the Rolls Royce B81 engine and automatic gear box and the Cletrac steering.

Listed in the requirement document back in November 1958 is a section on why the contract should go to industry rather than a government facility such as ROF. The answer was very simple: GKN designed FV420 on which FV432 would be based; although the terms of the contact allowed the War Office to place build orders with the ROF if they so wished.

An early document shows that the first vehicles would have B80 engines, Rolls gearboxes and twin doors at rear, with subsequent development of multi-fuel engines and new steering combined with the gearbox. The language of these documents is very formal and almost seems to belong to a forgotten age.

Stage two was to include the installation of a new engine, probably a diesel, and also a new and simpler transmission. First off would probably be required about 1960 with production in 1962. In the end the first production vehicles rolled off the line in 1962/3. The company had also been awarded the contract to design and produce WO/57/Vehs/A/5969 GS (u) 9, a light load carrier. This would become known as the FV431 and although prototypes were built and trials carried out the vehicle never entered service.

While discussions for the new vehicle were taking place, it was stated on 15 September 1958 that different layouts were to be considered. One of these was identical to the 432 shape we know but with only four wheel stations per side. Until recently it was thought that only the original five-wheel version had been built, but photographic evidence now shows the four-wheel version in operation at the REME training area at Bordon in Hampshire. The vehicle was delivered to Bordon as a non-runner so immediately became a challenge to the fitters to make it work. This they did and it was used as a general run-around vehicle and sometimes a recovery push vehicle. Its fate is unknown, which is a great shame, as it should really be preserved. In outline it resembles the shape of the FV432 but it is only 4.56 metres long compared to the 5.105 metres of a normal FV432 over track guards.

The new APC was known as the FV432 and for a short time was known by the name of Trojan, which seemed apt with the section hidden in the back like a modern wooden horse of Troy. The use of the name Trojan was short-lived and there are two stories as to why that was. The first is the more functional boring one. At the time that FV432 was being tested under the name of Trojan there was a commercial van by the same name and the manufacturers were not happy that their name had been adopted by the War Office for the new vehicle without their permission. They threatened legal proceedings unless the use of Trojan was stopped. The War Office agreed to this and from then till the present day the vehicle has been known as the FV432 and to the troops 'the 43'. The other version, which is slightly more amusing and could also be the truth as there is documentation regarding this in official records, is that in the United States and Canada it seems that a leading brand of condoms are called Trojan and the powers that be, knowing British soldiers' sense of humour and that it would not be long before jokes about being in a condom appeared, the name Trojan was discreetly dropped.

The trials proved satisfactory, as we shall see later, and the vehicle entered service and has been used by almost every branch of the army in one or other of its many configurations. One of the most outstanding features of its original design is the longevity that seems to have been built into it; it has completed over forty years service. It is now due for a major upgrade in its power pack and transmission.

The main reason for the retention of the FV432 was that immediately after the first Gulf War the government reduced the size of the armed forces (yet again) and a fall out from this was the drastic cut-back in Warrior production. However specialist vehicles still were required for under-armour tasks. The solution? – FV432 would soldier on until replaced by the new Multi Role Armoured Vehicle, MRAV. This was expected by around 2008 but no later than 2011. However in July 2003 the UK announced its decision to withdraw from the MRAV programme to pursue the Future Rapid Effects System, FRES. The last FV432s due out of service because of the introduction of FRES were scheduled to be around 2015 but in the summer of 2005 the MoD announced that FV432 and CVR (T) would be in service till around 2020, to be replaced by a vehicle known as Ajax. This must be a fitting testimonial to the vehicle and its original design and for a vehicle that was due out of service around the mid-1980s.

Over 3,000 vehicles of all types had been built when production ceased in 1971. Of those many have now been withdrawn and disposed of with some ending their days as hard targets and a few as gate guards. Many though have fallen prey to the cutting torch of the scrap merchant. The oldest 432 came into service on 1 May 1965, the youngest on 1 February 1975.

The beginning of it all, a Mk IX First World War tank similar to the type used at the end of the war to transport troops. Although a failure due to sickness, it was a start. *(Common user licence)*

Part of the Ram tank conversion, showing how it really was a simple case of removing the turret to create a very basic APC. Clearly seen is the disadvantage of having to leave the vehicle by climbing out of the top.

One of the only known pictures of the FV432 with the four wheel layout; it is visually identical in shape but is a couple of feet shorter. It has had a wooden pusher frame fitted to the front for its roles a pusher/tug. *(Via Tom Bell)*

The Ram tank that formed the basis for the RAM APC.
(Peter Breakspear, courtesy Tank Museum)

Head on view of the four wheel FV432, showing clearly the wooden pusher frame; nice to speculate as to its eventual fate. *(Via Tom Bell)*

If you think that the interior of a FV432 is cramped then how about this: the interior of a Russian BMP. Although contemporary of FV432, they were classed as infantry fighting vehicles as they could fire their weapons from inside. *(John Walker)*

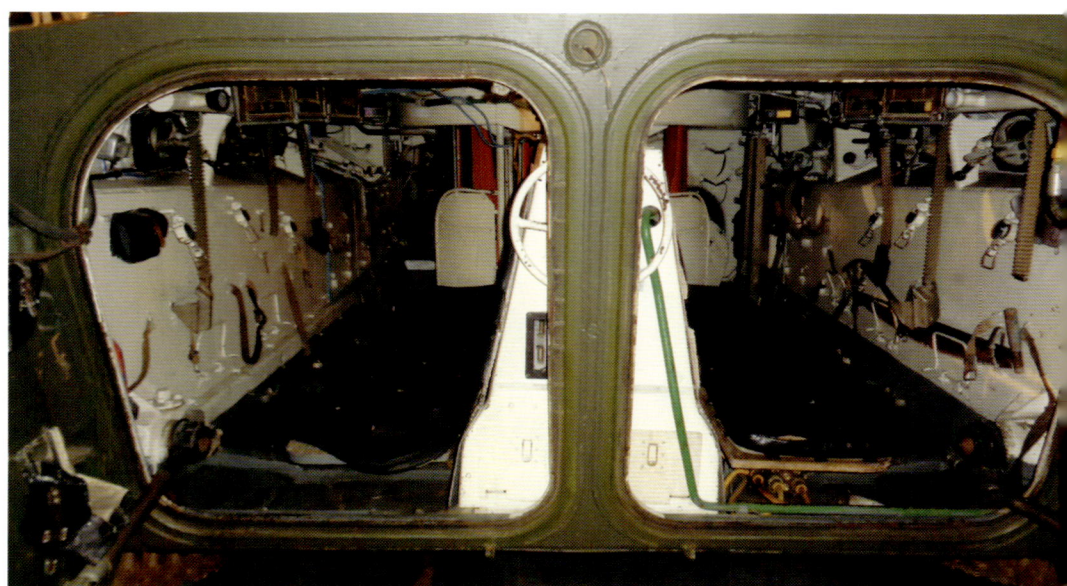

Side view of BMP showing the pistol ports, its low turret mount, a low pressure 73mm gun and above that a rail for Sagger guide weapon. A little more armament than the FV432. *(John Walker)*

Close up of the BMP showing how low it is and the section pistol ports, the bulges on the inside the doors are the fuel tanks! *(John Walker)*

The Oxford carrier shown in the swimming role, and using a screen system similar to that which would be fitted to the early FV432. (*Tank Museum*)

CT120, more commonly known as the Oxford carrier. Although time has moved on, the design still requires all troops leaving the vehicle to leave from the open top. (*Tank Museum*)

Front right view of the FV420 showing the open top and the driver's and commander's windows. One would hope that some sort of armoured protection would have been provided if it had gone into service. (*Tank Museum*)

(**Above**) Right side of the FV420 carrier. The way the sides lift can be seen and also the very large windows in the crew area, for which hopefully armoured shutters would have been provided. *(Tank Museum)*

(**Below**) Side view of the Oxford carrier showing its small size and not very practicable method of entering or leaving the vehicle. *(Tank Museum)*

(**Opposite, above**) The only known survivor of the FV420 programme. This vehicle has been bought by a collector with the aim of a full restoration. *(Rob Griffin)*

(**Opposite, below**) Inside view of the M75 showing how spacious it was. It seems there is plenty of room for the crew's 'tipple'. *(Common User Licence)*

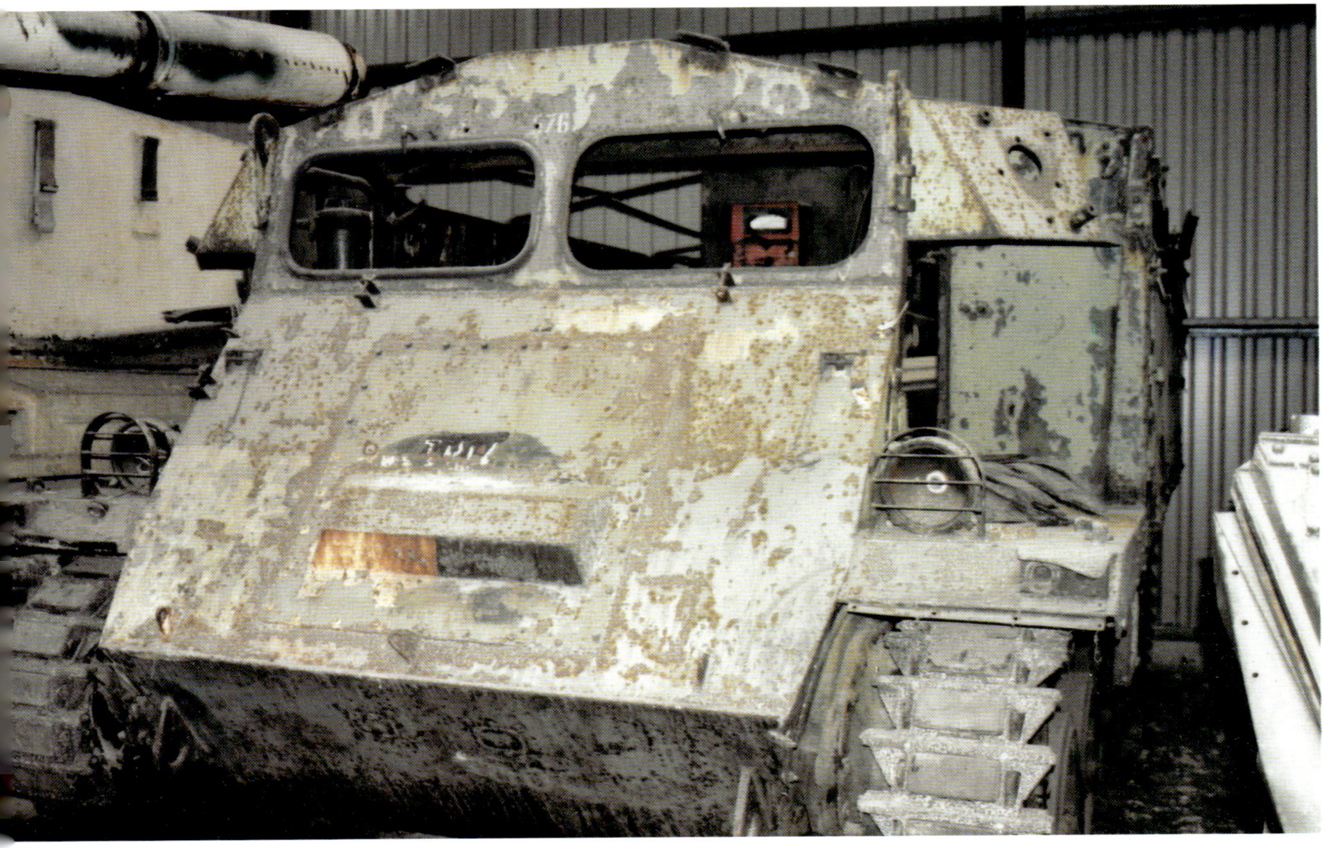

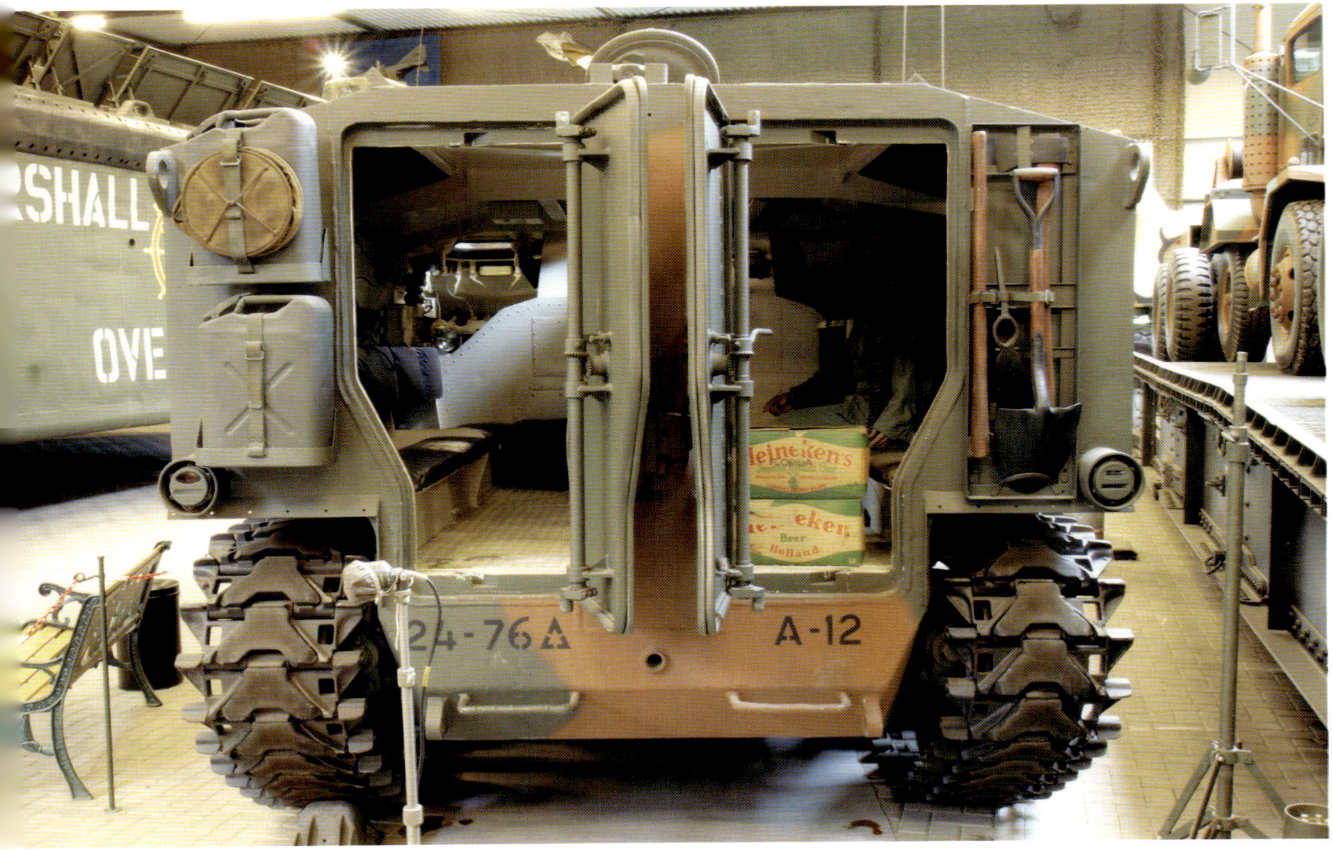

RSHALL
OVE
24-76
A-12

Side view of the M75 showing that, although having the same number of road wheels as FV432, it is a much larger machine. *(Prime Portal)*

The little Carden Lloyd carrier which in truth could only manage three crew at best; little protection and load capacity but it was part of the long climb to have an APC in service. *(Peter Breakspear, courtesy Tank Museum)*

M113, the competitor for the Australian new APC. Sadly it really outperformed the FV432 in almost all phases and thus became the Australian APC. *(Common User Licence)*

One of the first FV432s showing the early large NBC pack. In the early days this was always painted in the yellow and black stripes as a warning to other road users that it projected out and they may hit it!

The American M75, the vehicle that set the layout for APCs to present. The engine has been moved to the front and to one side, and this allows the space at the rear to be used by the crew. (*Prime Portal*)

Showing just how cramped it is inside the Russian BMP. The seats are almost level with the hull bottom so that would have been uncomfortable, plus if closed down and firing their weapons the smoke and fumes would have awful. As can be seen very little crew comfort is provided. (*John Walker*)

One more vehicle in the long evolution to FV432. This is what became known as the Bren Gun carrier, and again it is a very small vehicle and not really suited as an APC type of vehicle. *(Peter Breakspear, courtesy Tank Museum)*

Another view showing how very basic and simple the conversion from RAM gun tank to Kangaroo APC was. One would like to think that the section did their best to make it just a little more homely.
(Peter Breakspear, courtesy Tank Museum)

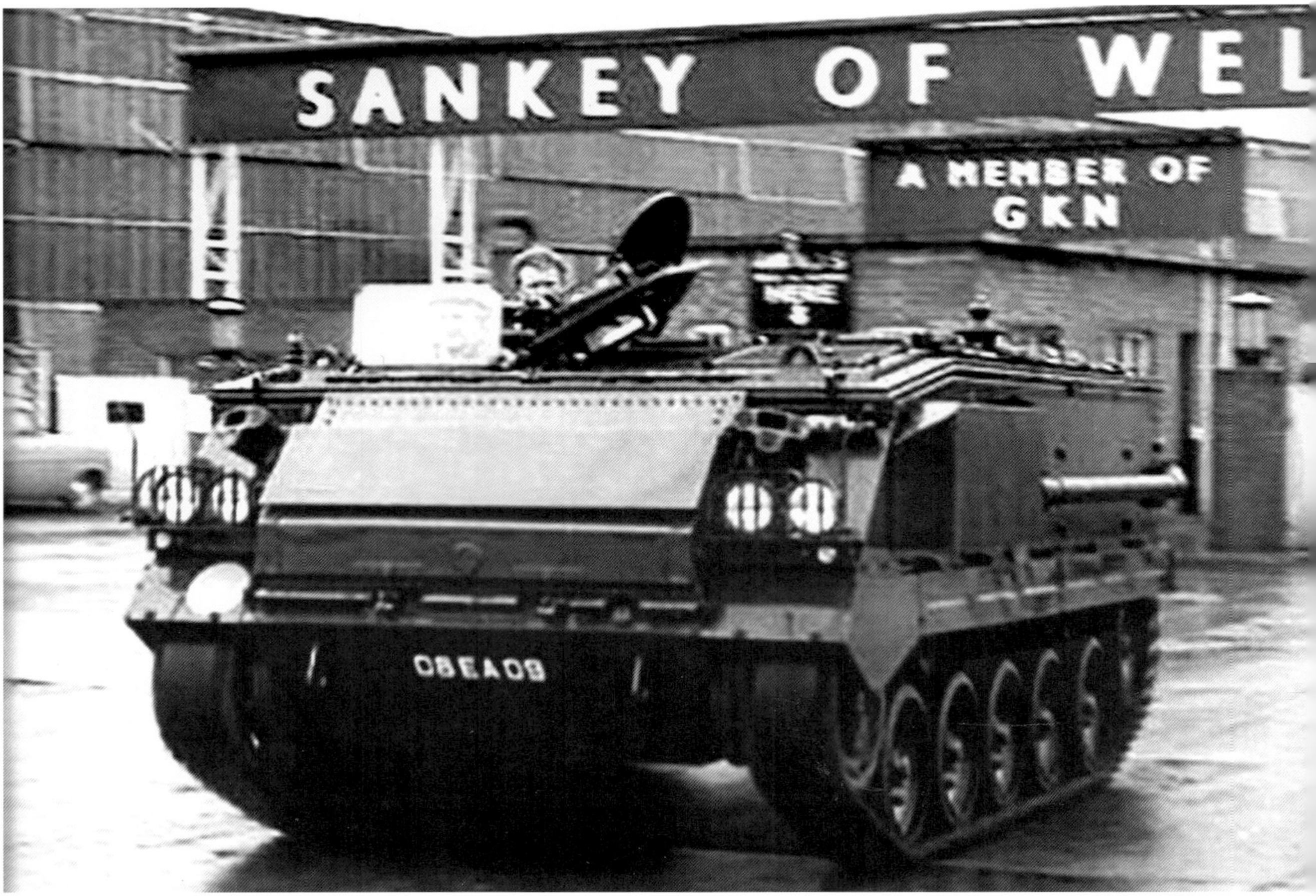
SANKEY OF WEL
A MEMBER OF
GKN

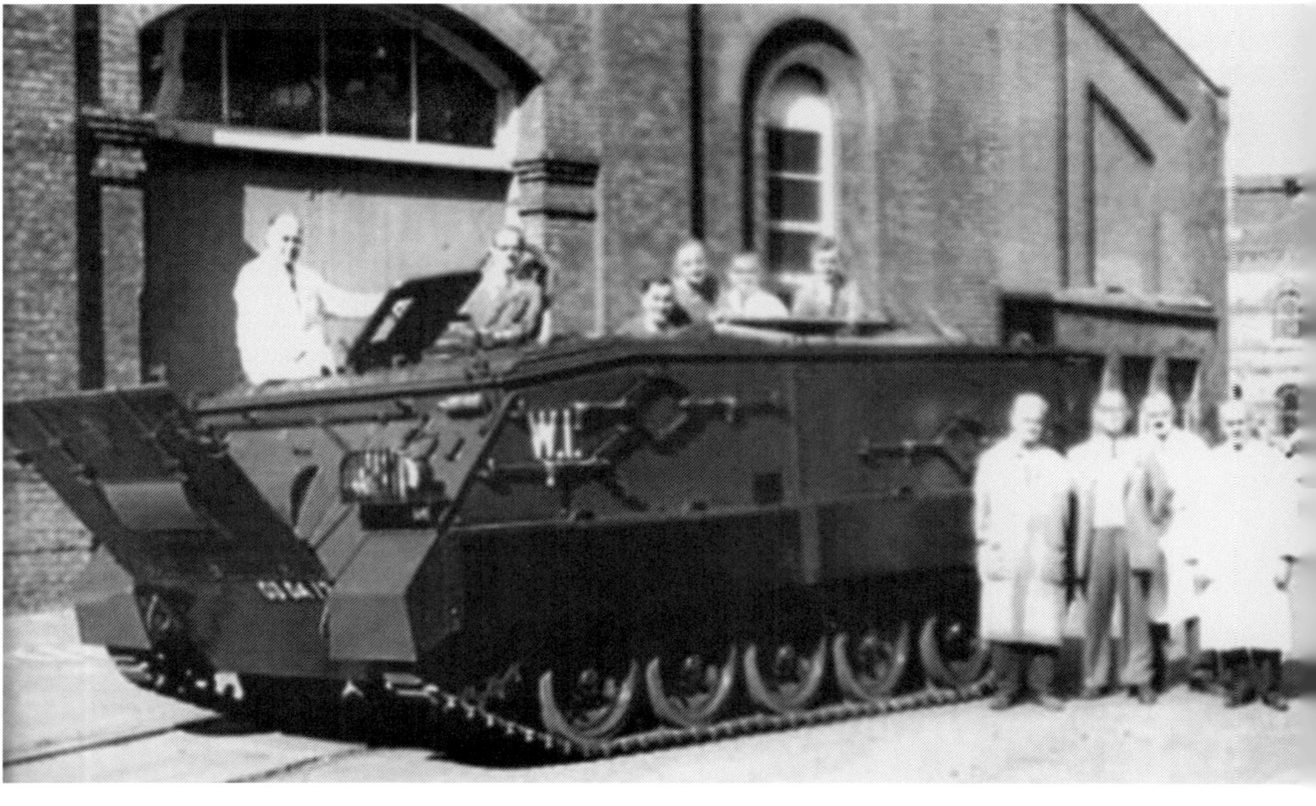

(**Opposite, above**) This previously unpublished image shows an early Mk 2 FV432 leaving the GKN Sankey works. Notice it has the early armoured exhaust box on the front left, and the flotation trim vane on the glacis. (*John Walker*)

(**Opposite, below**) A rare unpublished shot of W1 straight from the builders. Apart from the proud construction team, several things to note, the very large and boxy front dust shield and side skirts. It has the original steering from FV420, as evidenced by the raised portion on the glacis. Instead of the buoyancy aid it has a simple panel trim vane but note that this is shaped to fit over the steering bulge. (*John Walker*)

(**Above**) One of the first FV430. Notice the bulge on the glacis plate, similar to that on the FV420; this was to give space to the steering lever arrangement. The UN paint scheme is rather optimistic though. (*Rob Griffin*)

The steering lever arrangement as described in chapter one, so very complicated and not liked by drivers, was soon replaced with a much simpler system for production vehicles. *(Rob Griffin)*

After all the trials and tribulations, the Mk 1 FV432 finally appeared in its petrol powered version, the oval access panel and the exhaust cover on the hull top can be clearly seen in this retired FV432. *(Rob Griffin)*

Chapter Two

Description

As we have already seen, an enclosed troop carrier was needed by the British Army. After many false starts the army got the Carrier Full Tracked FV432 Mk 1-2 – so let's see what they got for their money. We will be looking at the Mk 2 but any variations that were particular to the Mk 1 will be mentioned.

The hull is constructed of armour plate, which will give protection against small arms fire and shrapnel from shell bursts. It is not designed to keep out anything like a main armament round from a tank gun. The vehicle sides and rear are vertical with the upper and lower glacis plates sloped. The main roof section supports the mortar hatches, commander's cupola, driver's hatch and the engine louvres. The sides of the roof section slope to meet up with the hull sides and contain the two fuel filler ports, one at right rear and one at left rear. The original front glacis plate has a large access panel located in it (slightly different on Mk 3) secured by six bolts which when opened allows the crew to carry out any maintenance on the steering box. The glacis plate also used to have the buoyancy trim vane used for swimming mounted on it. This was so heavy to remove that most crews used to leave it in camp when on exercise as swimming was only ever carried out at special training camps. In its place most crews obtained a Chieftain tank commander's bin and mounted that in its place. This gave a bit more stowage space for all those little extras that one needs for the rigors of two weeks exercise!

Either side of the access plate were located the lighting assemblies. These contained twin headlamps, although only the outer were true vehicle lights. The inner lights were normally fitted with infrared filters that, in conjunction with the IR headset issued to the driver known as CUBS, enabled him to drive in the dark. The lights were mounted on a flat plate and below this were located the indicators and side lights. Immediately above on either side are located the smoke grenade dischargers. Each discharge holds three grenades: an explosive charge fires them forward creating a smokescreen which hopefully allows the vehicle to escape. On the right hand top of the glacis looking at the vehicle from the front, one of the hand-held bromochlorodifluoromethane (better known as BCF) fire extinguishers was located. Moving down the left hand side, a large exhaust silencer is bolted to the front left with an exhaust pipe running down the side finishing level with the rear of the vehicle; a curved extension was provided which originally was used when swimming to carry the exhaust above the flotation screen. On the Mk 1 the exhaust exited on the hull top; as the Mk 1 was Rolls Royce petrol driven it depended on plugs and points the same as a family car, and instead of the exhaust box a large oval access panel was located. This usually was only retained in the closed position by a couple of bolts as the petrol engine was notorious for plugs and points issues, so the less work to remove the panel the better.

Moving to the rear, entry to the vehicle is normally by the large heavy rear door that is hinged on the right and opens outwards. However, unlike Warrior with its hydraulic-operated door, this door is opened by muscle power alone and many an accident has befallen the unwary. There is a classic sequence in an army training film on the cooperation of armour and infantry were the 432s come crashing into a wood and the back doors are thrown open for the section to de-bus. Except for one vehicle that has parked slightly nose down, the door crashes open and keen young infantrymen start to jump out only to be met by the door returning to the closed position due to the angle of the vehicle. The camera lingered for a few more seconds then switched to another scene; this of course was well received by tankies watching the film.

The door has a very basic metal stay that can be used when the vehicle is stationary to hold it open. Let into the door is an armoured glass vision block fitted with a metal spring-loaded flap that can be used to prevent light shining through the block during blackout conditions. This tiny block, which measures 150 x 80mm, is the only means that the section in the rear of the vehicle has for viewing the outside world; in that respect it is as much use as an ashtray on a motorbike. The door is also fitted with a blackout switch, which also serves to carry power to the number plate light and the convoy light. It consists of a fixed contact plate on the top left of the door which when the door is closed mates against a plunger housing mounted on the hull which has spring plungers fitted into it. These provide power when the door is in the closed position and the contacts are depressed. They also serve as a blackout system for when the vehicle interior lights are in use; any opening of the rear door will immediately extinguish all the internal lights. Also located on the rear of the door are a further two BCF extinguishers. On each side of the rear panel either side of the door are located two stowage bins. On the Mk 1 these were jettisonable petrol tanks that could be used during an approach march and then jettisoned just before combat, never popular and their replacement by the stowage bins was welcomed.

Moving down the right hand side of the vehicle, there are various brackets and attachment points for stowage and radio masts. The dominating feature, located more or less centrally, is the NBC (Nuclear, Biological and Chemical) pack access panels. On the Mk 1 and Mk 2 early versions the system was enclosed in a prominent box-like structure which projected from the side of the vehicle with twin doors to gain access; the later version is almost flush with the hull side and has a single door. For all versions though, once the door/s are opened access is then given to the fans and filters; in peace time paper particulate filters are fitted, but for full NBC operations these would be replaced by charcoal filters. The system could also provide, according to the MoD, cool fresh air; this was optimistic as to do that requires an air conditioner unit and that was lacking, but it was better than nothing.

Located along both sides and front and rear are mudguards. The rear ones have a large rubber flap that is supposed to help keep the dust down, in reality they usually got torn off in the first few days of an exercise so again they joined the growing list of kit left in the stores; the front ones also usually joined them as well. The side panels also were very flimsy and again were usually left behind. The saving grace for all the panels was that they were easy to fit or remove. The only time that an FV432 could be seen with all the panels fitted was for its REME inspections or formal parades. Towing eyes were fitted front and rear, to be used for towing the vehicle, or they could have an attachment such as the mine plough fitted. Also located at the right rear are power sockets that can be used for engineers' tools.

One of the big problems with any tracked vehicle is keeping the correct tension on the tracks. Due to wear the track pins start to deform and the holes in the tracks start to change shape from round to oval. This amount of stretching has to be compensated for otherwise eventually the track will become so slack that the nightmare of crews, the throwing of a track, will occur. There are two solutions to maintain correct tension, one is the removal of a link and the other is having in the system an adjustable wheel that can take up a certain amount of the slack track before the need to remove a link occurs. The removal of the link is only carried out after the track adjuster has taken up all the adjustment.

On the FV432 the rear idler wheel is the track adjuster. It is mounted on a cranked axle arm with one end pivoting on a bracket mounted on the hull sidewall while the other forms a stub axle which carries the idler wheel hub. Movement of the arm to the rear will tighten the track and movement forward will slacken it. There have been two methods of adjusting this arm on the FV430, both made use of a ram connected to the crank which when pressure was applied would push the ram to the rear thus tightening the track. Later vehicles have a grease nipple at the forward face of the ram and using the vehicle grease gun, which was capable of producing pressure of 500psi, grease would be pumped into the ram. To release the pressure a relief screw is located just below the grease nipple, and the weight of the track will then pull the wheel forward.

Early vehicles used a system similar to that used on the tanks in that a large openended ratchet adjuster was placed over a nut on the forward face of the ram. The crew would then turn the nut by use of the ratchet, which in its turn moved a threaded shaft that was connected to the ram and thus tension was applied to the track. To release tension the spanner was reversed and the nut slackened off.

The track is supported on its top run by two double roller assemblies each side secured to the hull side plates. The rollers are secured to a hub that is mounted on a two-ball race bearing on a spindle fitted into a support bracket. The spindle is secured into the bracket by means of a dowel the end of which protrudes and is used to support the track support rail that is used when splitting the track.

The track comprises ninety links when new and is of the single pin type, although interestingly in the early days of design a double-pin track that was solid rubber was tested. The pins that connect the tracks are hexagonal and fit into hexagonal sleeves bonded into rubber bushes in each link. The position of the bushes in the leading and trailing edge of each link are offset by ten degrees; this causes the track to curve inwards and helps to relieve the strain on the bushes. The track pins are not hardened and may be retained in one of two ways. The early versions were retained by the use of a spring circlip which was forced over the end of the pin and locating in a groove cut in the pin. The current version has a nylock nut at either end, which is retained by the nylon collar in the nut cutting into the thread on the pin. To remove the old-style pin, the track is slackened, the circlip is prised off using special pliers, and then using the track toolkit the pin is knocked out. This is not as easy as it sounds: quite often the rubber bushing bonded itself to the pin and no matter how hard it was hit it was not going to come out, and often the REME would have to come and flame cut the link out. To try to alleviate this, track clamps were issued and they were used to draw the track together to relieve the tension on the pin. The new pins were much better, as all you had to do was to remove the nylock nut on the outer end of the pin, fit a special ratchet type tool, and then simply keep using the ratchet until the pin was drawn from the link. To rejoin a split track the clamps could be used to hold the two ends of the track so that they nearly lined up, then a new pin, complete with circlip or nut and well-greased, would be knocked through and another circlip or nut fitted on the end.

If the track was to be replaced completely, only one side at a time would be done as if both tracks were removed there would be no means of braking the vehicle. When new track was to be fitted new sprockets would be fitted as well. The sprockets could also be used as a winch to help move the new track onto the suspension. This was achieved by fitting a special rope to the end of the track furthest away from the vehicle with the track laid out in front. A track support rail would be fitted to help support the track as it was removed and replaced; it locates onto the protruding dowels on the top roller mountings. One crew member would take a turn around the sprocket with the rope, then the vehicle would be started up and the low range gear (1–2) selected; by pulling the steering lever on the side of the unbroken track the vehicle would move in a straight line. The crewman controlling the rope would hook the rope behind the slowly turning sprocket and this would winch the track onto the sprocket. Once the track had engaged the sprocket the rope was then unwound and paid out across the top rollers where crew members would keep it taught to help the track onto the top rollers. This would continue until the two ends of the track were near enough for the track clamps to be fitted.

The hull carries the suspension, which comprises five double road wheels on axle arms, fitted in the trailing position from the front of the vehicle. Each arm is attached by splines to a torsion bar of which there are ten running transversely across the hull. This leads to a slightly staggered set-up of the road wheels. The upward movement of the axles' arms is limited by bump stops attached to the lower hull plates. Also fitted are four friction-type shock absorbers to the front and rear stations either side. The use of transverse torsion bars leads to a height penalty, as the crew floor has to be raised to cover the torsion bars; this is why tanks such as the American M60 are high.

The road wheels are interchangeable and are also the same as the rear idler; this eases slightly the logistic problem of supply. The twin wheels are located onto the hub by two diametrically-opposed locating pins on the hub which is fitted to a stub axle on the axle arm that is attached to the torsion bar. Each hub is oil lubricated and provided with a filler plug on the outer face. The axle arm pivots in bearings in a housing welded to the hull wall thorough which the torsion bar is located. The other end of the torsion bar is attached to an anchorage in the axle arm housing on the opposite hull wall. Friction-type shock absorbers are fitted to the front and rear stations with the front one being anchored to the top of the final drive casing and the rear ones to the rear top roller bracket. Upward motion of the individual axle arms is limited by the use of a steel and rubber bump stop bolted to the hull wall.

We now can enter the vehicle and see the layout and equipment. Normal entry for the section is via the large rear door; the driver and commander could enter from their hatches in the roof. Looking either side of the rear area, the seating arrangements for the section can now be seen. Seating is basic, consisting of four padded bench seats that can be raised to the vertical position and mechanically locked to give more room for loads. Behind each seat area is the overhang over the tracks known as the sponson. This area contains space for the crew to stow some items of equipment. However the area is not totally clear: on the left are two half-gallon fire extinguishers, and if the vehicle is fitted for the ambulance role then a set of batteries that normally would be located on the floor are moved onto the sponson to allow one of the stretchers to be fitted; on the right the forward position is taken up with the fan controls for the NBC equipment. Stowage is held in place over the sponsons by means of wire grills that are held in a channel by wing nuts that can be lifted out to obtain access. It can be seen from this that stowage of kit had to be carefully thought out to avoid having to rummage through loads of equipment to find a particular item. Space was also found under the bench seats, and again grills could be fitted to retain equipment, although in practise they were rarely used. The rear part of the crew area also contains the two internal fuel tanks; one located either side of the door. Into this area, all section equipment, weapons, ammunition, and any other items required for the exercise or operation had to be fitted.

On the rear of the door was probably the most important item on any British AFV, the Boiling Vessel, better known to generations of soldiers as the 'BV'. The FV432 was issued with two of these vital tools The BV is very simply a box with a heating element in the base, this covered by an inner wall which is isolated from the outer wall by insulating material. The lid was a lift-up-and-off type which gave access to the inner body into which tins or boil-in-the-bag rations could be placed. Eleven pints of water could be boiled but an inner tray could be used very much like a bain-marie in a kitchen. The BV was an improvement over the standard issue petrol cooker, but it did need the engine running to work.

Above the crew compartment are two large circular hatches known as the Mortar Hatches. These consist of four segments that can be folded back, two either side, and engage in clamps located on the roof. Failure to check that the clamps were engaged could lead to the hatches flying back on any unfortunate standing up in them. They were fitted with a rubber seal to prevent the ingress of water when closed; this failed miserably in most vehicles, leading to a constant dripping of water into the compartment.

Looking forward on the left side of the vehicle is the power pack bulkhead, onto which are fixed the two internal fire extinguishers. To the right of this are the driver's and commander's seats. The driver sits in the front right of the vehicle and has access (as we have seen) via his hatch or through the main crew area. To his left are the access panels to the power pack, which can easily be removed. On the access panel there are covers that can be opened to enable the driver to check the main engine oil level and the transmission oil level. In the event of oil being required the dipstick holders for both are also the oil fillers. Just forward of the engine oil filler is the engine speed hand control. This consists of a knurled knob which can be locked in place once the desired engine speed has been reached by a locking wing nut. This control is only used when the vehicle is static, for charging batteries, for using power tools, or for warming the engine before moving off.

At the base of the bulkhead is a location for a battery box that contains two 100-amp/hour batteries which provide power for the ventilation system. When the vehicle is converted to the ambulance role this battery box is moved onto the left sponson and all the necessary wiring is already built in to enable this to be completed easily by the crew. Two more sets of batteries are located in the forward area that is occupied by the driver and commander. One set is fitted beneath the driver's seat and, although provided with a cover, is always at risk of being covered in debris. The third set is located on the sponson on the driver's right hand side.

The gear range selector lever for the automatic gear box is located in a quadrant on the sill on the driver's left. The lever operates within a gate marked with the gear ranges 1–2, 3–4, 3–5, 3–6, Neutral and Reverse. To allow reverse gear to be selected a spring loaded plunger located at the right rear of the quadrant has to be pulled out to allow the selector lever to engage reverse. Also located within the quadrant is a micro switch that is operated by the selector lever when in the neutral position. This allows the engine to be started in this position only, in much the same way as on a civilian car.

The power pack is to the driver's left. This is a composite unit that, once the engine decks and all the connections, which are of the quick-release and self-sealing type, are removed, the whole assembly can be lifted from the vehicle and either exchanged for a replacement or, by using umbilical extensions, run on the ground to find faults. All the components are mounted in a fabricated frame with the engine located on the left. The transfer gearbox is bolted to the flywheel housing and to the input end of the automatic gearbox that is mounted alongside the engine thus bringing the drive to the front of the vehicle. The output flange of the gearbox is connected by a double universal coupling to the steering unit. In front of the gearbox is the engine oil tank, which has a flexible filler that extends to the filler cap on the sill to the driver's left. The radiator is mounted on top of the frame at the front in a sloping position to allow it to fit under the sloping air louvre above it on the roof. Two cooling fans are mounted at the rear of the radiator. These sit in a dished cowl which fits under the air intake louvre. The heat exchanger is mounted transversely midway above the engine, with the engine oil and fuel filters mounted behind it. A two-stage air cleaner is mounted to the left alongside the radiator with, to its rear, a hydraulic fluid tank which supplies fluid which is pressurised by a pump mounted on the rear of the engine and is used to provide the drive for the cooling fans.

The engine fitted to the FV432 Mk 1 is a Rolls Royce B81. This is a petrol engine and (as we have seen) needs plugs and points with all their problems. The Mk 2 vehicles onwards have the Rolls Royce K60. This is a multi-fuel, direct fuel injection high-speed compression ignition engine operating on the two-stroke cycle principle. A tachometer (rev counter) located on the driver's instrument panel indicates the output shaft speed and is sometimes used as an indication for gear changing by less experienced drivers.

To steer and brake the vehicle the layout is very different to that normally expected in a tracked vehicle. While most AFVs have a variation of the normal driving controls, the FV432 does not. Due to the auto gearbox, there is no clutch or gear-change pedal, just the ratio selector. There is no footbrake or handbrake in the conventional sense. The driver has two steering levers directly in front of him and located on top of each lever is a button. Unless using the button the thumbs should not touch it, as we shall see. To move off, the driver selects his gear ratio, then, pulling back on the steering levers, the buttons will pop up. The levers in this mode are acting as the parking brake. To move off he will allow the levers to travel forwards. As the vehicle moves off, his right foot is on the only conventional pedal in the cab, the accelerator. To steer he pulls back on the relevant lever, again avoiding the button. When the direction change has been completed he releases the lever. To stop he pulls back on the levers together, endeavouring to maintain a straight line. Once the vehicle has been brought to a rest, he can now apply the parking brake. By keeping rearward tension on the levers he depresses the buttons and allows the levers to move forward slightly, all being well the parking brake is now applied. Now it can be seen why it is not a good idea to have a thumb on the button while driving.

The driver's hatch is hinged on the right hand side and when it is closed he has a single periscope for driving. This can be replaced by an image intensifier for night driving, and a wash-wipe system is also fitted. Various controls for lighting, horn, warning lights and a full restraint harness, which hardly gets used, completes the driver's area.

The commander sits immediately behind the driver. Should internal communications break down, the commander can simply tap the driver on the shoulder, and this is what many infantry commanders did in the early days. The commander has a seat that can be raised so he can sit with head out in the prescribed position of head and shoulders only above the cupola. It can be lowered so he can sit completely below the cupola, or it can be swung up and locked in the vertical position allowing the commander to stand up, very much a personal choice. The commander's cupola is basic to say the least. It can rotate 360 degrees and is equipped with three No. 32 periscopes, one of which has a wiper blade that is operated by a simple pull wire by the commander. His hatch can be locked in the vertical position and this gives a good base to secure the map, using elastic bungee cord.

Armament of the basic APC is very much that. A locating base on the cupola allows a 7.62mm GPMG to be mounted. In the earlier days a 7.62mm LMG (better known as the Bren) was the weapon used. Other variants, as we will see, have a more potent punch.

(**Opposite, above**) This shows the height penalty in using torsion bar suspension, the actual hull floor can be seen between the boxes that cover the torsion bars. It also, as can be seen, is a trap for water and debris. (*Rob Griffin*)

(**Opposite, below**) A view of the driver's cab. His seat has its back reclined which enables easier access if coming from the rear of the vehicle, the large battery box cover on the right and the steering levers in the centre. Just visible is the only pedal the driver has and on the left is his gear selector lever. (*Rob Griffin*)

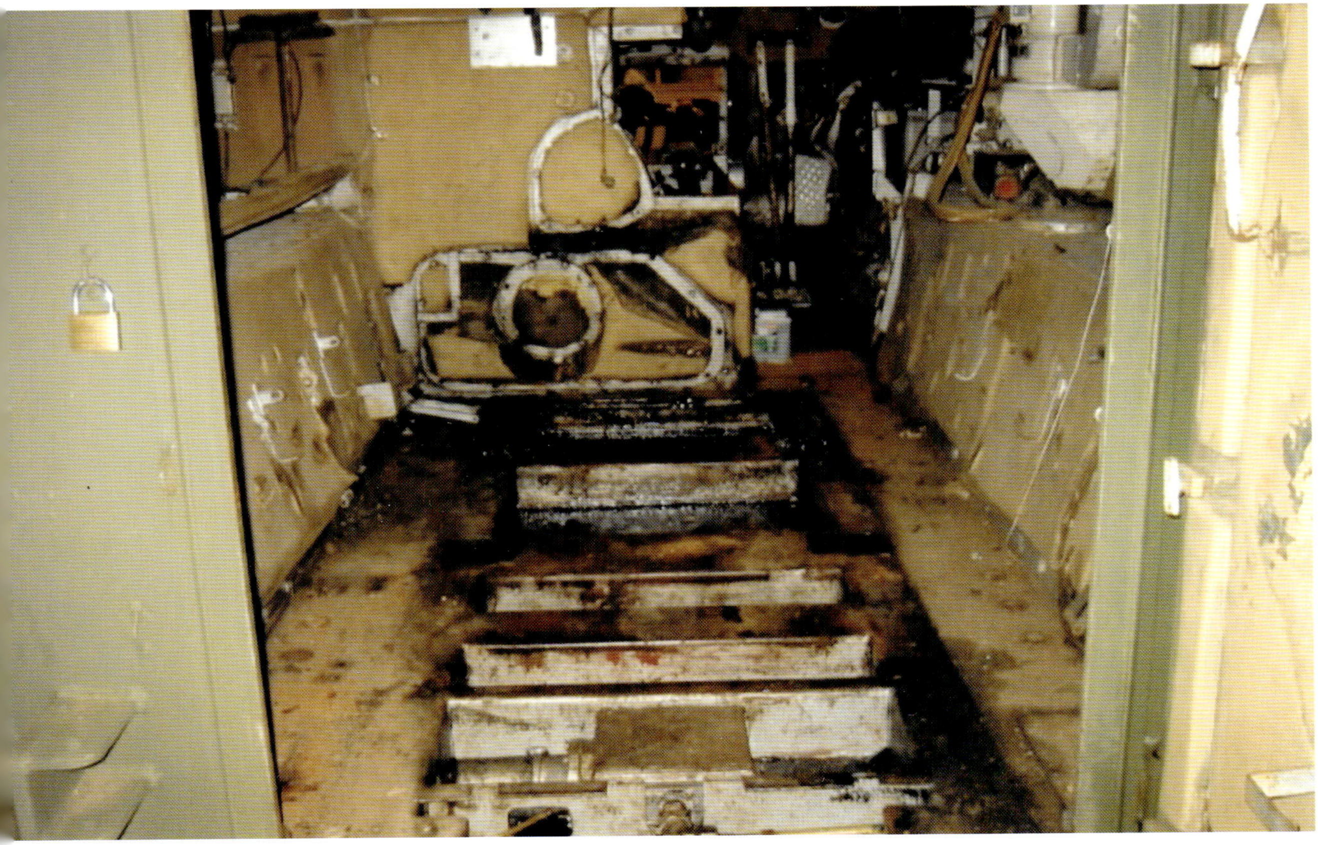

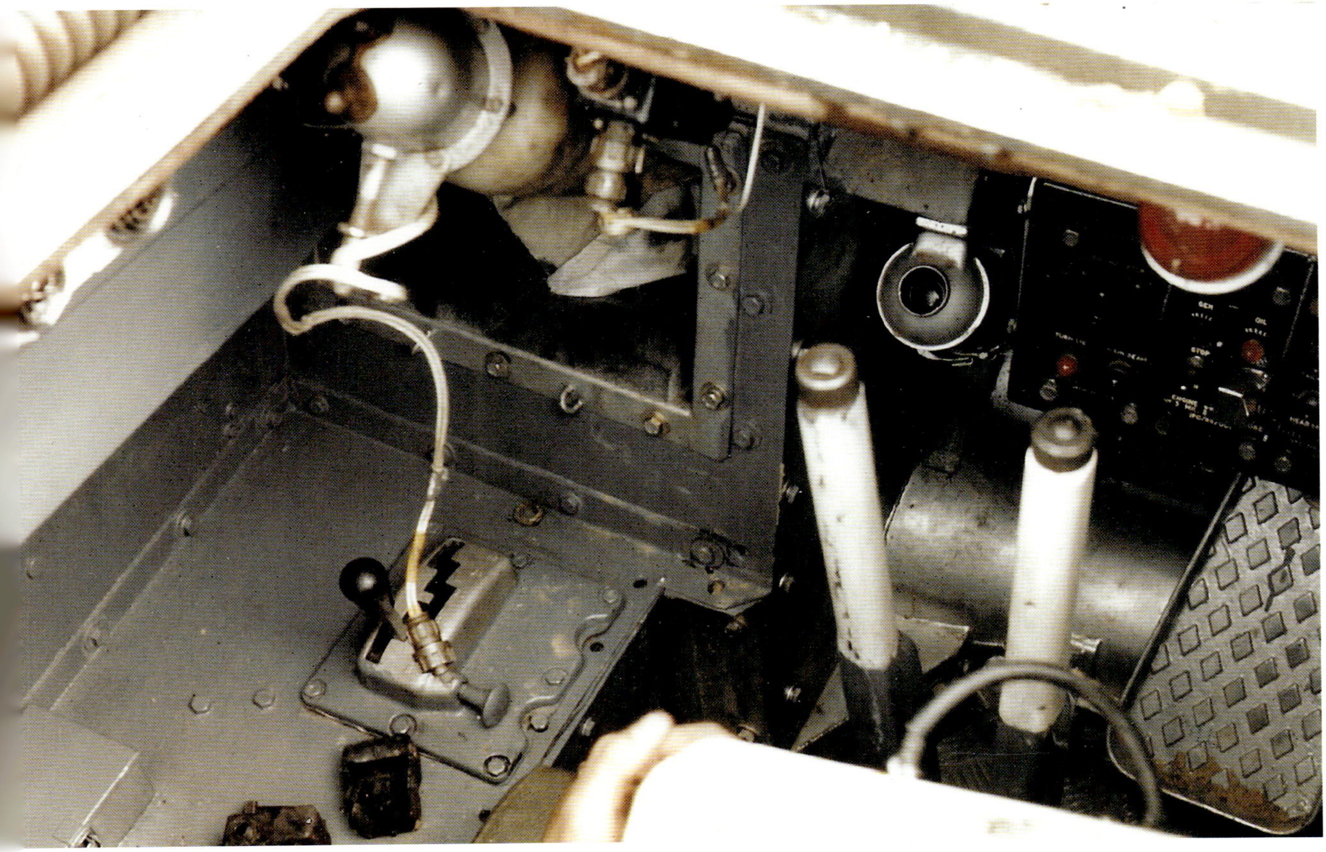

The driver's spring loaded hatch. Notice the spring and locking lever, the sight would fit into the rectangle space at the front of the hatch and the green object to the right is the wiper motor. (Tim Babb)

The much maligned GPMG mount. It can be seen how this mounting will expose the firer, with no protection at all. It would take until the introduction of the Mk 3 Bulldog FV432 for this to be rectified by fitting a remote operated weapon station. (Plain Military)

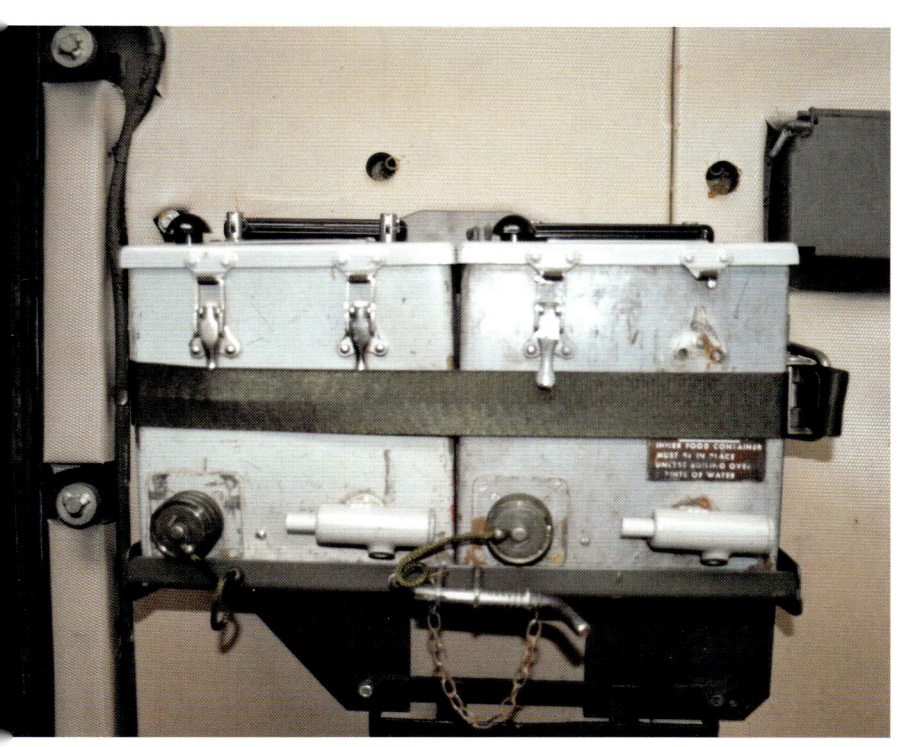

The all-important boiling vessel. A very simple item but so important for crews, it provides up to eleven pints of boiling water and saves making use of the petrol cooker. If required they can be removed and the tray swings up to give more room. *(Rob Griffin)*

The cupola showing just how simple it actually is. The mount for the GPMG can be seen on the left of the image. The three periscopes with the right hand having a glass cover over it; this is the one that is fitted with a hand operated wiper blade. *(Plain Military)*

(**Above**) Overall view of a FV432 ambulance showing the location of the exhaust box for the diesel power pack on the front right and its pipe fitted with the extension. It also has some of the new stowage issued on various rebuilds. *(Daniel Novak)*

(**Opposite, above**) Looking into the back of an ambulance version, the stretcher frame can be seen and immediately above it is the NBC controls and fan housing. *(Tim Babb)*

(**Opposite, below**) Looking down into the driver's cab we can see his full harness on the backrest, the battery box cover and forward the steering levers with the locking button visible on top. *(Plain Military)*

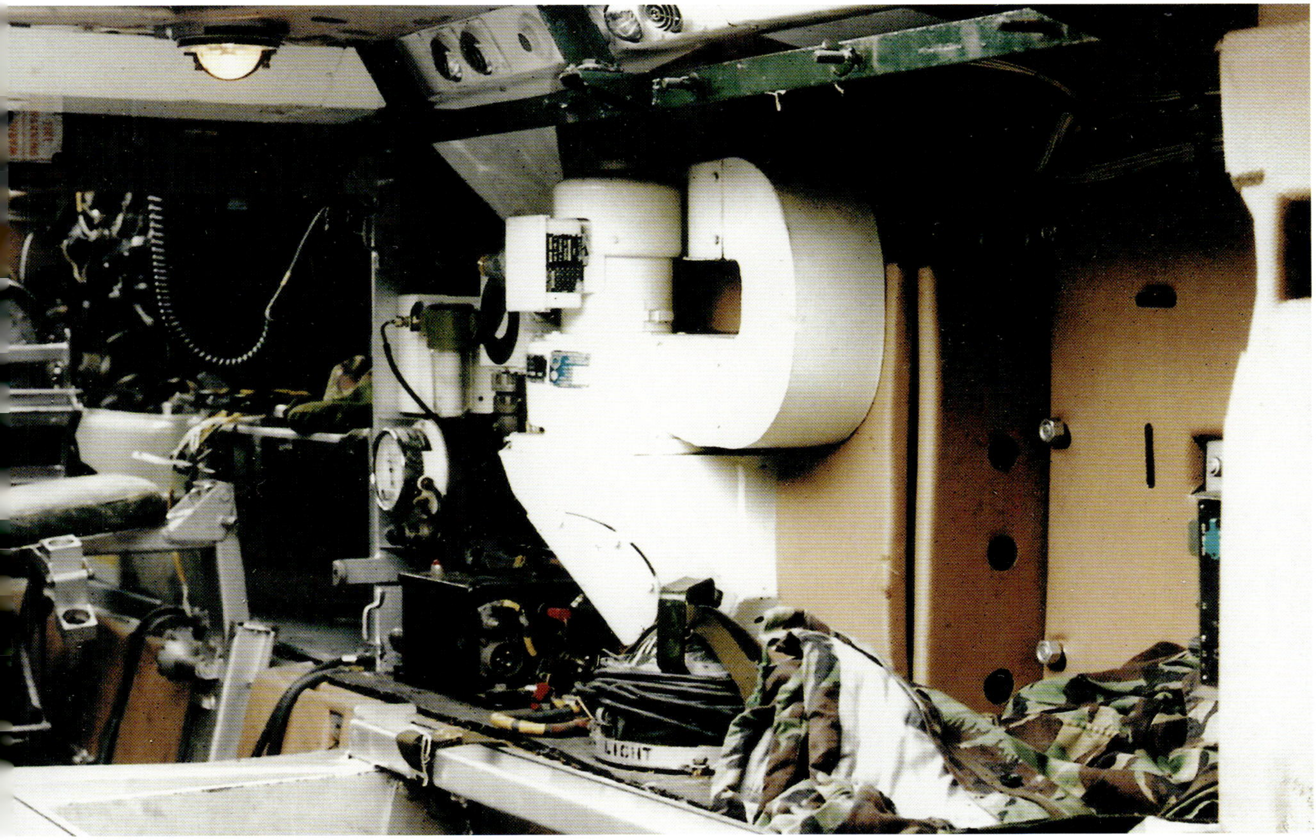
LIGHT

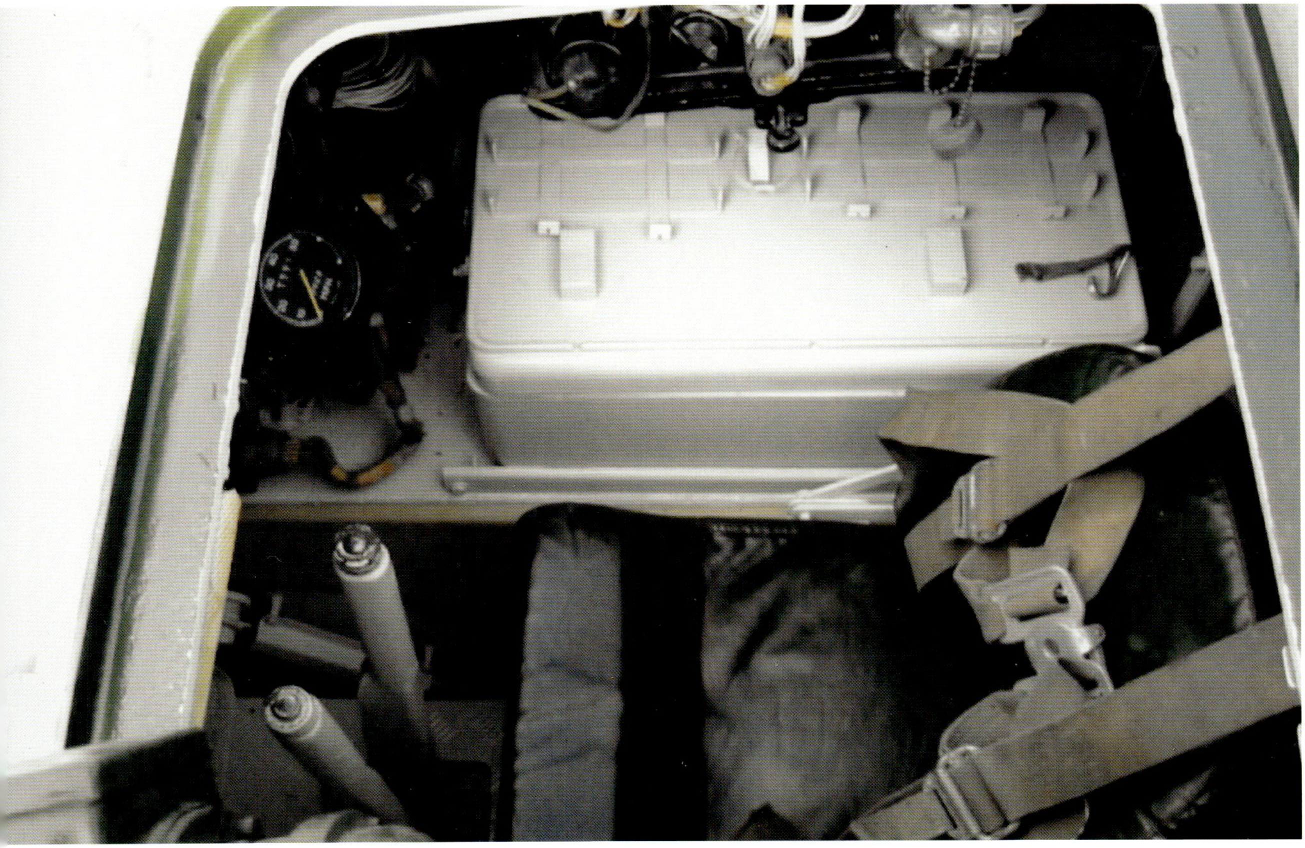

A very muddy vehicle but clearly visible, located horizontally behind the rear idler wheel, is the adjuster ram. This version is the type operated by pumping grease into the ram, the nipple can just be made out under its layer of mud. *(Tim Babb)*

View showing a rather pristine condition rebuilt FV432. How long will it last like this once back in service? *(Plain Military)*

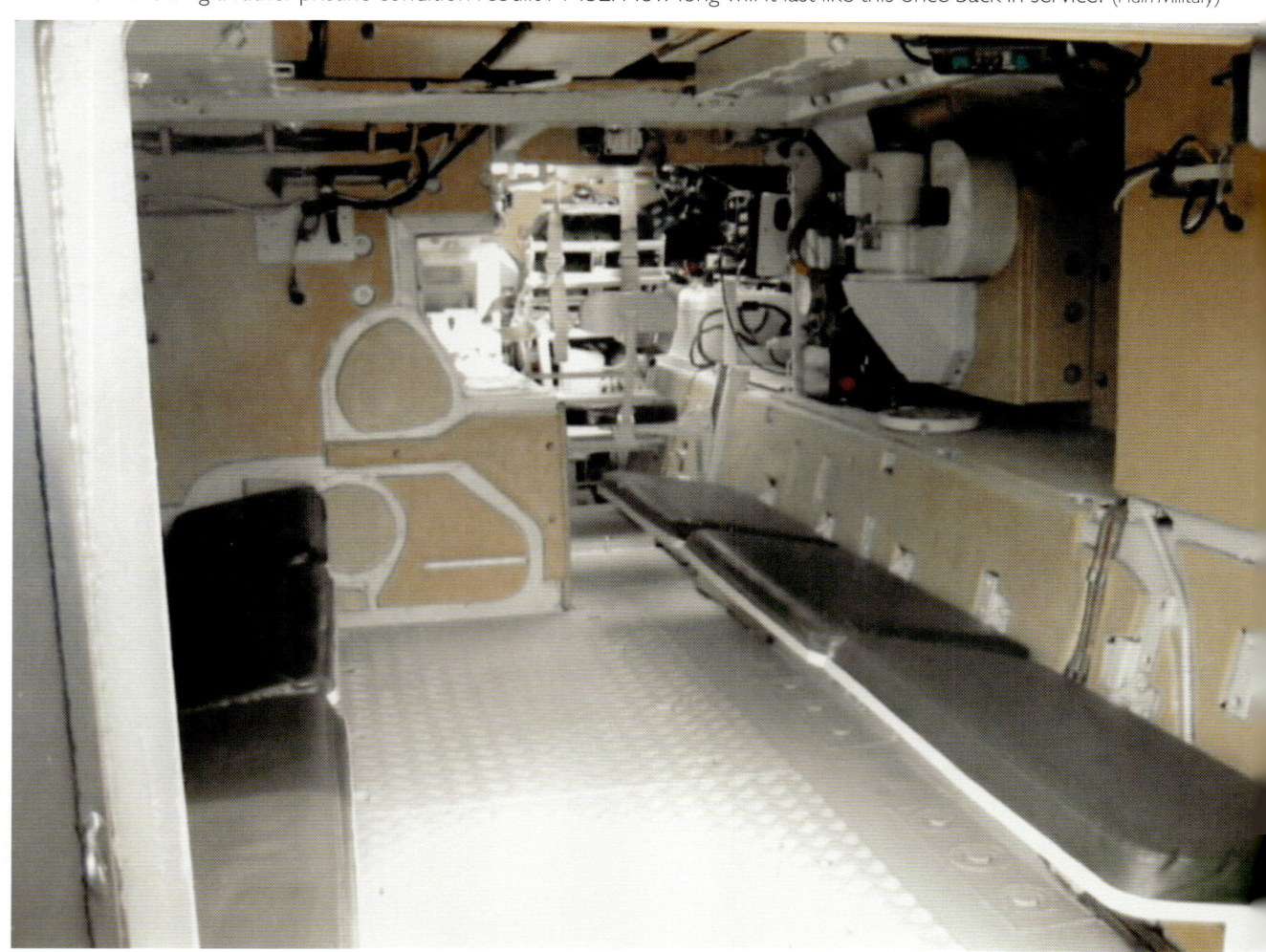

A view in the workshops showing the difference between a standard Mk 3 Bulldog FV432 and the sand coloured version with its up-armour pack fitted, note the tactically bright red fire extinguishers. (*Plain Military*)

With the front panel open the steering box can be seen and either side of it the connections for the steering levers are visible. (*Rob Griffin*)

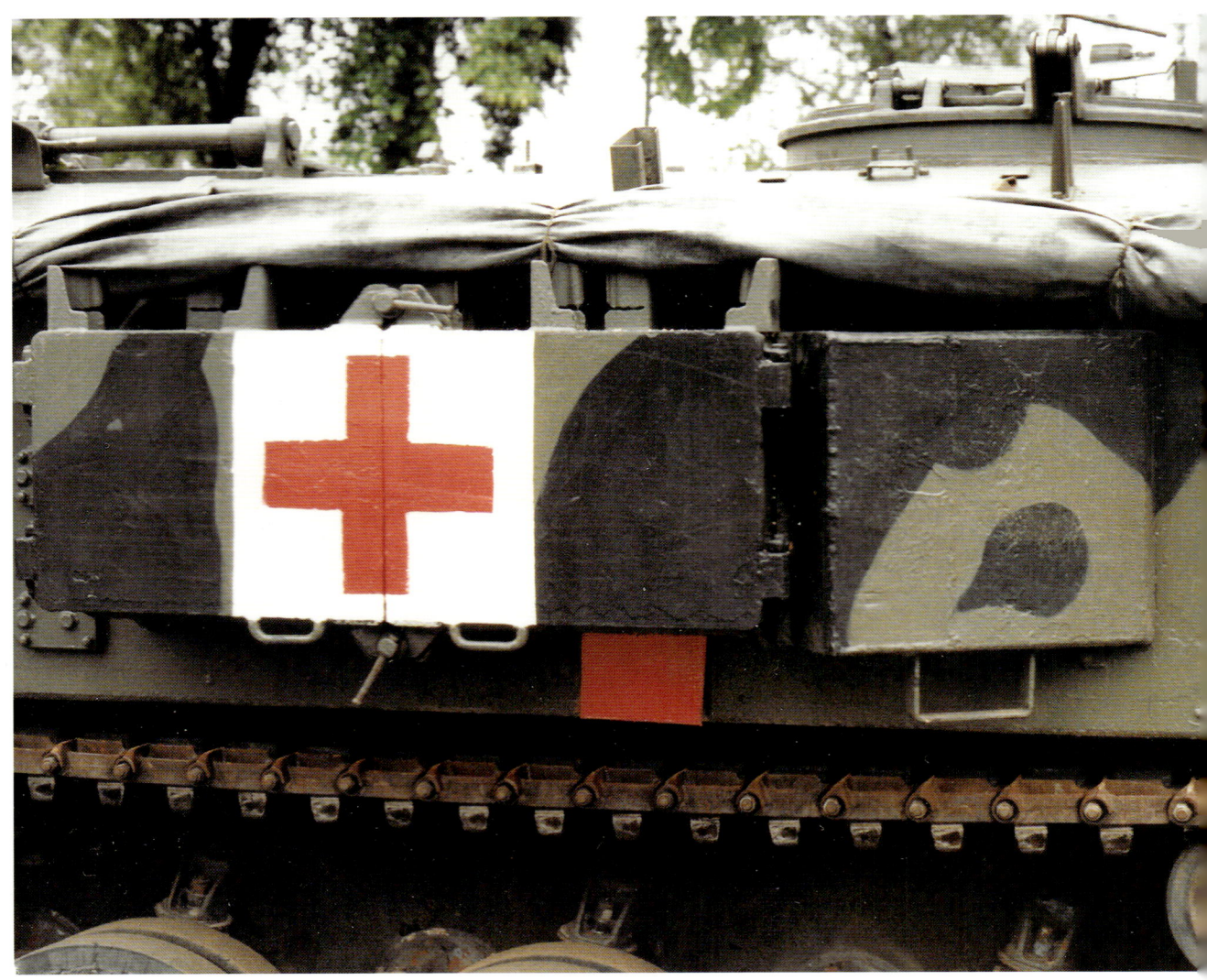

(**Above**) The original large NBC box showing how much it actually protrudes from the hull side. Located on the top can be seen the brackets that would hold a spare track link, one to each bracket. Below the NBC box is a red rubber flap, behind that is a fire extinguisher handle that allows the crew to activate the vehicle fire extinguishers from outside. *(Tim Babb)*

(**Opposite, above**) The basic frame of the driver's seat minus its back and seat squab, the seat can be raised or lowered to allow the driver to operate either closed down or head out. *(Rob Griffin)*

(**Opposite, below**) This shows how the road wheels are mounted on trailing arms, and visible behind them are the rebound pads. Note the sag between the top rollers. *(John Martin)*

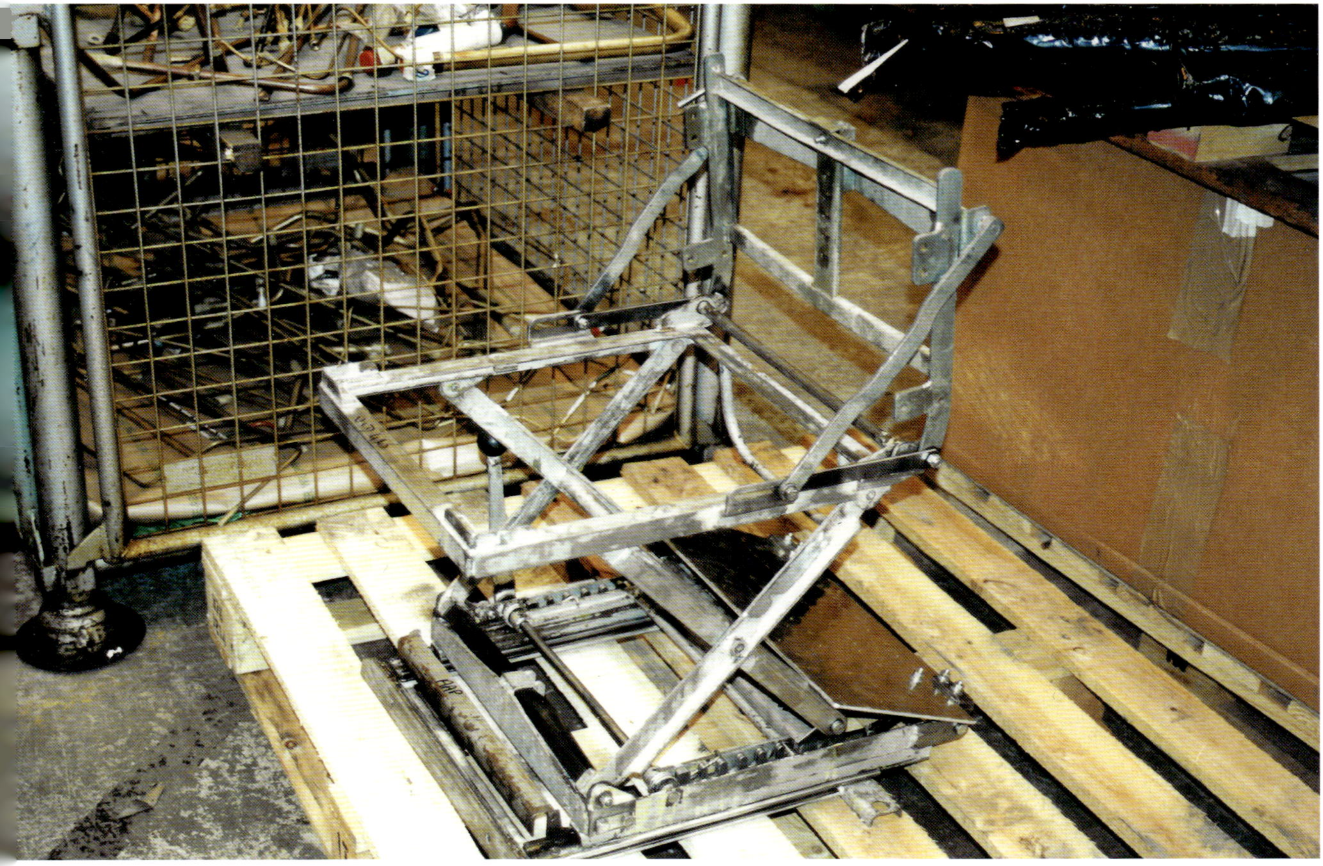

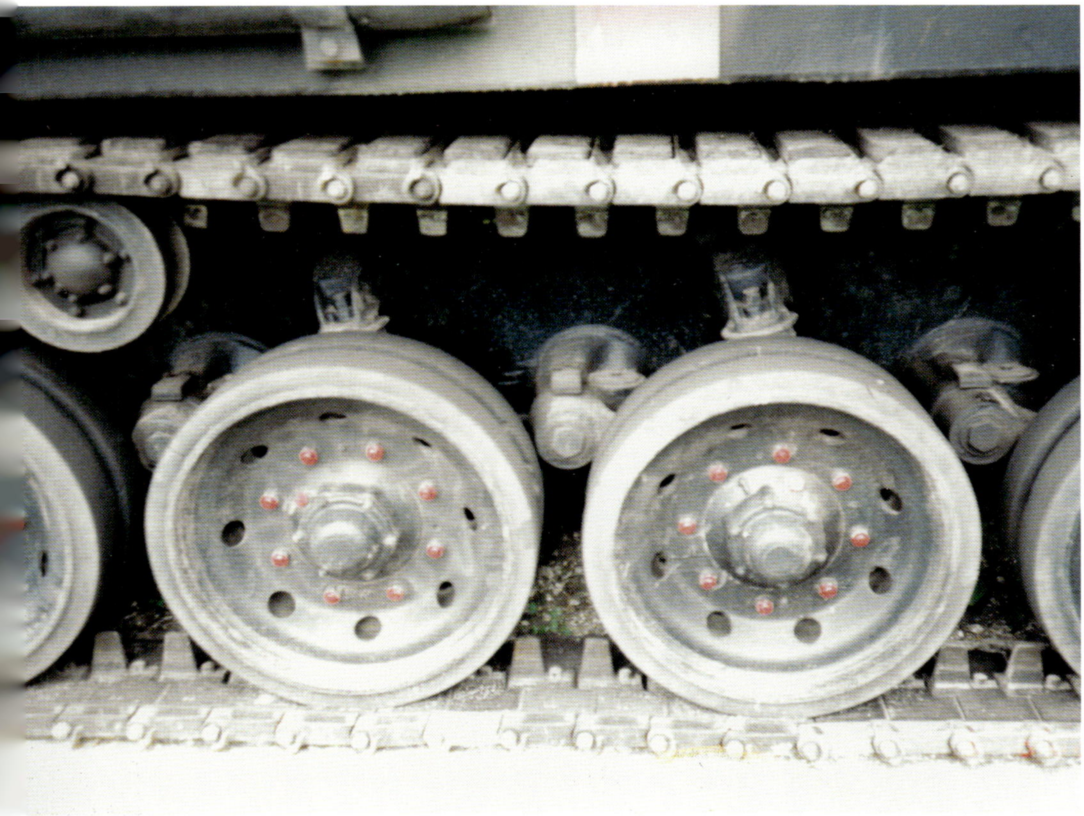

Refurbished FV432 showing the double road wheel and the new rebound pads behind. Also note the nuts on the end of the track showing it is the later type. *(Rob Griffin)*

(**Opposite, above**) The later style NBC pack. Notice how it is nearly flush with the hull sides and only a single door and no track stowage on the top. *(Rob Griffin)*

(**Opposite, below**) A wheel arm awaiting its turn for refurbishment at the base workshops. The right side is where the wheel would be attached and the left will fit onto the torsion bar splines. *(Rob Griffin)*

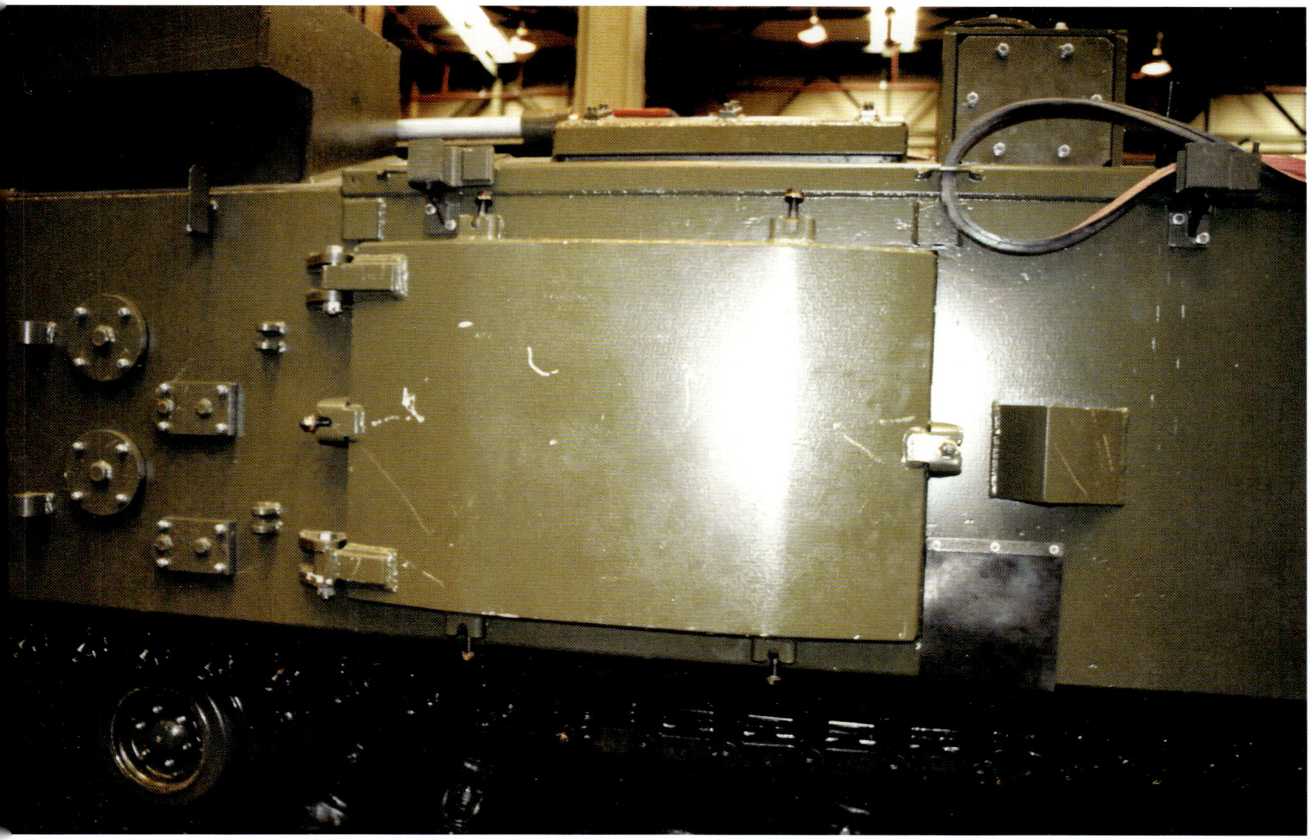

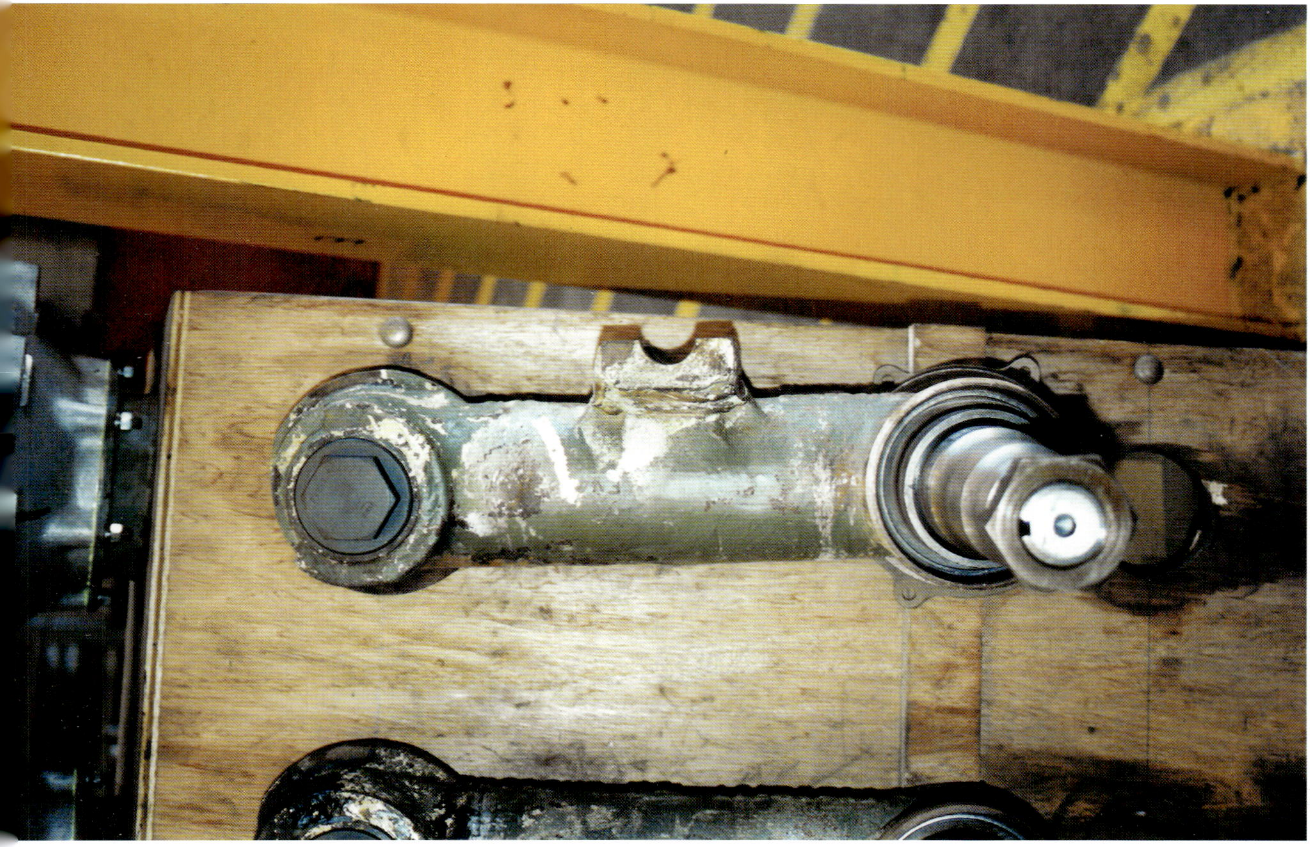

A later modification to allow easier erection of the carbon fibre camouflage poles; a pole is simply fitted into one of the tubes and then bent in the direction of the next set of fittings, this method speeds up the process. (*Rob Griffin*)

Looking forward towards the power pack bay. On the wall can be seen one of the control boxes for the Clansman radios that are fitted, to the left a good illustration on how the cages are located over the sponsons. (*Tim Babb*)

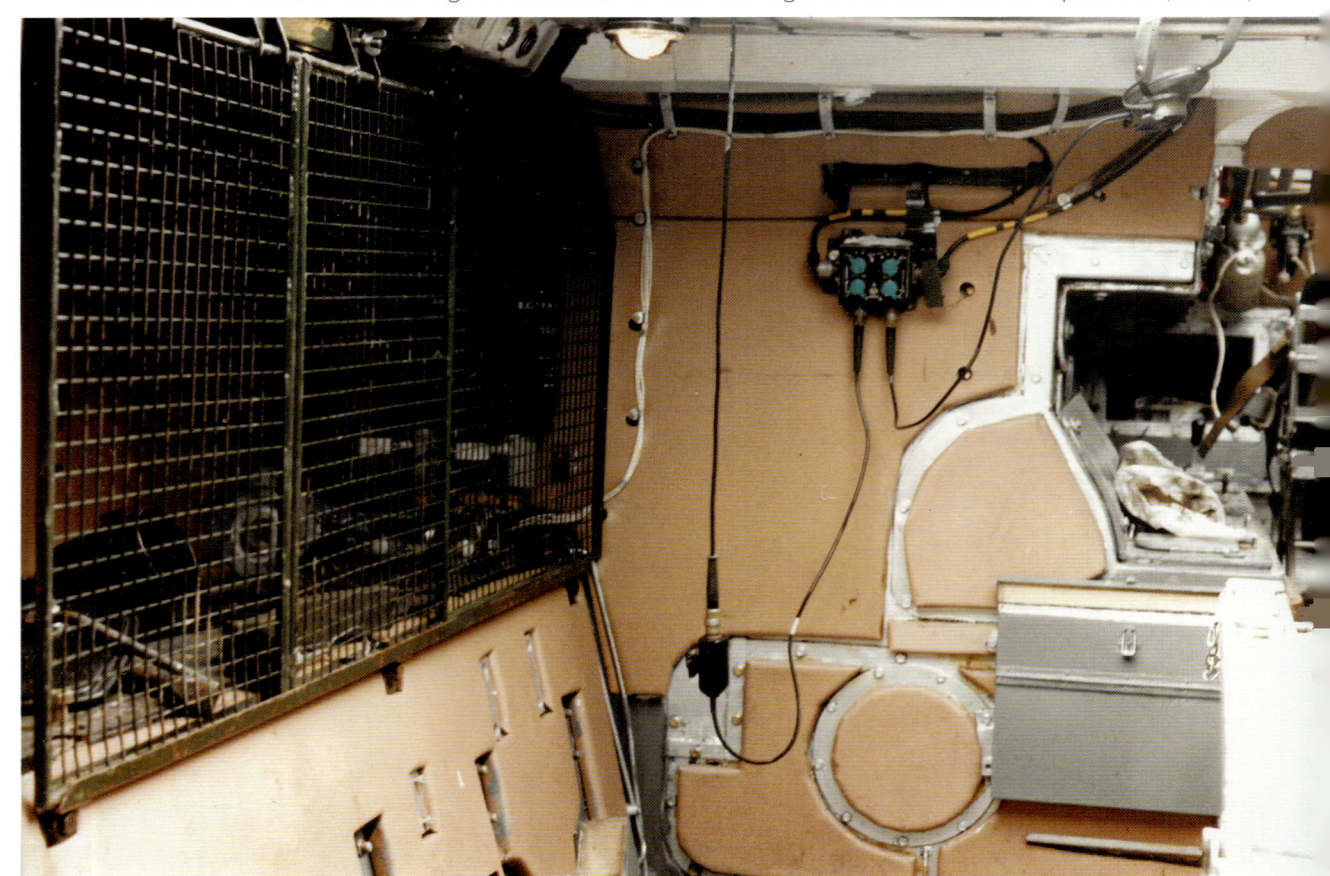

With the engine louvres lifted, the twin fans that give the FV432 its distinctive whine can be seen. The two round caps are air cleaners. This setup is in a training establishment as the forward louvres are replaced with dexion mesh. *(Rob Griffin)*

The rather worn well of an FV434 showing how much the area is using what would have been the crew compartment; FV430 has been successful in being adapted for man roles. *(Rob Griffin)*

The front of the vehicle showing the drive sprocket and the foremost top roller. The sprocket hub has been cut out to allow mud to be squeezed out, preventing a build up around the hub; if this is not controlled the risk of a track jumping the sprocket is increased. *(Tim Babb)*

The twin rear bins which replaced the external detachable fuel tanks for the Mk 1; these bins proved a boon for storing vehicle kit. *(Rob Griffin)*

The gearbox out of the vehicle. The long levers either side are for connecting to the steering lever linkage. (*Rob Griffin*)

The power back removed from the vehicle. If required it can be connected to the vehicle systems using umbilical leads to bridge the gap. This is useful when trying to trace a fault. (*Rob Griffin*)

(**Above**) Another disadvantage of torsion bars, the covers over each location, because they are welded and watertight they act as superb water and oil traps which all has to be cleaned up during a refit, and nothing better than a plastic bucket. *(Rob Griffin)*

(**Opposite, above**) How workshops mount the vehicles once all the suspension has been removed. This vehicle has been blasted as can be seen by the pattern etched onto it. Of note can be seen the locations for the torsion bars, rebound pads and the large round opening for the final drive. *(Rob Griffin)*

(**Opposite, below**) This vehicle is in the process of being stripped down to a bare shell, cleaned and then rebuilt. *(Rob Griffin)*

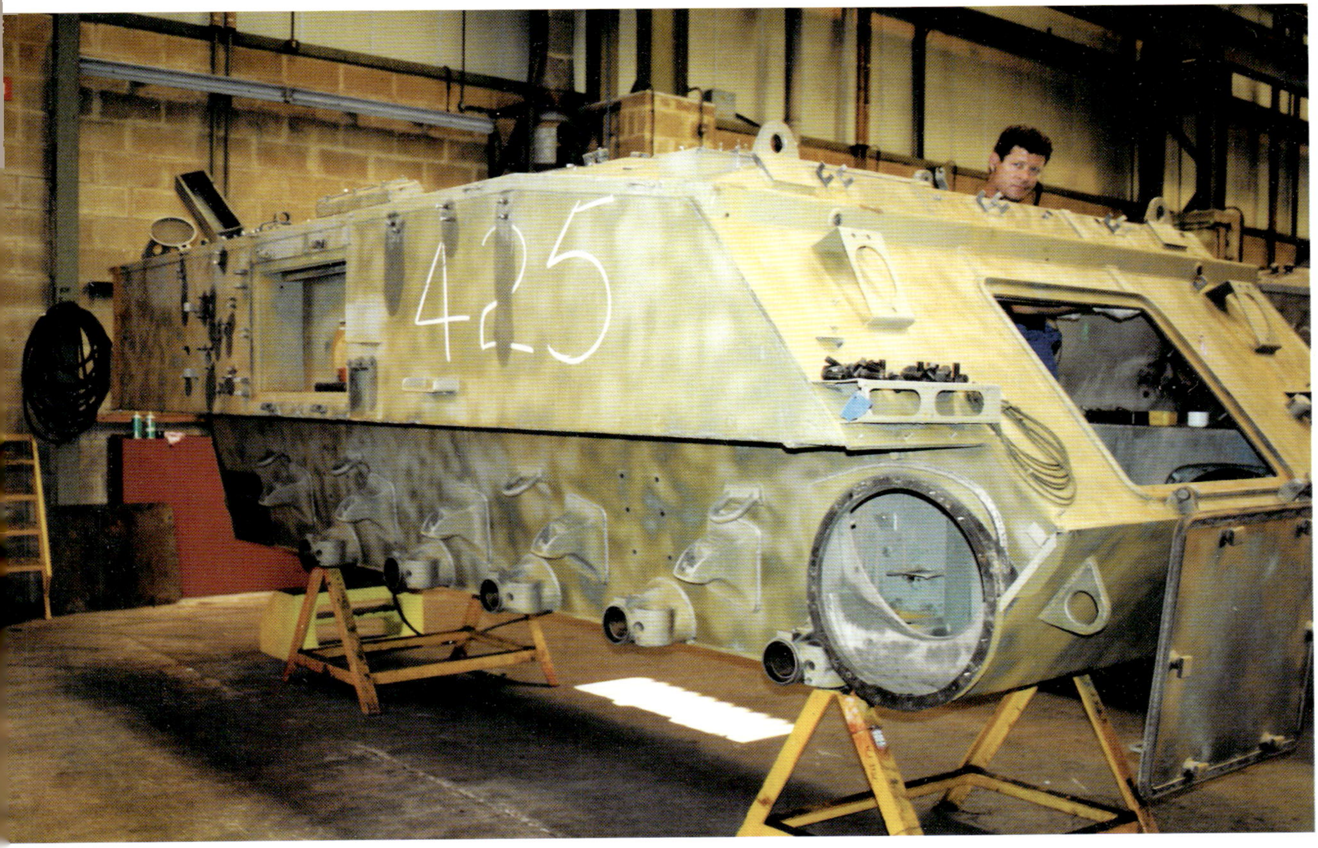
425

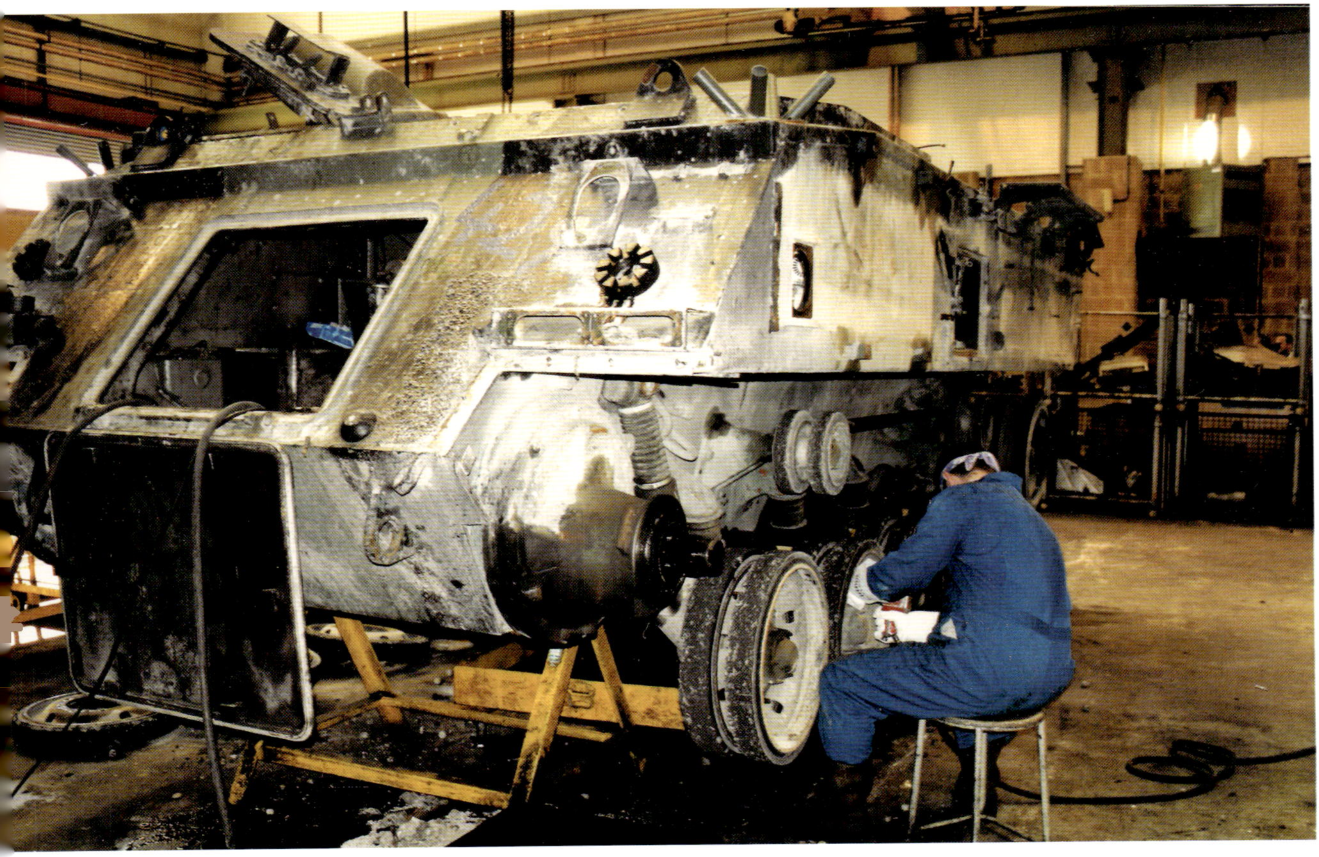

The ultra-tactical red fire extinguisher, although when in service these will be covered or, at one time, a green sleeve was issued for them. *(Rob Griffin)*

Getting there; this vehicle is well on the way to being completed, note that it has its rear mud guard and rubber flap fitted. These will be removed once at its new unit and kept in the stores. *(Rob Griffin)*

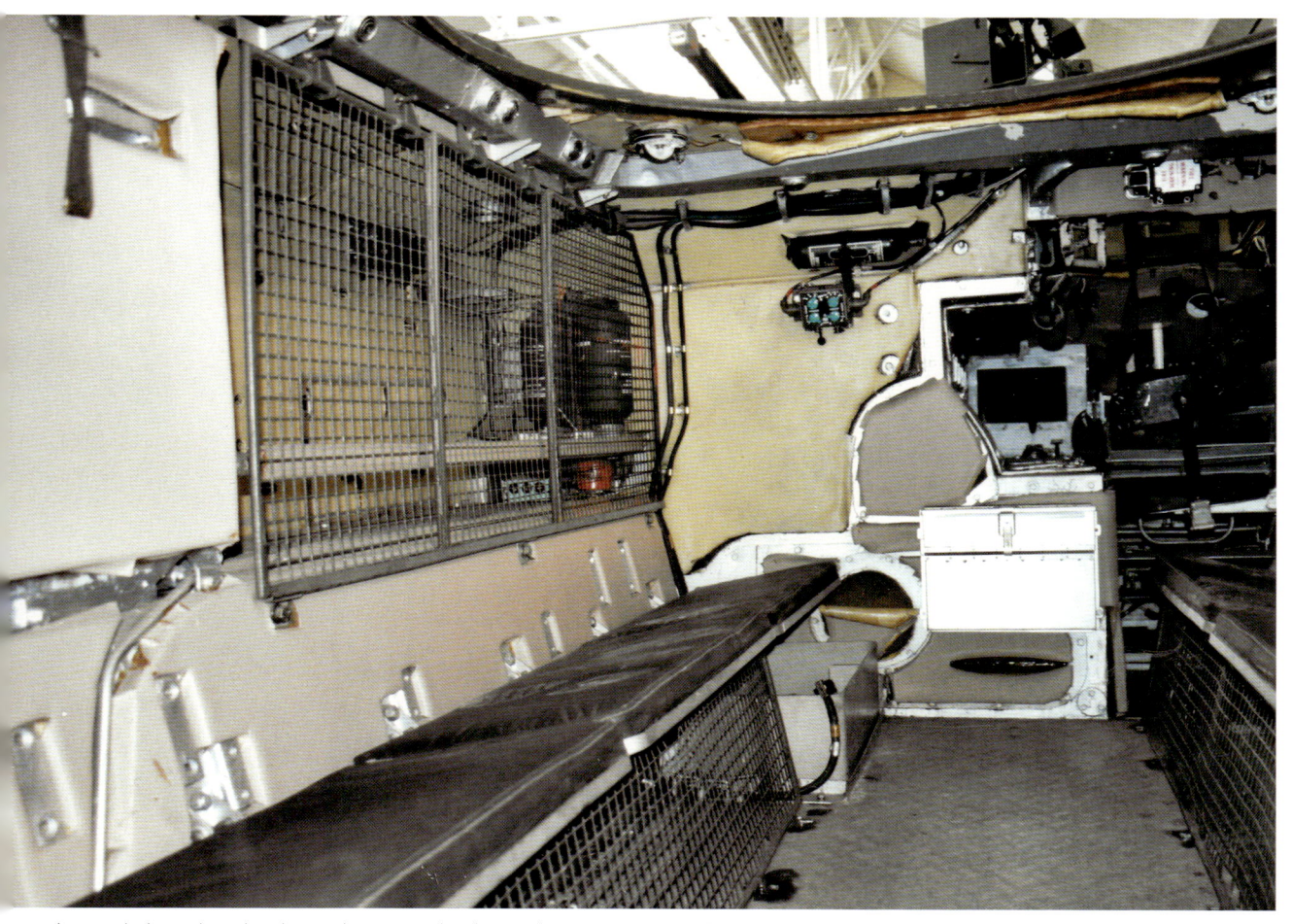

A good shot showing how the cages both on the sponsons and under the seats are fitted. *(Rob Griffin)*

Straight from being rebuilt, this power pack is awaiting fitment into its new home.
(Rob Griffin)

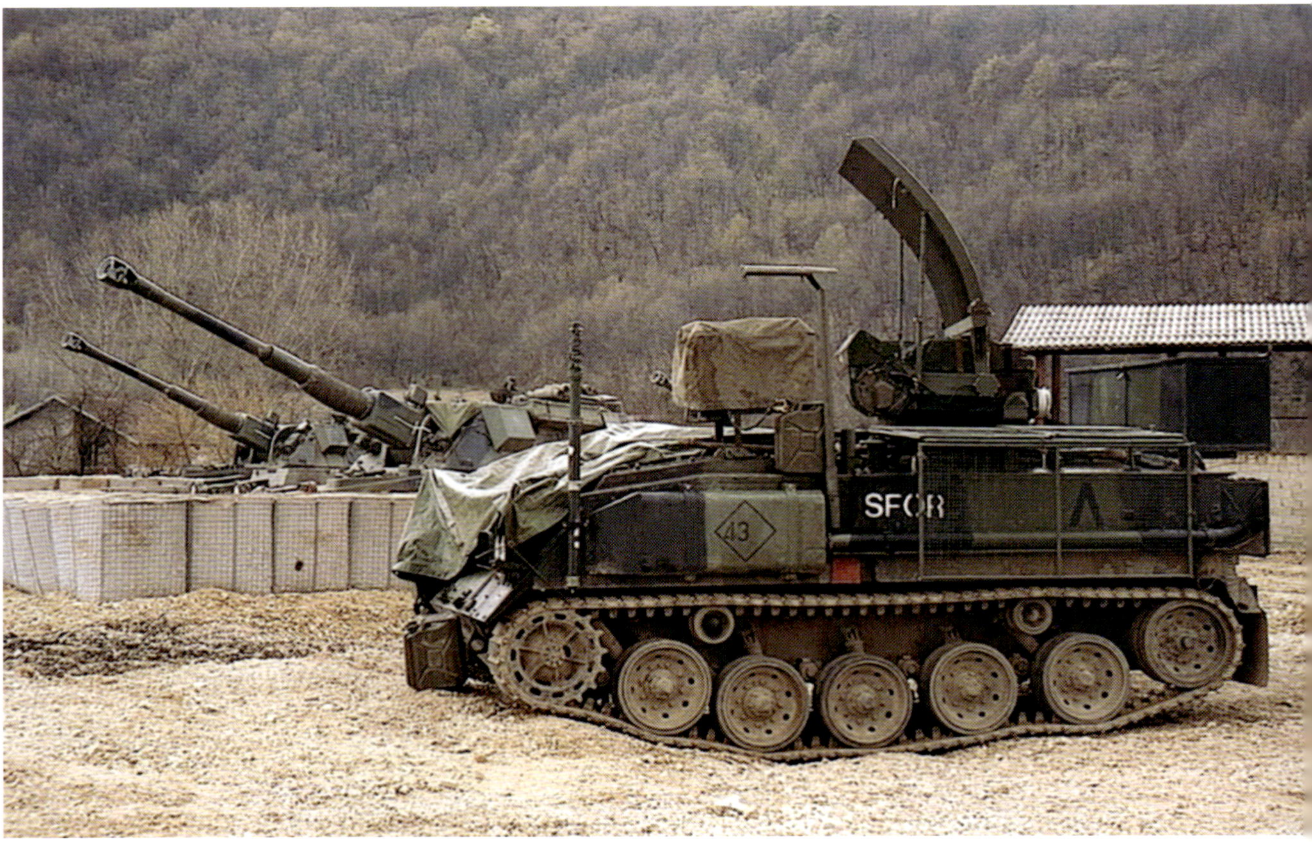
SFOR
43

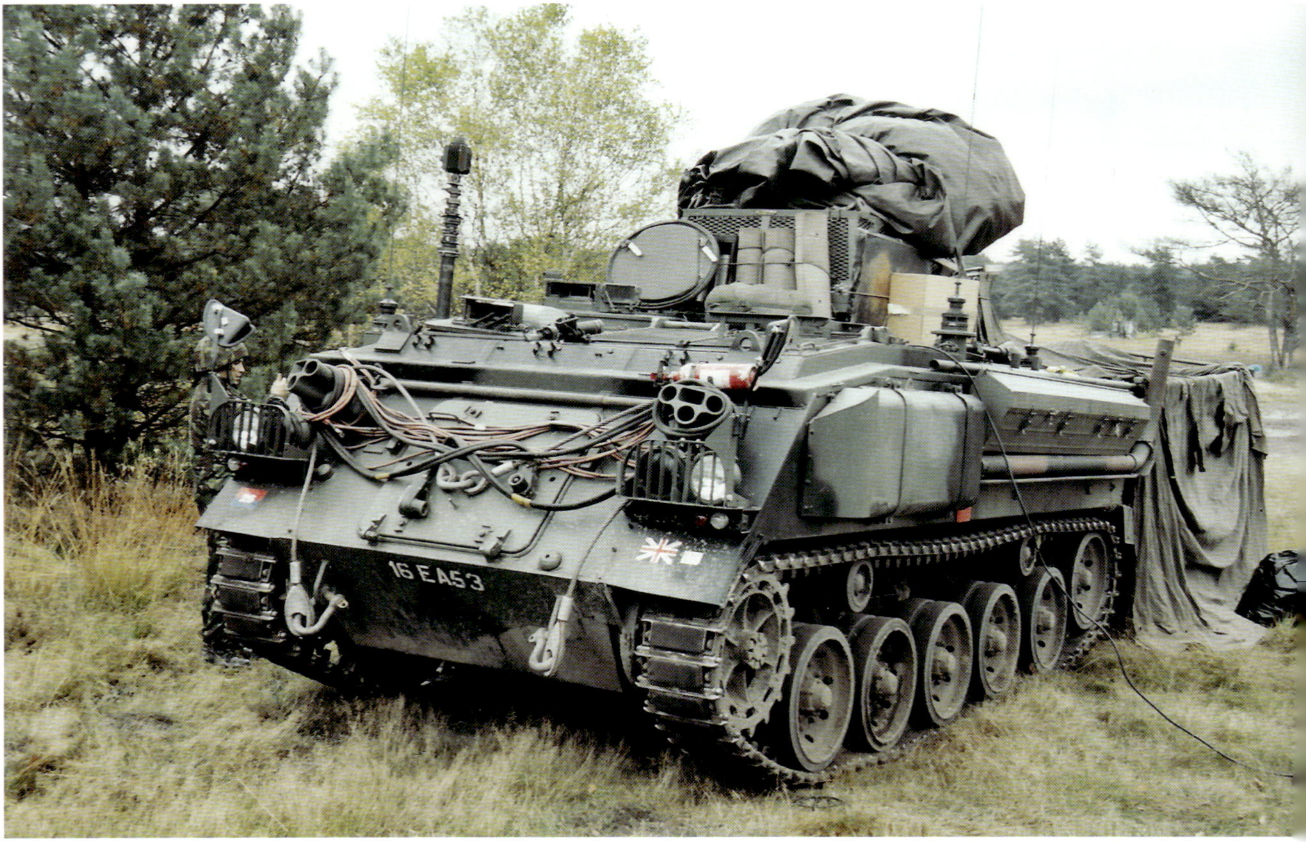
16 EA 53

(**Opposite, above**) Cymbeline mortar locating vehicle working in close conjunction with AS90 SPG. Once Cymbeline has a firing solution, that will be passed to the guns and then counter fire will be launched, this can take place very quickly, which surprised the belligerents in Bosnia. (*Author's collection*)

(**Above**) Although taking place on a privately owned vehicle, the principles of a pack lift are the same. In this shot the pack is slowly being lifted from its location while the steering box can be seen behind the open cover. (*Author's collection*)

(**Opposite, below**) It seems as if this vehicle has managed to include the kitchen sink. It only goes to illustrate the amount of equipment and personal kit taken on exercise or operations, Notice the mast on the front right; fitted to the top is a VHF pot which shows this vehicle is fitted with Clansman working VHF radios. (*Author's collection*)

Chapter Three

Trials and Service

Once a vehicle design has been proposed and it seems that it has potential then a full-size wooden mock up is produced; from photographs, some of the mock-ups are totally realistic. Quite often they will have some components fitted to them to give an idea of the layout. However, just because a design has made it to this stage it does not mean it will go any further and British Armoured Vehicle development is littered with projects that fell at the first fence.

After viewing a mock-up, the various interested parties may well request various changes to be made. These always come down to a compromise due to cost or requirements. If we could all have what we wanted in a vehicle it would be very large and heavy. Once the final design has been approved then an order for several pilot models will be placed, and this will not necessarily be with the company that will build the production vehicles. These pilot vehicles will be used to test all aspects of the new vehicle. Some may be designated as firing vehicles (if fitted with weapons) and will spend most of the time on the range testing all the weapon systems and, importantly, letting the user try to create a handbook for each item of equipment. Some vehicles will be used for mileage tests and others will be used for assessing cross-country performance. Often the automotive test will use a similar vehicle to provide a datum to work from. One or two vehicles will have a most unglamorous trial period: they will be designated for firing trials, as the target not the firing vehicle.

The next stage will be to evaluate all the data from the trials and review the design to see if any major changes are required. Once this has been done then prototype models will be built and issued to the user for what is known as user trials. Some of these will be carried out by units who will one day receive the vehicle, while more thorough testing will be carried out by individual corps units such as ATDU at Bovington and the ITDU at Warminster. The results of these trials are perhaps the most important as sometimes the user may have a different outlook on the layout of a vehicle or its requirements. That is not to say that they are left out of the design process at the beginning, it's just that once the vehicle is there in the flesh and blood some things take on a different aspect.

Once the trials are over and the design is finally confirmed the tender will go out for production of the vehicle and as always the best bid wins. These days though the government is asking the builder to provide a set period of time for support and training as part of a full package; the contract for Challenger 2 was the first major contract awarded in this style.

The document WO351/4 gives details of the troop trial reports of the new vehicle and also the vehicles used in the trial. They were all fitted with the Rolls Royce gear box and the following vehicles were used: 03 DA 05 W9, 03 DA 07 W11, 03 DA 08 W12, 03 DA 11 W 15 (CV) and 03 DA 21 W5.

The trials were carried out by the 1st Battalion Royal Ulster Rifles supported by LAD 5 infantry workshops REME. The trial period covered January to March 1962 and five vehicles were used, plus Centurion and Saracen as comparison vehicles. It was found that driver fatigue was less than in the Saracen and Centurion. Forward visibility was found to be good but that to the rear was poor, although the latter is not so important in an AFV where reverse is usually controlled by the commander. The location of the dipswitch (on the instrument panel) was thought to be dangerous as it meant that on road moves at night the driver would constantly be taking his hands away from the control to operate it; the preferred location was on the floor, which is where it was for civilian cars at the time.

These vehicles did not have a wipe or wash facility on the driver's sight; mud covered them as can be imagined and it is surprising the problems something as simple as mud can cause. Track pads were a problem and 612 were lost during the trials. During closed-down operations 25 per cent of passengers felt nausea and headaches while mobile; this disappeared when opened up again. Trials also covered closed-down static, for 24 hours with little physical activity, but this seemed to cause no adverse effect mentally. In the end it was felt that familiarity with the vehicle would solve a lot of the headache problems.

Seating was generally felt to be good but problems arose if troops were wearing 58-pattern webbing with kidney pouches (these are right at the rear of the belt near the kidneys hence the nickname). None of the trial vehicles were fitted with heaters and it was felt that this was a requirement (not till the Balkans war did this arise, a mere forty years later). Debussing was via the single large rear door which was felt to be cumbersome and should have a better system fitted, especially as if the vehicle was stopped on a forward slope it was hard to push the door open and could be dangerous.

At the end of the trial the users were very enthusiastic about the FV432 and recommended it should be brought into service once the three main problem areas were rectified, these being track pin and pad unreliability, replacing the Lucas fan system, and reducing external noise.

It then was found that serious cracks up to 50mm long had occurred in W9 and W15 and also later in W11 and 12. This was investigated in full and a conclusion was reached that it would not be a problem with the production vehicles although checks would be made to ensure that the cracks did not reoccur.

One other aspect that sometimes is overlooked when studying armoured vehicles is the problem of bodily functions when closed down for a long time and like it or not these are just not going to disappear. When you are confined in a small space with up to ten of your comrades, this is where friendships can be placed under great strain! During the trial period the crew were not permitted to carry out any such functions in the FV432. It was thought that a hole in the floor through which a pipe could be fed attached to a funnel would be sufficient and would protect the NBC seal. For defecation it was suggested that a fibreglass seat could be built using disposable tie-neck bags. This in a similar form is what is used for the CVR(T) series, while Warrior goes one better and has one of the crew seats fitted with a removable centre section that covers an inbuilt chemical toilet.

It was also felt that the driver should have a boom mike or a throat mike that could be switched to 'live' and then back to normal thus freeing up his hands for driving, as the current audio equipment consisted of a headset and hand-operated microphone; this would come with the introduction of Clansman radios.

The report numbered WO 189/132 covered a trial on the effect of attack by HE and chemical weapons on the FV432. In the period April-October 1965 trials were carried out to see if the effect of HE bombs or shells would affect the overpressure system employed on FV432 and the effectiveness of the filters used. One concern was that an explosion might be great enough to force agents through the normal gaps that would be found in the vehicle but normally protected by the overpressure system. To test the system, experimental HE bombs with GB (nerve agent) were exploded at various positions outside the vehicle and the measure of agent was taken both inside and outside. The vehicle was tested both in the pressurised mode and unpressurised. For all tests dummy soldiers were used to crew the vehicle. All available types of filters currently on issue to the FV432 were tested in several combinations. It was found that with the vehicle fully closed down and both types of filter fitted the protection was high, although it showed that the air inlet was a weak spot. The end conclusion was that the over-pressure system was most effective at preventing leakage through the normal fissures mentioned. One side effect from the bombs was noticed and that was the damage sustained to the rubber aerial bases. It was felt that if one of those were blown completely away it would offer a route for the entry of chemical agents.

FV432 went through many different trials for acceptance and these trials were carried out in cold and hot climates as both give different problems to the vehicle and to the user. In the period 8–30 March 1966, 10 EA 95, 10 EA 94 and 03 EA 85 took part in trials in what was then the British protectorate of Aden. One purpose of the trials was to test radio communications in desert areas, but more appropriate to the vehicles as regards maintenance was the trial of a graphite grease dispenser, which was meant to automatically lubricate all those components that required grease. It failed the trial, as it required too much pressure to operate and it was found just as effective to have a crewman carry out servicing using a standard issue grease gun. The vehicles however managed to acquit themselves well in the hot sandy conditions.

One trial which must have been spectacular, no matter what the outcome, was the attempt to improve the FV430 series' exit from water obstacles. This was covered in the report WO 194/1009 Assisted Egress from Water by FV432. The trials took place in March 1963 and ran through till June 1963. The aim was to test the theory of using rockets to assist the vehicle exiting from water obstacles. To do this the vehicle was equipped with Starling 2 series A rockets producing 2,400lbs of thrust. These burnt for only three seconds with an almost instantaneous build-up of power on firing. They were located on two positions forward of the hull and one on the rear. Up to five rockets were also tried fitted to the belly plate. Twenty-five runs were made with rockets in varying different locations, with correction rockets fitted for some runs to try and keep the vehicle travelling in a straight line. One aspect was that the driver's ears suffered from the noise despite having hearing protection and this was a matter for concern as it meant that perhaps a new headset design would have to be produced. Successful operation of the system was dependent on the vehicle maintaining its water speed as it touched the bank. Also it was required to change into 1–2 range as soon as the vehicle touched the bank, so a part-time juggler might well have made a good driver. The vehicle had to have an extended periscope fitted so that the driver could see the bank, as no forward vision was available with the flotation screen erected. Drivers were encased in wetsuit, mask and helmet with transistorised telephone. It was felt that many of the problems with judging distance could be overcome by training, although it was appreciated that the required amount of training would never be available due to other restraints of training within the various units, and not least the cost of the rockets themselves. The final conclusion reached was that while it was proved that rocket assistance could help overcome the obstacles that were beyond the normal capability of the vehicle, the control of the rockets was affected too much by the human factor, i.e. the control of firing the rockets by the driver. This and the expense of purchasing the rocket meant that the project was not accepted. One other aspect of the rocket trials that seemed to have been ignored was the tactical limitations to the use of the system in the dark hours. One can just imagine enemy troops overlooking a river in darkness, when all of a sudden the mother of all firework displays lights up their front. Would they have fallen to the floor in fits of laughter or remained coherent enough to take action?

Another report, WO 194/430, covers the Adaptation of FV432 to carry Vigilant ATGW. It was felt that the guided missile would provide the lighter armed infantry troops a real chance to take on the expected masses of Soviet armour that they were trained to face.

During the mock-up stage, the user acceptance of FV432 was carried out at FVRDE during February 1960. FVRDE were requested to investigate the use of the current ATGW VIGILANT on the FV432. It was accepted that modifications to the vehicle would be required and the vehicle would be employed in three roles: direct fire, indirect and separated. It was concluded that the missile conversion kit could be supplied so that any FV432 could be converted to the role by a REME base workshop. It was to be crewed by five men: driver, commander/controller loader, assistant loader and 2nd controller. Eighteen missiles were to be carried plus two in the launcher and the remainder under armour. Vigilant had a range of 1,500 yards with a minimum of 200 yards; time of flight to max range, 12 seconds.

The mortar hatches would be removed and the space used to house the launching assembly. This consisted of a circular plate carrying a rack and roller support path. Three or more roller units would be attached to the underside of the vehicle's fixed roof to support the plate and allow it to traverse by means of a simple hand traverse mechanism. Carried on the plate would be two independently operable armoured launch boxes hinged at the rear and part balanced by torsion bars. Each box would contain one Vigilant missile in its own carry box. The box would be placed into the launch box by the loader once the front and rear closure lids had been removed.

In the up position the armoured box provides protection for the missile box inside it. The rear of the box seals the hole in the mounting plate thus providing continuity of the NBC seal. On raising the box a flap at the rear opens automatically to allow the venting of the rocket motor gases. Once the missile has been fired the box would be lowered and the empty container removed by the loader before fitting another one.

The controller's sight was the one item it was felt would need most development. A controller system was proposed, either the 'Tommy Gun' version (so called because it resembled the famous gun and something very similar was used by the commander of Rapier) or a special in-vehicle version. This was the preferred option, with the Tommy gun version being used in the remote role. There were no requirements for any specialised electrical services to supply power for Vigilant, which made the conversion easier.

It was noted that Vigilant was similar in size to the proposed Swingfire missile then being developed and it was felt that a similar launcher for Swingfire could be produced or maybe one standard launcher that would take both missiles, although this was not certain at the time. The report also points out that the Swingfire missile mentioned had no connection to the well-known Swingfire heater unit that was a commercial item at the time!

In the end the conversion was abandoned in favour of the FV438 fitted with Swingfire, but as the reader will see in the description of the FV438 later many similarities exist between the vehicles. This was a wise decision as Vigilant had a short range compared to Swingfire which could engage targets out to ranges of 4,000 metres.

One aspect of the FV430 that was not popular was the exposed position of the commander when using the pintle-mounted machine gun. During 1966 a trial was carried out at FVRDE at Chobham to design and introduce a cupola for the FV430 commander. As we will see later the REME actually did this in Aden but this was classed as a local modification whereas the FVRDE cupola would have been an issue item.

The cupola was to be designated the Cupola AFV No. 16; it was primarily designed for the FV430 series but could also be adapted to the Saracen, Ferret Mk 2 and the American M113. It had all-round vision in the form of periscopes, which were inclined away from the cupola to prevent the sun glinting from them. It was armed with a 7.62mm GPMG, either the L7 or L8 version, and is mounted on the outside of the cupola looking as if it is a pintle-mounted weapon. Having the gun outside means that there was no chance of toxic gas entering the vehicle, a rather forward-looking idea for the period. With an elevation of −10 to +45 degrees the machine gun is traversed and elevated by hand-operated mechanisms. It is sighted by means of a unit power periscopic sight coupled to the elevating linkage. Periscope wipers and washers are provided for use in inclement weather. The really good feature of the cupola is that the gun may be cocked and any stoppages cleared from under armour – a very desirable feature that is not included in many vehicles and was only considered in the failed 21 cupola for Chieftain. Incorporated within the firing circuit is a sensing switch that will cut off the electrical supply when only a set number of rounds are remaining. This, when activated, will leave sufficient rounds hanging in the cupola enabling the commander to attach a fresh belt to the remaining links before carrying on firing. Sadly any remaining photographs of the cupola are of poor quality.

The cupola itself is made of armoured steel with all vertical walls 16mm thick and all horizontal plates 13mm thick. The gunner is carried around when the turret is traversed by means of a seat attached to the turret ring. Fitting the cupola does not affect the integrity of the NBC seal.

The first production cupola was due to be fitted in December 1967, but the project was cancelled and thus the commanders of FV430 vehicles lost a good piece of equipment. The reasons for the cancellation are vague but cost is mentioned and also there is a hint that it would be too complicated for the infantry, a slur that it took the introduction of Warrior to kill.

Due to the cost of producing modern AFVs it is in the interest of the producing country to sell as many as possible. One contender for purchasing the FV432 was Australia. Due to the very close relationship between the UK and Australia they were asked to comment on projects. One such project was the WOPS 26 common user tracked vehicle policy; this was of interest to Australia as it was looking for a new APC to replace its White halftracks and Saracens. Other countries were also producing or looking to produce similar vehicles, with Canada working on the ill-fated Bobcat and the USA on the M113. In June 1960 Australia issued its WEPS 26 (weapons and equipment policy) which was similar to the UK WOPS 26. This document firmly laid down the Australian requirements for a new APC. A direct consequence of WEPS 26 was a signal to the Australian Army representative in London enquiring on how soon a Trojan APC (as it still was called then) could be supplied and how long before bulk supply could commence. The DRAAC considered that a prototype vehicle would be better as the purchase quantity vehicles would need modifications to them to bring them to the Australian required standard. The British Director General of Fighting Vehicle was sympathetic to the Australian case to carry out trials and once Trojan had finished its UK trials it was intended to pursue trials in other climates. Given previous co-operation on other projects Australia would provide ideal conditions to test the vehicle in hot-wet and hot-dry climates.

The Australians for several reasons agreed this but the main one I think was that it saved them from purchasing a vehicle and thus two prototype Trojans were shipped to Australia in September 1962. In contrast the purchase of two production M113s from America was very simple and straightforward. A request to the American government and payment of US$25,000 each and the vehicles arrived in Australia in October 1962, thus setting the scene for the evaluation of the British FV432 and the American M113.

The trials would be conducted by a specially formed unit of the Australian Army, No. 5 Tropical Trials Unit (5TTU). The area to be used was the hot-dry trial area at Mount Isa in central Queensland and for the hot-wet trial, the Innisfail area north of the Queensland coastal zone. The automotive road trial would use the road between the two areas for their part of the trial. The FV432 that were sent were 03 DA 10 and 03 DA 17, which with the benefit of hindsight were not the best to have sent as they still had the original hanging from the roof steering and not the production steering levers.

Of interest on the shipping of the vehicles, the FV432s arrived on the SS *Iberic* in more or less good condition but due to poor seals on the mortar hatch, seawater had accumulated in the crew area and had caused some deterioration of the interior. In contrast the arrival of the M113s on the SS *Monterey* were in perfect condition. The vehicles were initially sent to Bulimba for crew training then by rail flats to Innisfail. The trials commenced with the road move from Mount Isa to Innisfail, a total distance of 1,100km. The road had some stretches of bitumen but was a mostly dirt road. When not using the tarmac road, clouds of fine dust followed the journey. Part of the trial consisted of physiological testing where the crews would spend long periods of closed down operations during a 32km circuit. Once this phase had been completed the vehicle then returned to Innisfail again by road but this time loaded to their full combat weight.

The hot-wet phase was conducted in jungle terrain about 34km west of Innisfail. Both vehicles managed to negotiate the circuit until it started to rain when first the FV432 struggled to negotiate the inclines and then eventually all the vehicles struggled. The FV432 drivers complained of lack of power to their vehicles. One indication of the difference between the two types was during the crossing of an extremely boggy area. The M113 attempted it and crossed successfully, followed by one of the FV432s, which immediately became bogged. This was followed by the second FV432, which also became well and truly stuck. To add insult to injury the last M113 passed both stuck vehicles and successfully crossed the area.

During transit through the jungle the M113 had the edge over the FV432 by the virtue of having no projections on its hull side. The 432 with its NBC filter box suffered damage during this phase including the external fuel tanks; both types had great problems with aerial breakages at this time. To ascertain the deterioration of the vehicle in jungle, both types were left for fourteen days, with two covered in canvas and two left to the elements. On examination both M113s were dry inside and had not suffered due to the time in the jungle. The same could not be said for the FV432 with water accumulating inside due to no drainage system to remove it. The 432 that had been left uncovered suffered an accumulation of leaves and twigs in the air intake, which caused the vehicle to start to overheat later on.

During the limited swampy area trial, one of the M113s sank so far that its roof was underwater and it took the combined efforts of the other three APCs, an M543 wrecker and a bulldozer to extricate it. The flotation trials were carried out in Mourilyan harbour with one type of each vehicle loaded to combat weight. Preparations for the M113 were simple and quickly carried out whereas those on the 432 took longer. This was due to the fact that the 432 had to erect the flotation screen whereas the aluminium hulled M113 had natural buoyancy. Once in the water the 432 was the faster of the two but it was felt this was outweighed by the fact the driver could not see where he was going due to the screen. The screen also had problems in that it was easily holed and also caused problems when trying to leave the water again due to lack of visibility.

Entrance and exit from the vehicle was tested by a platoon of fully equipped infantry. It was found that the full width hydraulically operated rear ramp of the M113 allowed two men at a time to exit, as opposed to the single narrow door of the 432. Also on entering the M113 the infantry just walked up the ramp but on the 432 they had to climb into it. It had become clear that the FV432 was not suitable for use by the Australian Army and the winner was the M113. Other factors against the 432 were the continual problems with its tracks and the high load of servicing it. Areas where the 432 was considered better included the interior padding, the forced air ventilation system was considered an advantage, but other problems such as the steering levers were not popular and caused blistering of the drivers' hands. The M113 had vertical steering levers, which were popular and would eventually be fitted to the FV432. It was concluded that with modifications the FV432 could be operated in a hot-dry climate but would not be so suitable in hot-wet area. The final mileage for the FV432s was W14 (03 DA 170 4,752km and W1 (03 DA 10) covered 5,003km. On 16 May 1963 the FV432s were loaded onto the Port Launceston for their journey back to FVRDE in England with their Australian crews glad to see them go.

W1 (03 DA 10) later was used in the development of the Swingfire equipped version of the 432, the FV438, then later it was designated as a hard target and sat on the range quietly rusting away after an eventful career. The end result meant that Australia purchased the American M113 instead of the FV432, leaving India as the only other country to employ the vehicle and that only as a command post to control its Abbot self-propelled guns.

The report of November 1986 covered the camouflage set for vehicles. This was the new equipment that consisted of a set of very flexible poles made from carbon fibre, a thermal cam net and thermal cam woodland, which is a plastic sheet that is used to cover the vehicle to provide a thermal screen. The original trial had been carried out by 4 Armoured Division in BAOR and as a result recommended that the kit be brought into service.

The trial was to see what difficulty an infantry crew in FV432 would encounter erecting the system. The vehicles used were an Mk 1 and an Mk 2 432; only the commander and driver were used for the actual task. This involved carrying out the task by day and then by night under normal operating conditions. They first of all had to hammer special pegs into the ground; these pegs had locations for the carbon fibre poles to be fixed into. The poles were then assembled to make a frame and fitted into the pegs. The thermal reflecting sheets were then attached to the vehicle and finally the net pulled over the framework. This is a better system than the old way of just draping the net over a vehicle as it allows you to form almost like a garage, so that if required the vehicle can be driven in and out. At the end of the trial it took the two crewmen 25 minutes to erect the system during the day and 35 minutes during the hours of darkness

The second part of the trial was to prove that the system could be mounted on the vehicle. It was felt that creating a garage was possibly fine for some arms but the ITDU felt that the priority for an infantry vehicle was to camouflage up as quickly as possible. To achieve this, six mounts were made to receive the poles and were mounted one at each corner and one either side of the centre line. The system proved a lot quicker with times of 18 minutes for day and 30 minutes for night.

Results of the trial proved that the thermal sheets as issued were too small for covering a basic FV432 and recommended a larger size be brought into service. It also highlighted the problem of stowing all the extra kit on an already overcrowded vehicle but the end recommendation was that the equipment be brought into service for use with infantry FV432 vehicles.

One other vehicle to be trialled was the only variant of the FV433 Abbot that was built although it never entered service. This vehicle was called Falcon, it was a standard FV433 chassis but instead of the turret containing the 105mm of the Abbot, had a special turret mounting twin 30mm Hispano-Suiza type 831L cannons. It was developed as a cost-effective vehicle to protect troops operating in the forward area against low level attack. It was provided with dual sights so the weapon system could engage air or ground targets. The guns had a rate of fire of 650 rounds per minute.

The ammunition is fed to the guns from the magazines located in the base of the turret through chutes into belt-feed mechanisms that are operated by the recoil action from the guns. All the empty case and belt links are ejected outside the vehicle, thus keeping the fighting compartment clear of empties. They are cocked and fired electrically with full automatic fire and single shot being available. The gunner was provided with a periscope gun sight and automatic lead angle display for anti-aircraft and an × 6 magnification to be used in the ground role. The commander has a similar periscope gun sight but does not have the anti-aircraft display; he also has two periscopes for normal viewing. The range data is provided for by laser ranging.

The power control system fits to the turret controls and drives the turret in traverse and the guns in elevation. This provides high speed traverse and the guns are also stabilised against vehicle movement. This means the system could be used while on the move, which would be of great advantage to the troops it was protecting. In the end the system was not adopted for various reasons, one being that it was found very hard to refill the ammunition containers easily and quickly. The actual hull of the vehicle survived and was to be found at the Vickers site in Newcastle painted yellow and has been used for many tasks while there including acting as a carrier for completed Warrior turrets.

Having looked at how the vehicle is tested before being accepted for use, let's now look at its use in service. Apart from a few specialised roles, the FV430 series can truly be called the workhorse of the British Army, serving in virtually all theatres involving tracked vehicles. As will be seen later it has been adapted for many roles and still carries out some of those today and will do until its eventual phasing out.

What is it like to travel in? Well the phrase 'pea in a pod' does spring to mind. It depends on how many are in the vehicle and the conditions that you are operating in. Nearly all the infantry 432s when working would try to travel opened up as much as they could so that the section had maximum fresh air. Travelling in them fully closed down is not a sensation for those who are claustrophobic. The noise is a constant rattle of the tracks punctuated by a change in note whenever steering is applied, coupled with the noise from the engine and smells of oil and diesel mixed up with close confines of human bodies become a bit fresh. There is also very little light apart from the cluster lights, this and the fact of the constant swaying and not being able to see where you are or even going can make for stomach churning nausea.

A few tales from ex-Lance-Corporal Arthur Graves, who at the time was a 432 ambulance driver with 29 Field Ambulance in Obernkirchen in BAOR. Arthur says that when they went on exercise the vehicle commanders were medics and the vehicle was set up either as two stretchers in an ambulance role or as a mobile MI (medical inspection) room with only one stretcher and seats on the left hand side. One of the vehicles, 07 EA 50, was fitted with an experimental heater running on petrol, this being several years before the requirement for a heater was acknowledged. In May 1968 they deployed to the Royal Engineers camp at a location outside Hameln (Hamelin of pied piper fame) called Ohr Park bridging camp. This was on the side of the River Weser, which is a very fast flowing river and is used for amphibious training for the Royal Engineers and other arms as required. Into the water was launched poor unsuspecting FV432 04 EA 82 and away it went in a flurry of foam and ribald comments. As it progressed across the river it was noticed that it seemed to be sinking, this was confirmed when it duly disappeared out of sight in mid-river, faster than a U boat in a war film. Luckily the crew escaped. Normally the engineers would send a diver down to hook up a towrope and the waterlogged vehicle would be winched back to dry land. This however was not possible due to the unusual height of the Weser at the time. It was left underwater for a week and eventually was lassoed by taking a winch rope from a Scammel recovery vehicle out and casting it into the river until it snagged on the vehicle. It was then winched up onto land where Arthur was first to get under the vehicle and fit the missing gearbox drain plug that had been left out by a certain MT sergeant, as he puts it, during pre-swim checks. Whether this was to protect the poor sergeant or not he omits to mention.

Arthur's first exercise driving FV432 was when he was attached to D Company, the Black Watch, on the Soltau training area in Germany. During a night navigation training exercise he was what is known as tail end Charlie i.e. the last vehicle. Night driving was done with the blackout switch on the driver panel on so the brake light would not come on when the brakes were used. The only light showing would be the convoy light at the rear. On having to cross a public road it was mandatory to put all lights on, then cross, and straight away turn them off again. This has the effect of blinding the drivers and leaving them with two bright spots in front of their eyes. The vehicle in front of Arthur crossed the road, turned all his lights off and then stopped, but had forgotten to turn the convoy light back on, so Arthur came shooting across the road, put his lights off and ran straight into the other vehicle. No one was injured by the accident. Arthur's vehicle damaged its buoyancy tank on the glacis plate (one reason why they were usually left behind in camp) the other vehicle suffered damage to its rear jettison tanks and lower tow eyes. These are by no means the exception and exercises always bring their fair share of damage.

An ex-Royal Signals and REME soldier John Sheen tells us of some of his exploits while working with both FV432 and FV434. He arrived at York barracks in Munster BAOR straight from training at Catterick. For a while he was the REME's driver but then the powers that be decided that all the command post FV432s in the brigade must be driven by a Royal Signals driver so John was duly 'volunteered'. He and his mate decided that this would be the end of their rather cushy present job so set out to fail. On the day of the driving test they did all they could to fail, like leaving indicators on, missing road signs and anything else that came to mind. When the QTO from the Green jackets asked the Highway Code questions they came up with the first thing they could think off. The end result of this was THEY PASSED!!! He ended up working in one of the brigade command posts.

Keith Read, ex-Gloucestershire Regiment soldier, tells of a new Second Lieutenant who on his first exercise could not work out why for four days the platoon hardly saw anyone else. It was then pointed out that you do not stand in the mortar hatches when using a prismatic compass to take a bearing. Anyone who has been taught how to use a compass will remember one of the first things they would have been taught, and that is before trying to take a bearing with the compass, move well away from any large sources of metal. I think that a FV432 certainly counts as a source of metal.

Bombardier Dave Story comments on his time on an Abbot, he says that the move to Abbots from pack howitzer was a move that he did not really want to make but the decision had been made for him:

> The change from Land Rover to an armoured vehicle was tremendous and it did have its perks, like the boiling vessel on the Abbot meant that we always had a supply of hot water and you could also cook your evening meal while on the move. This meant that if your night location was a tactical one there was no messing around lighting petrol cookers and getting shouted at for showing lights.
>
> If it was a training exercise and not ranges there always seemed to be plenty of room in the Abbot but as soon as we were due to have a range firing period the kitchen sink seemed to be stowed and there always seemed a lack of space. My pet hate was putting up the camouflage netting, it was bad enough in daytime but night was worse still. You were not supposed to show any light and make no noise. Well the Abbot must have been designed to defeat that theory as every part of it was a trap for the net; once it got caught it was no use losing your temper and tugging at it as that only made it worse. You simply had to go and crawl under the net till you found the obstruction, free the net from it and carry on, only for it to get hooked again and so the process went on till at last it was done. Then you heard the magic words de-cam we're moving.

I took part in several of what they call Exercise Medicine Man in the training area known as BATUS in Canada. We used value engineered Abbots out there and a lot of the normal kit we were used to had been removed in the value engineering. This was not too much of a problem though and we muddled through. Again camouflage nets were issued but this time they were desert ones, these are big and heavy and a pain to stow and have a backing cloth to them if I remember correctly, so we tried all sorts of tricks and devious plans to try and avoid using them, but were unsuccessful and like everyone else on the prairie we spent our time struggling with them and cursing all around.

BATUS is a large area of Alberta leased to the British to use for live firing and for your first trip it certainly is impressive. To sit on the gun line and hear the tanks call for supporting fire and actually fire live rounds instead of just simulating it is very exciting. BATUS is either hot and dusty or cold and muddy. As the exercises are designed in phases there is a break between each one and that means a trip back to the showers. This is great till you get in the truck to come back on the prairie and find that the dust kicked up by the vehicle covers you again so you look no different. The one Abbot I crewed in BATUS seemed not to want to play as it always managed to break down. So for several days we had not fired any ammunition, when we re-joined the battery there was our next allocation of ammunition, by dividing it between other guns we managed to take it all on. Next day we fired a few rounds then broke down, once we were repaired we re-joined the battery again only to find more ammunition waiting. This happened once more then we seemed to have a perfect period and disposed of the lot.

The exercises are hard and tax you but it makes you aware of what real conflict could be like. After three weeks on the prairie you come back to camp and have around five days to clean and service every vehicle and weapon before handing it all over to the advance party from the next battlegroup. Then the whole cycle starts all over again, in those days there used to be seven exercises a year but the last always fell foul of the winter so they scrapped that one.

Staying with the Royal Artillery, Jim Matthew of 19 Field Regiment says that when the regiment converted to tracks from being towed it was a major change not just of equipment but for the crews as well. To start, he found travelling in a closed down FV432 a bit claustrophobic 'and it was amazing that we were not seasick. After a while though you got used to it and the perk of having more room to fit and work the equipment was a major one for me,' he says, 'after trying to stuff it all into the rear of a Land Rover the spaciousness of the FV432 was a joy, although my infantry colleagues would probably disagree.' The crew also appreciated the luxury of the boiling vessel, and it is probably one of the better items of equipment that the Army has designed.

Camouflaging was a pet hate as well and this is probably universal through the Army and especially after they fitted 27-foot masts to our vehicle it was even worse. Jim recalls an accident caused by the nets: 'It was dark and as you know lights are really not allowed so there I am stumbling around on the top of the vehicles when I tripped and fell from the louvres and ended up being caught by my wedding ring. I was taken to hospital and was told that the ring would have to be cut off so they could treat my fingers, I protested and to my amazement they actually managed to stitch around the ring.'

In BATUS if a vehicle breaks down and cannot be recovered in time then the crew are taken away and the vehicle is left in the impact area to take its chances. So you can imagine how one infantry crew felt the next day when they came back to the vehicle to find a very neat hole drilled in both sides from a Chieftain 120mm round. That was the end of that vehicle and as far as I know it is still out on the prairie.

Prior to the first Gulf War Brigadier Richard Carey was doing a presentation of British equipment to be used. As the slide showing the 432 appeared, a German officer said, 'This must be the famous British sense of humour.' This confused Richard and he asked the German what he meant. The German said, 'Surely you do not expect us to believe that you still use such old vehicles.' Brigadier Carey replied that yes we do and to be honest we have certain affection for our old warriors.

Quite often on exercises with tanks the 432 crews do tend to be left out a bit, however one time this did not happen was during Exercise Crusader in the 1980s, at the time it was the biggest exercise of its kind and roamed over many different areas. One day my troop of tanks and a section of infantry were told to take up a position on the edge of a housing estate. We parked the tanks right on the edge in a field but the 432 crews parked next to houses, this normally provokes a furious outburst from the German owners but for one crew this did not happen. One local woman made a large flask of coffee for them and invited them in to use her bathroom and even cooked some of the rations for them. It all seems fine but the problem was the coffee, most Germans like their coffee very strong, so the crew gamely drank the flask thinking that was it, only to find another replaced it straight away. They then came round begging us to have a cup, we said just throw it away but they could not as they thought it would hurt her feelings. This went on all day, and while the rest of us had our fair share of visitors I have never seen a crew so pleased to leave a cushy location as they were that evening.

There are many more tales that could be told which could fill a book on their own but I hope that these few offerings have given the reader a feel for life in a FV432.

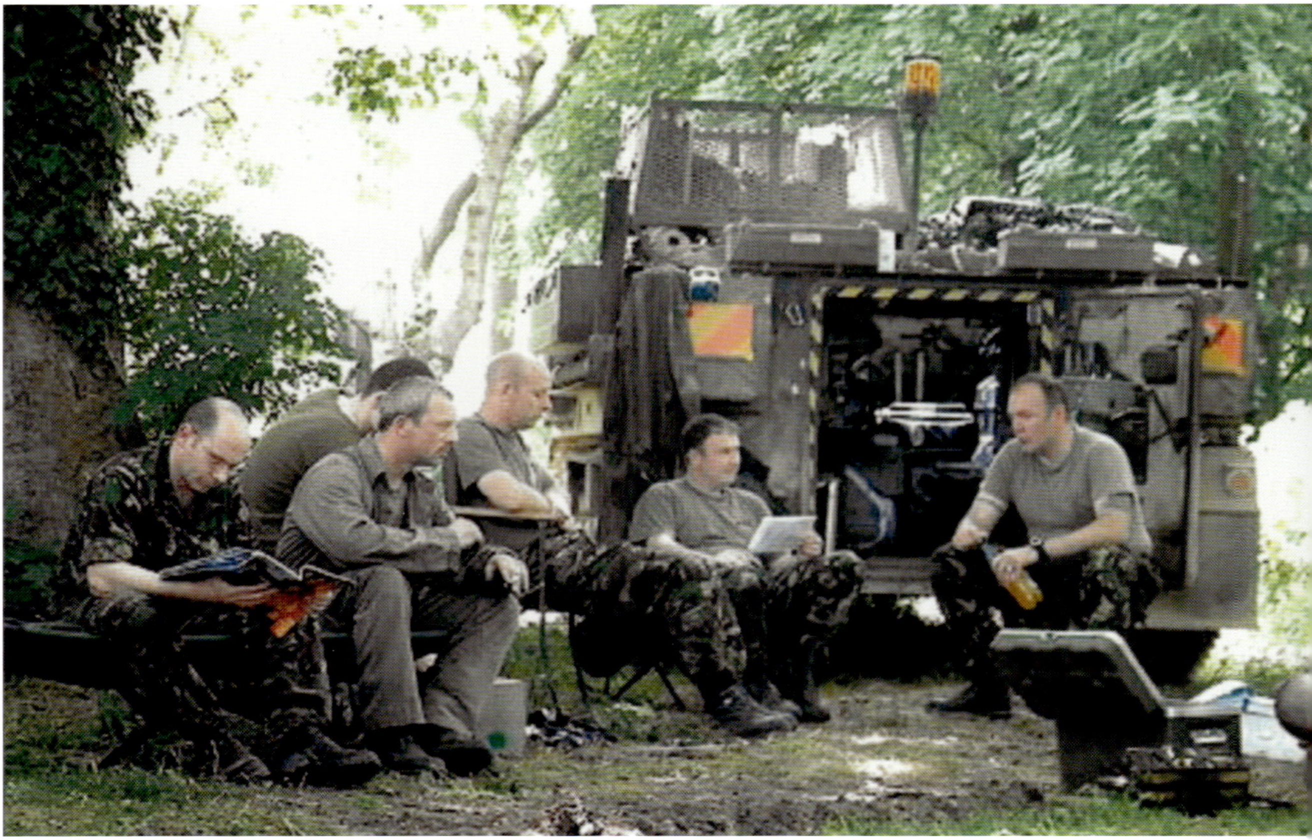

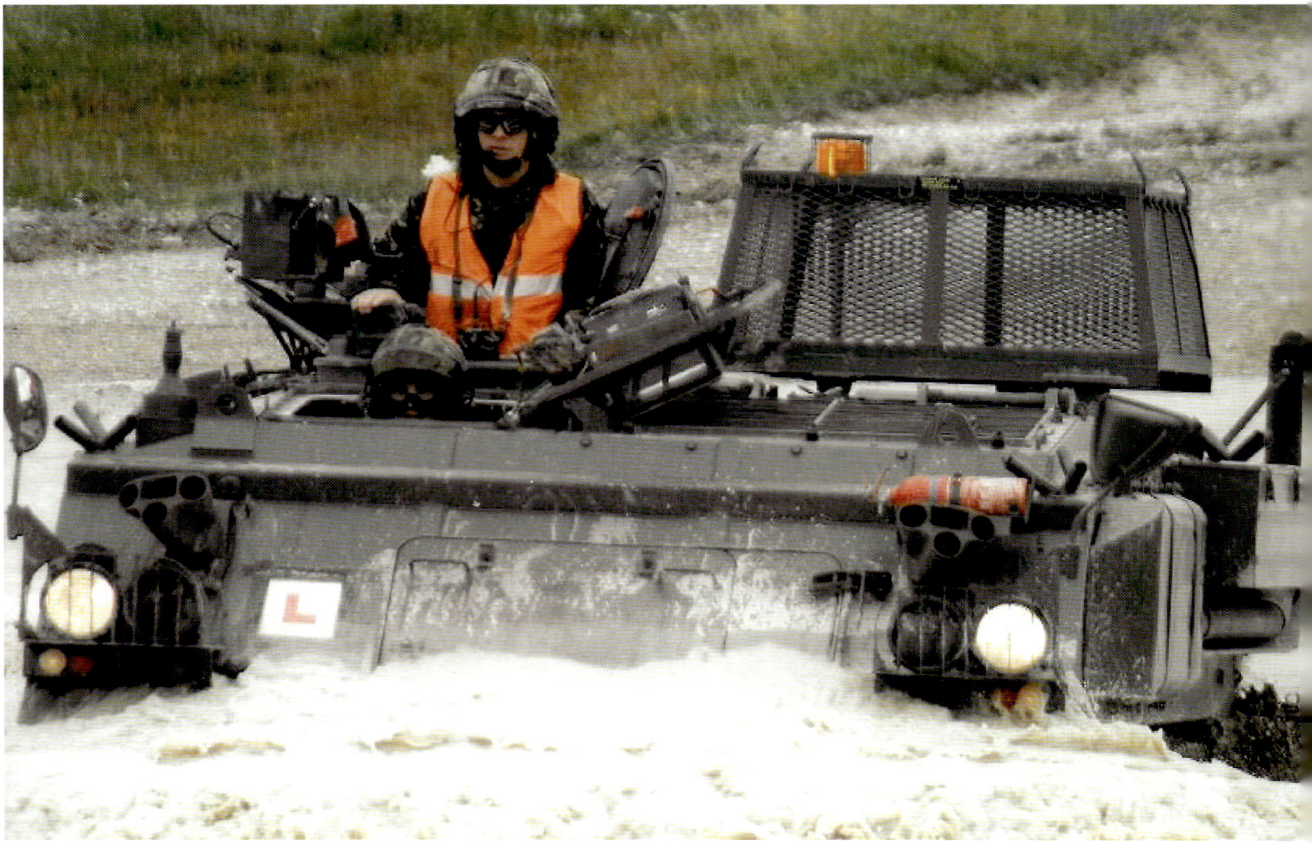
L

This crew could either be setting up or packing away. Note they have obtained a tank crew style bivvi that is fastened to the vehicle side, and in the background the BV and personal items.

(**Opposite, above**) A typical scene around the back of an FV432. This could be a briefing but looks very non-tactical with one soldier even reading a magazine. Note no personal weapons or equipment. The vehicle has the latest stowage basket and boxes.

(**Opposite, below**) Learner driver doing a deep fording drive in his FV432; when doing this, the worst thing you can do is ease off on the speed as the bow wave created will catch up with you and give you a good soaking.

(**Below**) A typical scene near any barracks in UK and more so when BAOR was active, a good plume of smoke being emitted from the exhaust.

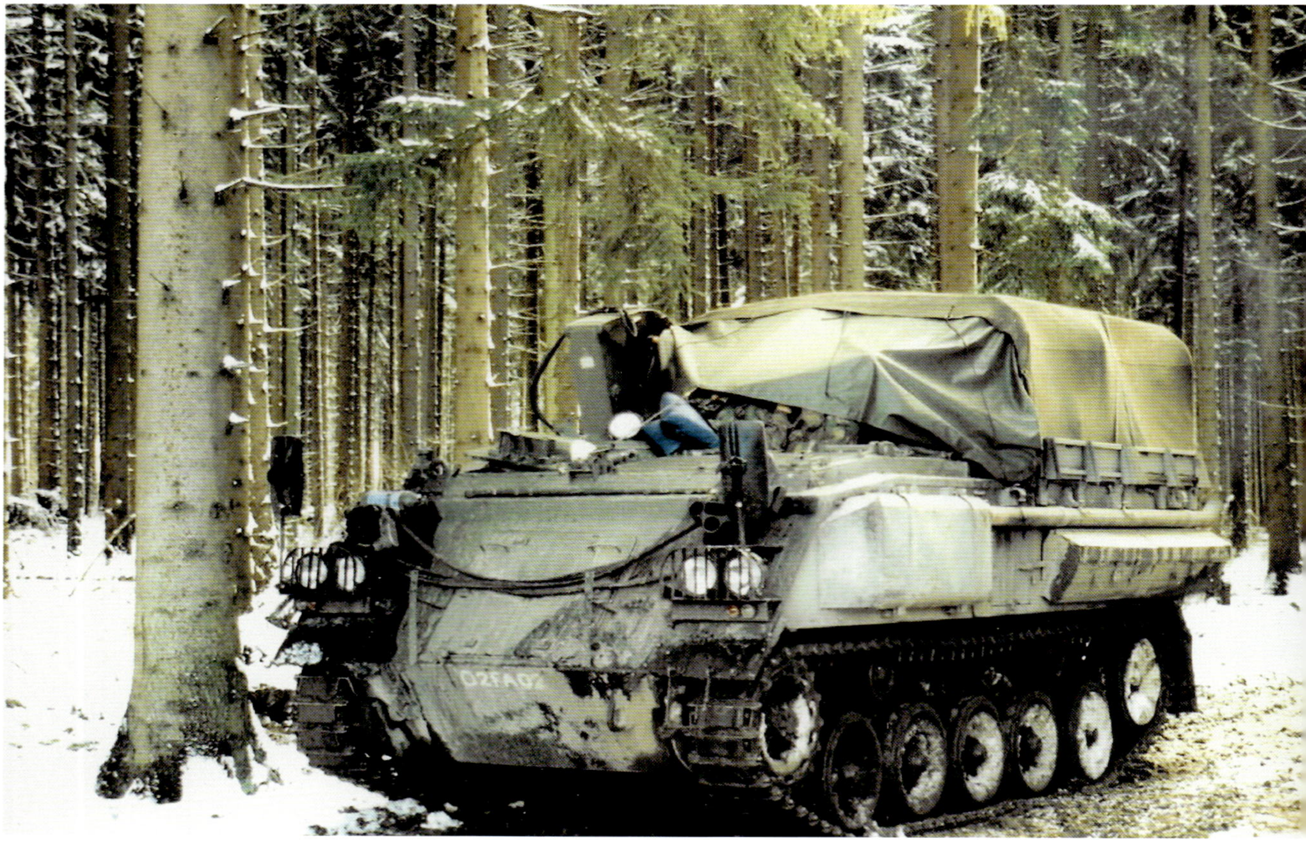

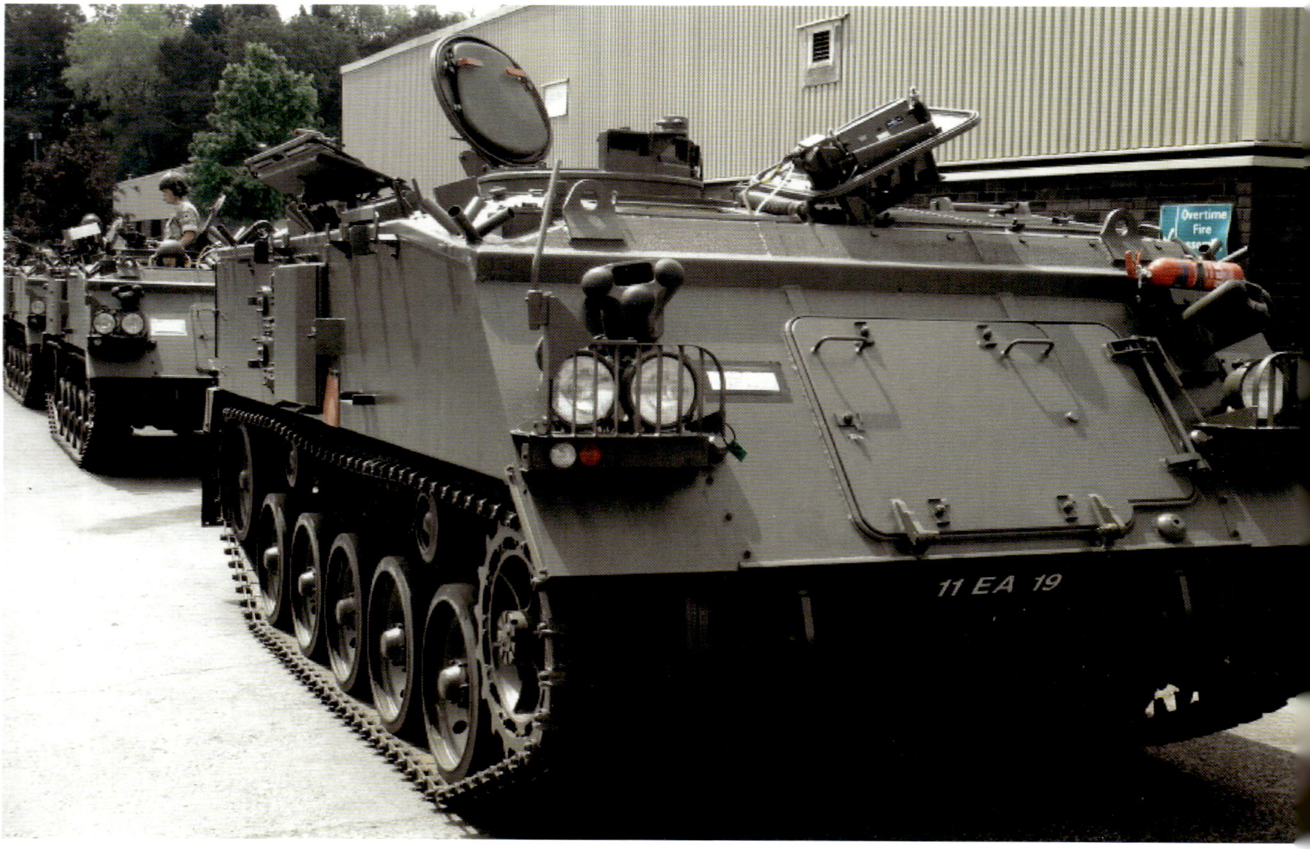
Overtime
Fire
11 EA 19

(**Opposite, above**) A typical REME FV434 variant with their trademark penthouse rigged over the load area and inside lots of home comforts.

(**Opposite, below**) A mint condition FV432 straight from the workshops at Bovington camp. Although this looks like a standard vehicle it is in fact the Mk 3, known as Bulldog, with its new power pack and transmission amongst the upgrades. A give away is the front access panel which is now in two parts.

(**Above**) Sometimes the stay in cover may be for a short time, so it would not be worth erecting camouflage nets; often a sheet is draped over the vehicle to hide its shape and cover any shine. That is just what this crew of an FV434 have done.

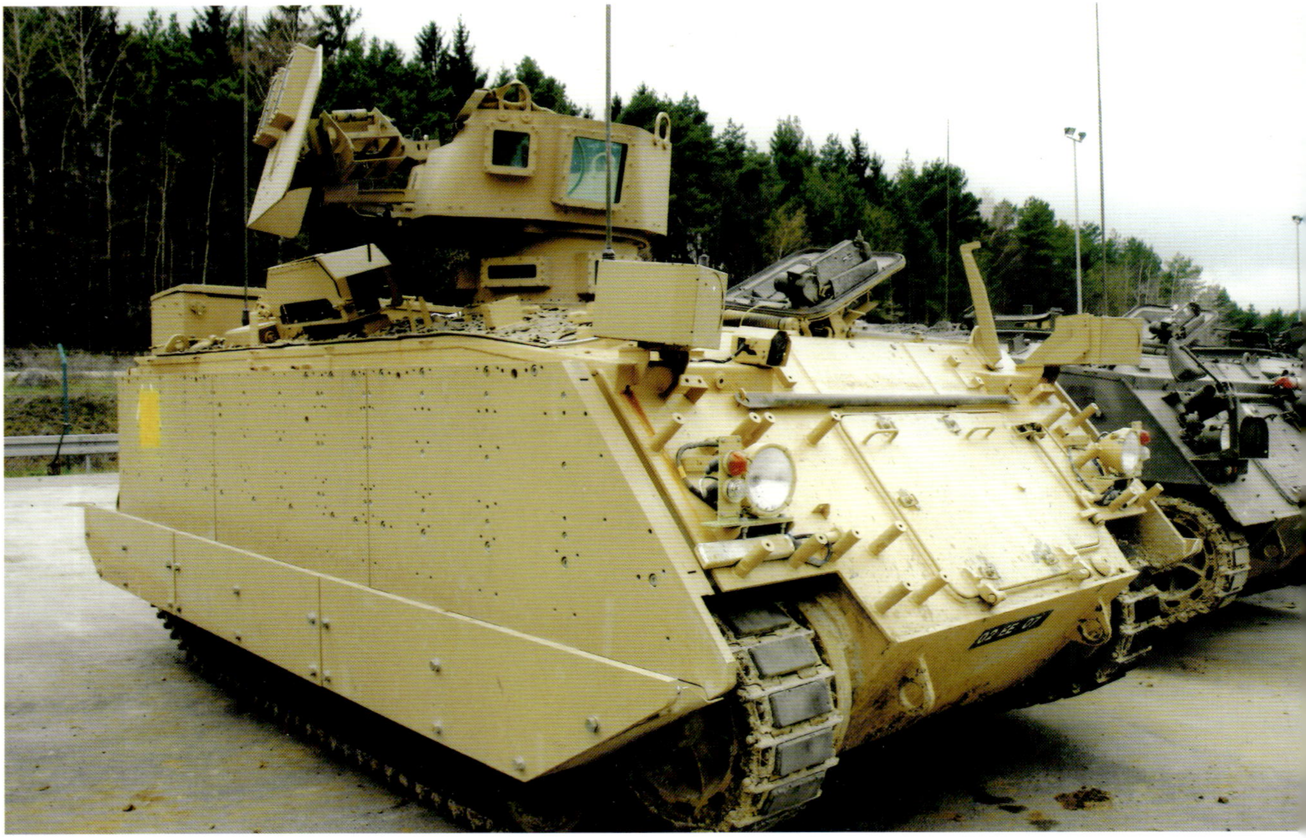

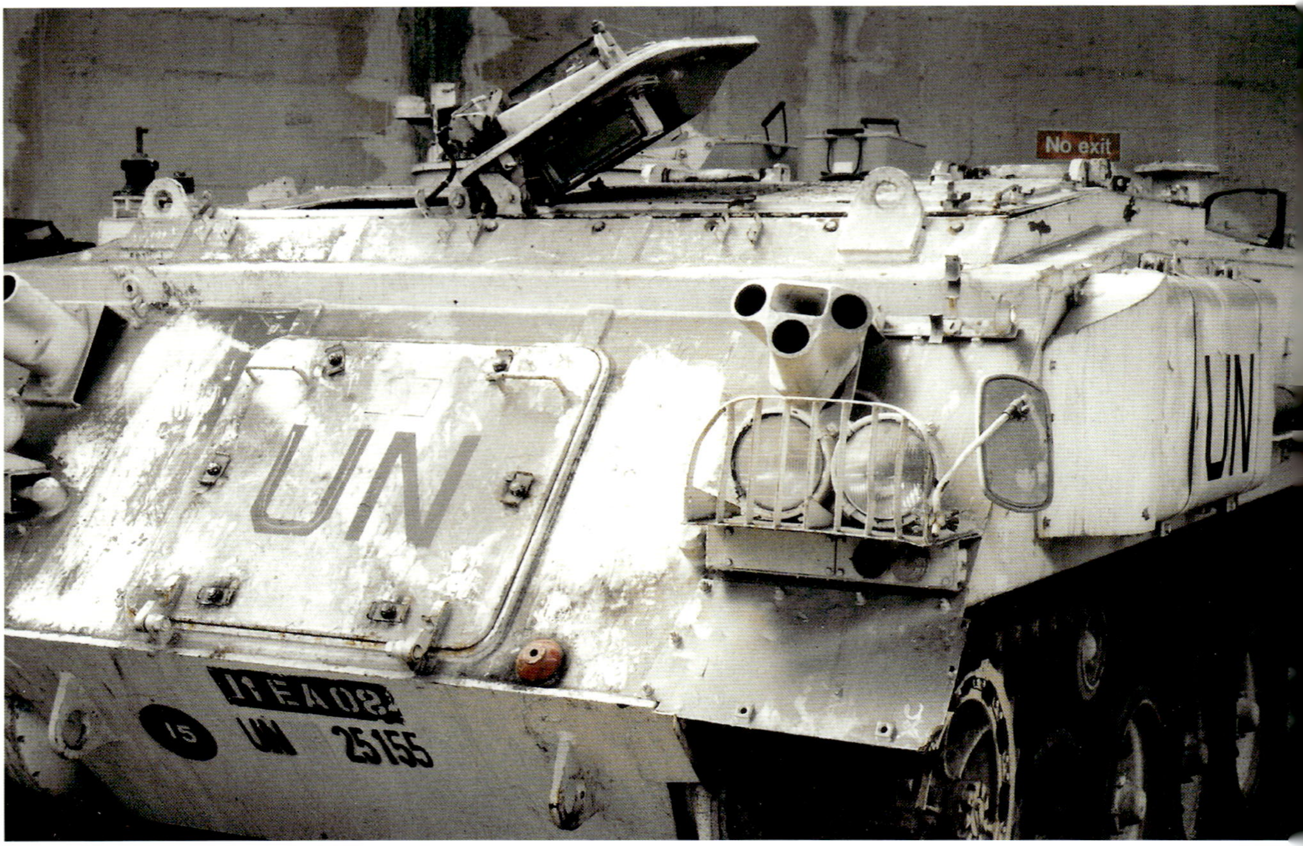
No exit
UN
UN
15
UN 25155

(**Opposite, above**) It's an FV432 but not as we know it. This is one of the variations on up-armour available to fit on the FV432. This vehicle has the full works: side armour, armoured cupola for commander, and anti IED fittings; compare it to the standard APC to its right.

(**Above**) To save on track mileage, tracked AFVs are often carried by rail, which is an easy task. The hard part is loading and unloading from the flat wagons, one mistake and the vehicle can slip off the edge, which is what has happened to this FV438 from Guide Weapons troop 4/7RDG, although they seem happy enough about it.

(**Opposite, below**) This white painted FV432 served with the UN forces in Bosnia, as can be seen it has been worked hard. Note the UN registration on the lower glacis plate.

(**Above**) This view shows how very little freeboard there was when swimming the FV432. The commander has opted to sit next to the driver to relay instructions, and also possibly to help extract him in the event of a sinking.

(**Opposite, above**) Oh dear, which lucky crew member will have to get out and attach the tow rope to the brackets which are well under water?

(**Opposite, below**) FV432 working with its running mate Challenger 2 on Salisbury Plain. Although Warrior has replaced it in the troop carrying role, FV432 still provides a lot of support to the battlegroup.

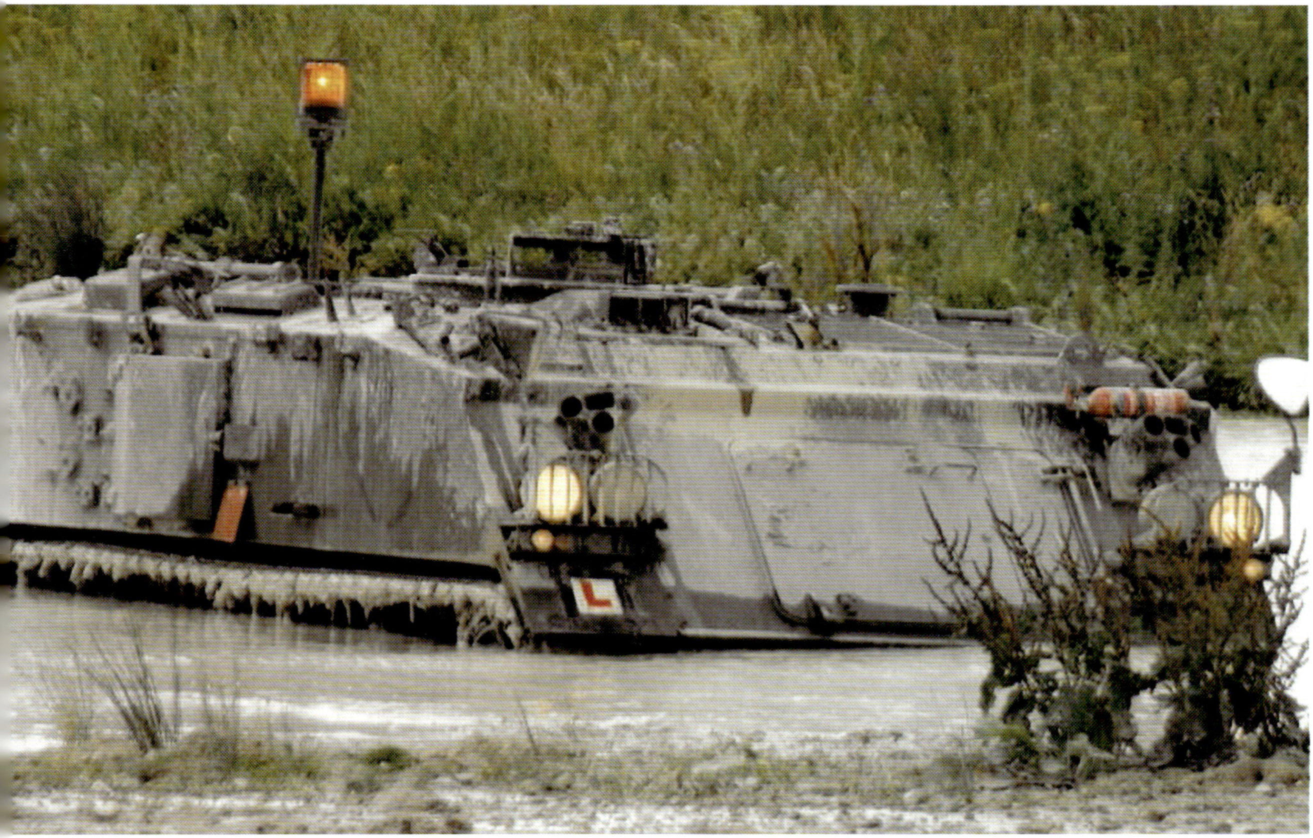
L

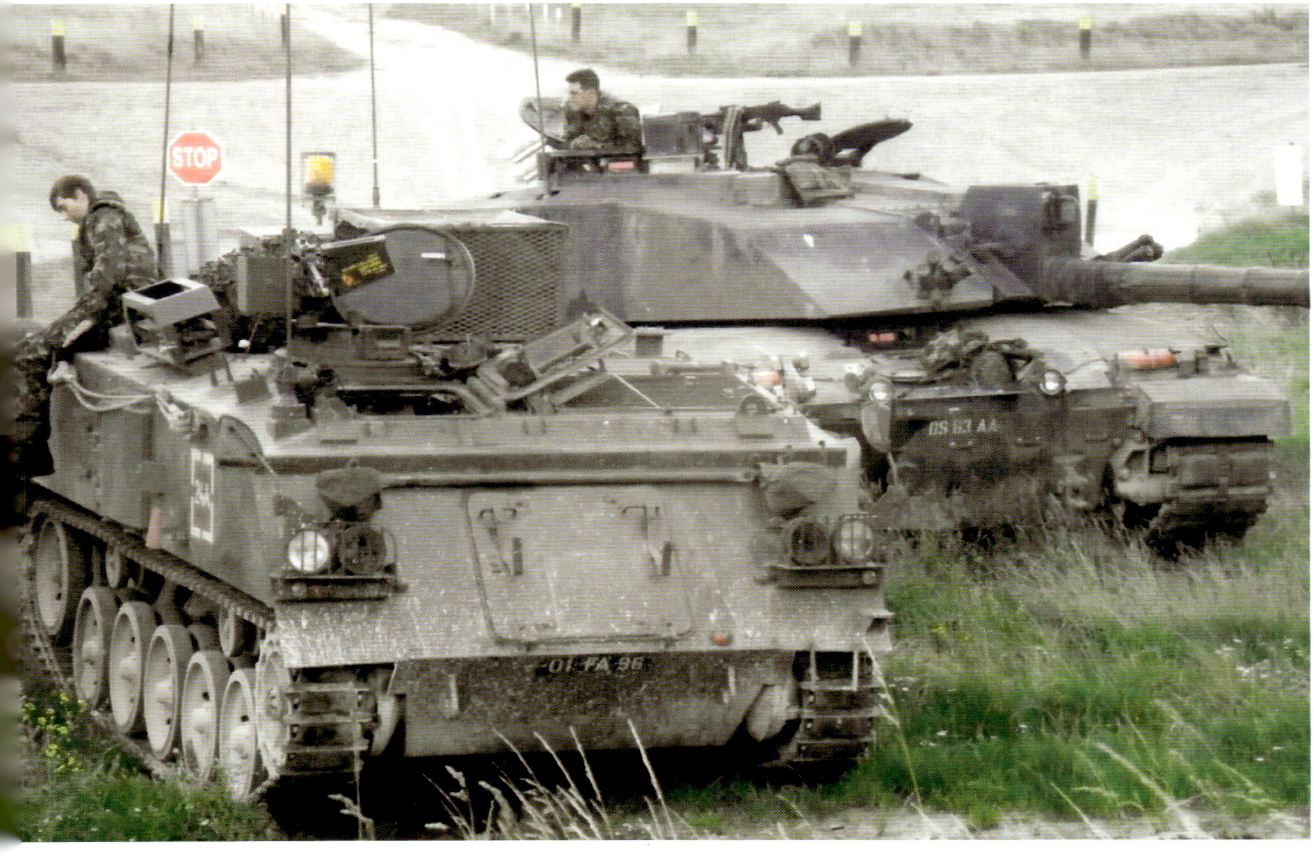
STOP
DS 63 AA
01 FA 96

A tracked vehicle crewman's worst nightmare is a thrown track, made even harder by the vehicle facing uphill. This is going to be a difficult one. The track has been split at the rear and the sprocket end, the rear part is held by the track rope being used in an unusual way, the rope has two arms which normally fit into the track, but here they have used one arm in each track to try to keep it together.

Two FV432 in Bosnia have set up a hasty command post. Both vehicles have been backed up so the open rear doors nearly touch the next vehicle, a sheet is then draped over the back of the vehicles to give a basic cover. Note the front vehicle seems to have some add-on side armour.

This rear view of FV434 shows, in great detail, the fittings carried to allow it to do its job. The jerry cans across the rear will contain various oils that may be needed in repairs. On the right side can be seen the A-frame recovery bars. The towing bracket can be removed and this allows access to more storage behind it.

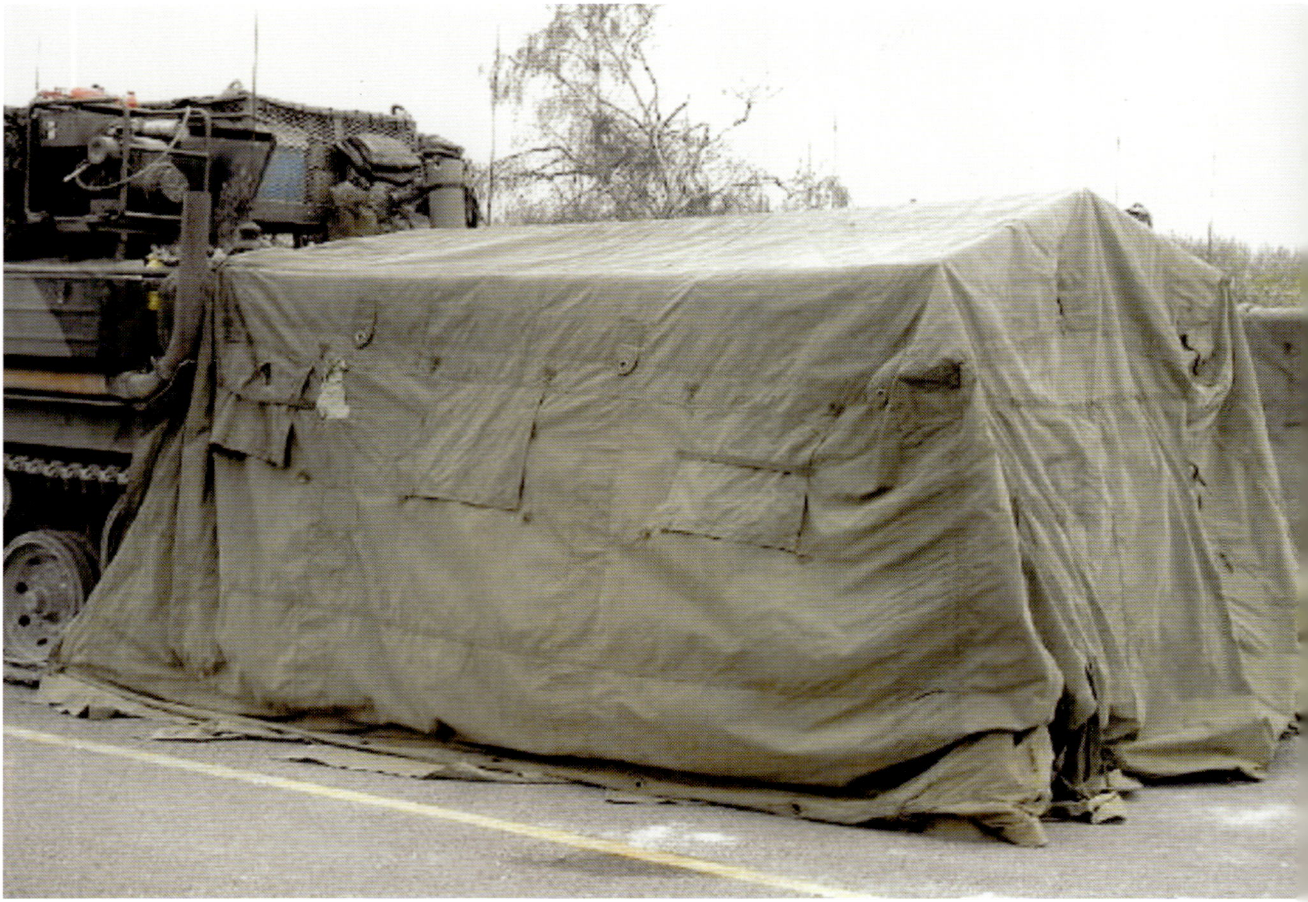

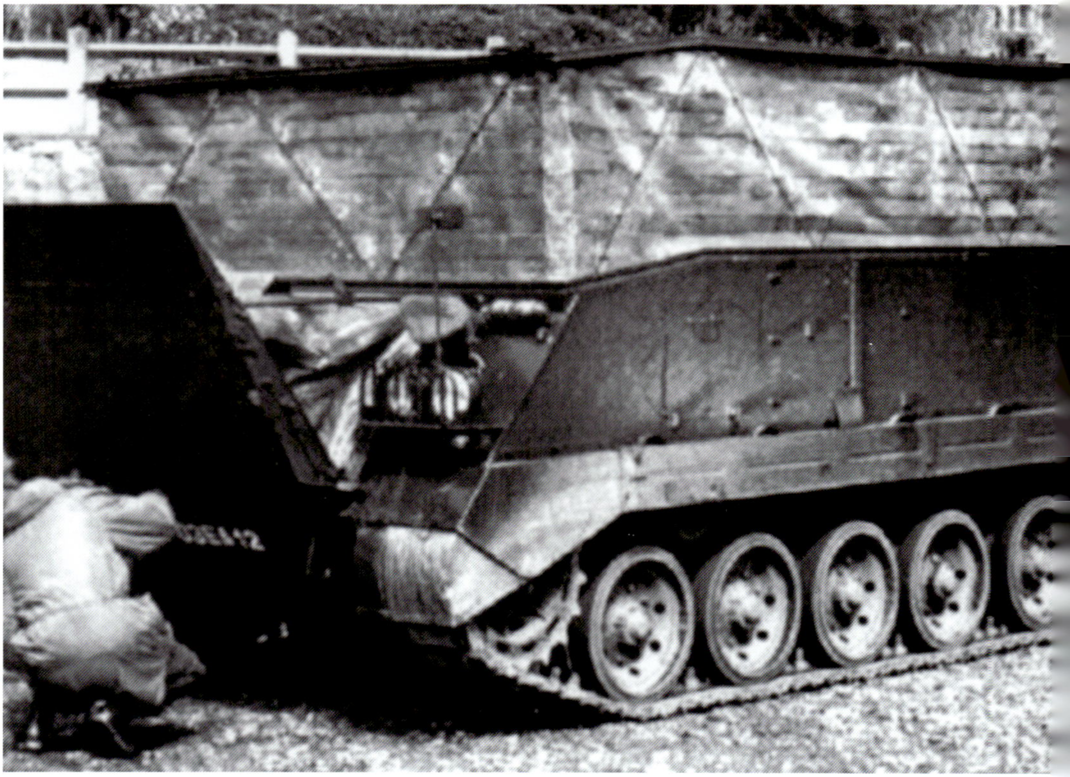

(**Opposite, above**) This FV432 has erected the penthouse that is carried by command post versions, this gives more room for table and maps to allow staff officers room to work. Note the cluttered appearance of the stores on the roof including the generator, however the crew will know where every item is in there.

(**Above**) This vehicle has the carbon fibre camouflage poles erected into the locating tubes on each corner, it can be seen that this will make camouflaging a lot easier as it will tend to avoid the snags that would occur without it.

(**Opposite, below**) A grainy shot showing the flotation screen in its raised position and the front mounted trim vane open. A crewman can be seen checking underneath for any missing drain plugs.

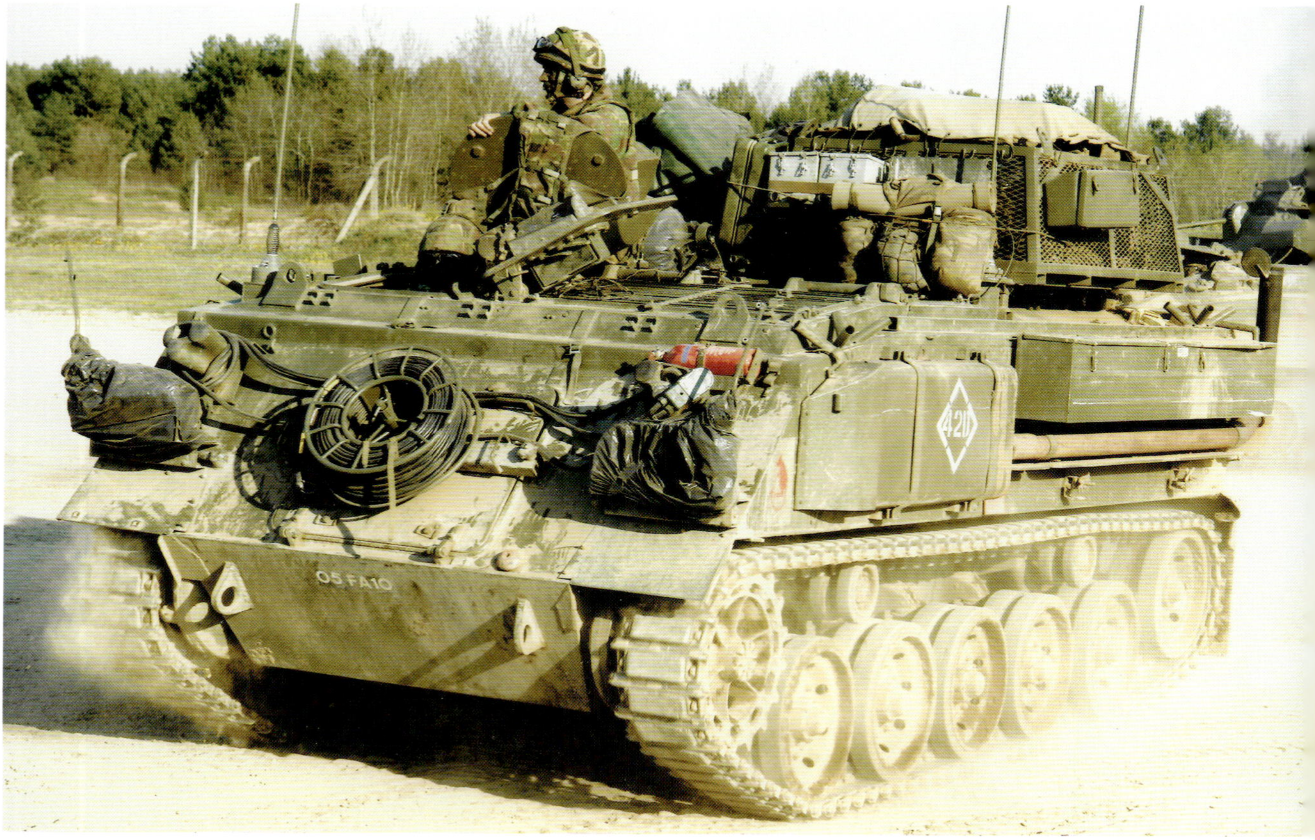
42U
05 FA10

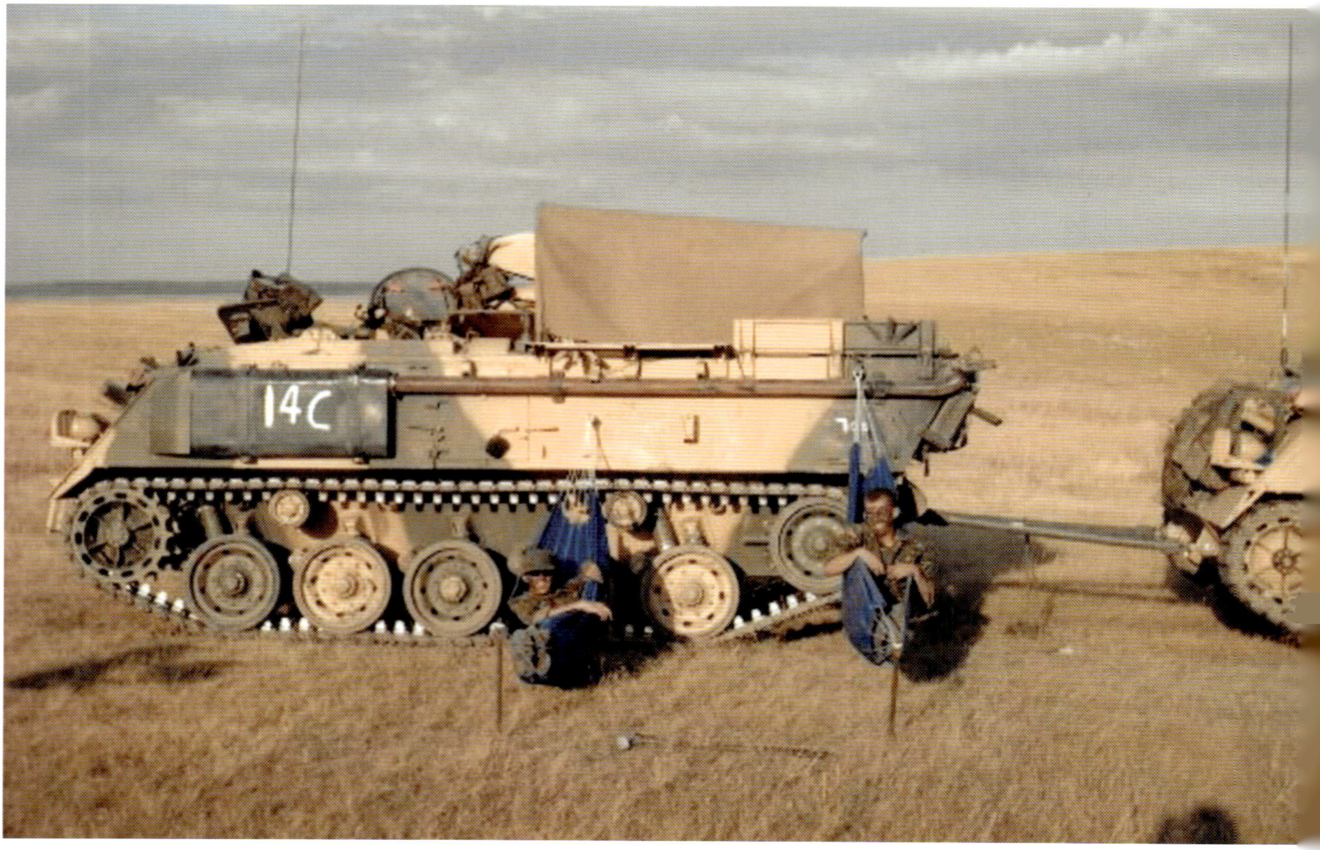
14C

(**Opposite, above**) A typical loaded vehicle on exercise on Salisbury Plain. It is evident from this image just how much equipment has to be carried. Note the boiling vessels located on the forward edge of the basket. The cable wrapped around both smoke dischargers is the inter vehicle slave lead, the military version of car jump leads. Notice how the headlights have been covered to prevent reflection.

(**Opposite, below**) When in BATUS and broken down, what better plan than to put up your hammocks and relax for a while. The FV434 makes a convenient place to secure the hammocks due to the fact there are very few trees out on the prairie.

(**Above**) Two FV432 Mk 2s moving along a typical Salisbury Plain track, which always produces the fine white dust when the area is dry. Note both crewmen are wearing helmets and the commander is manning the GPMG, this also shows how exposed he is when doing this.

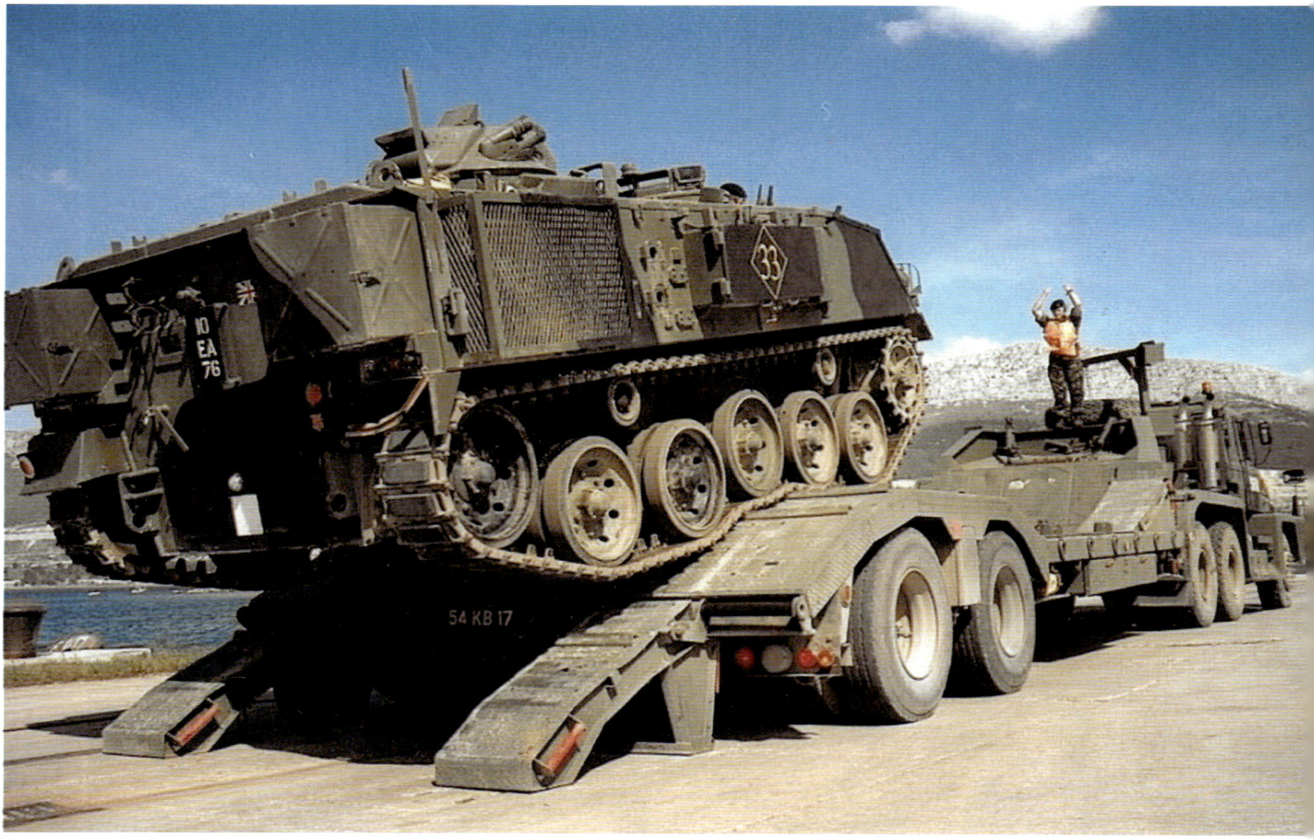
33
10
EA
76
54 KB 17

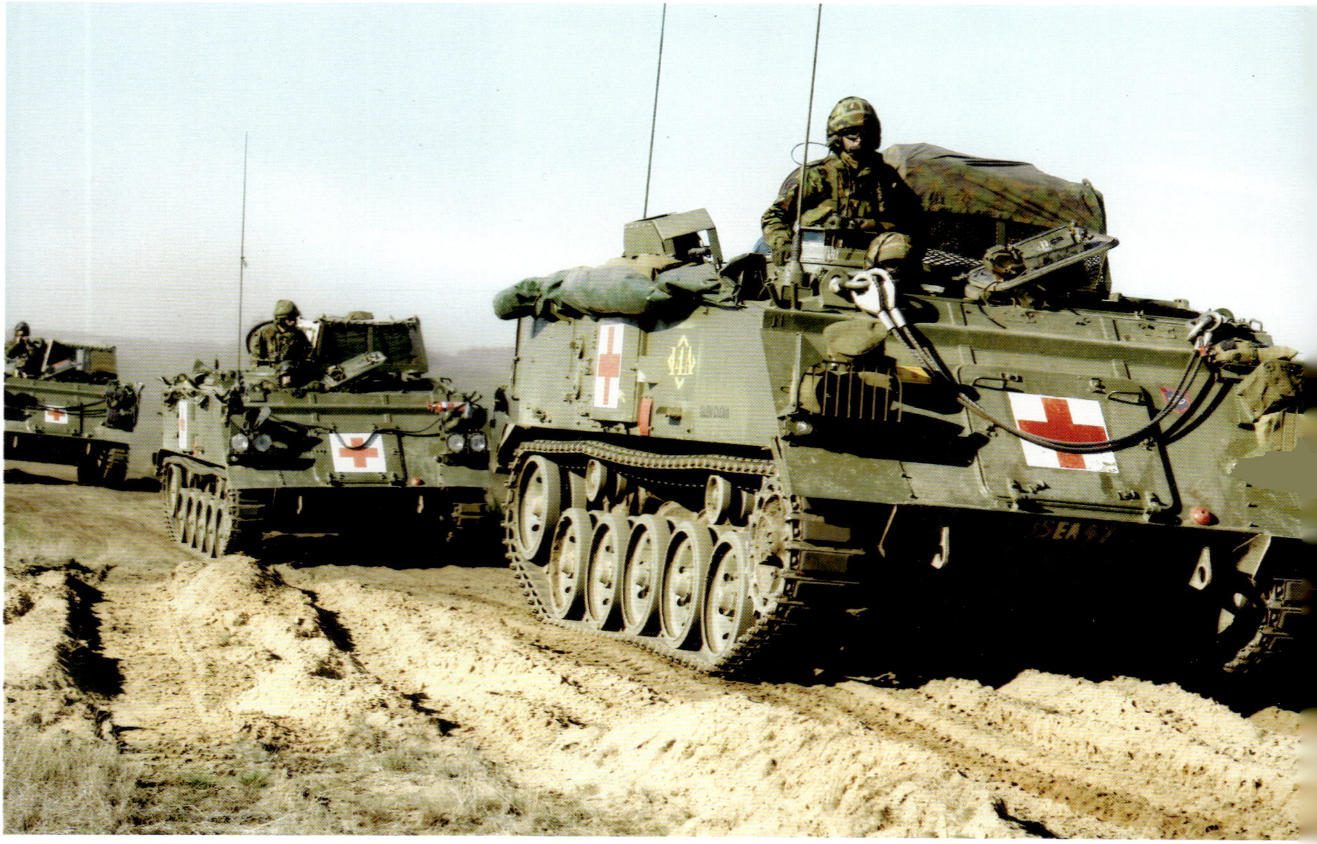

(**Opposite, above**) This vehicle is loading onto a Scammell commander tank transporter at the Croatian port of Split. It is most likely a new arrival and will be transported to its operational location by the commander.

(**Opposite, below**) A column of FV432s configured in the ambulance role. This could be part of armoured field ambulance set up. Notice how the red cross stands out, the lead vehicle has its tow rope slung for easy access across the front, and also the lack of GPMG as per the Geneva Convention.

(**Above**) FV434 with the usual penthouse rigged ready for home comfort. The bracket across the front of the glacis plate is used when lifting power packs. Look to the right front and you will just make out a set of civil-type air horns, local modification, I wonder.

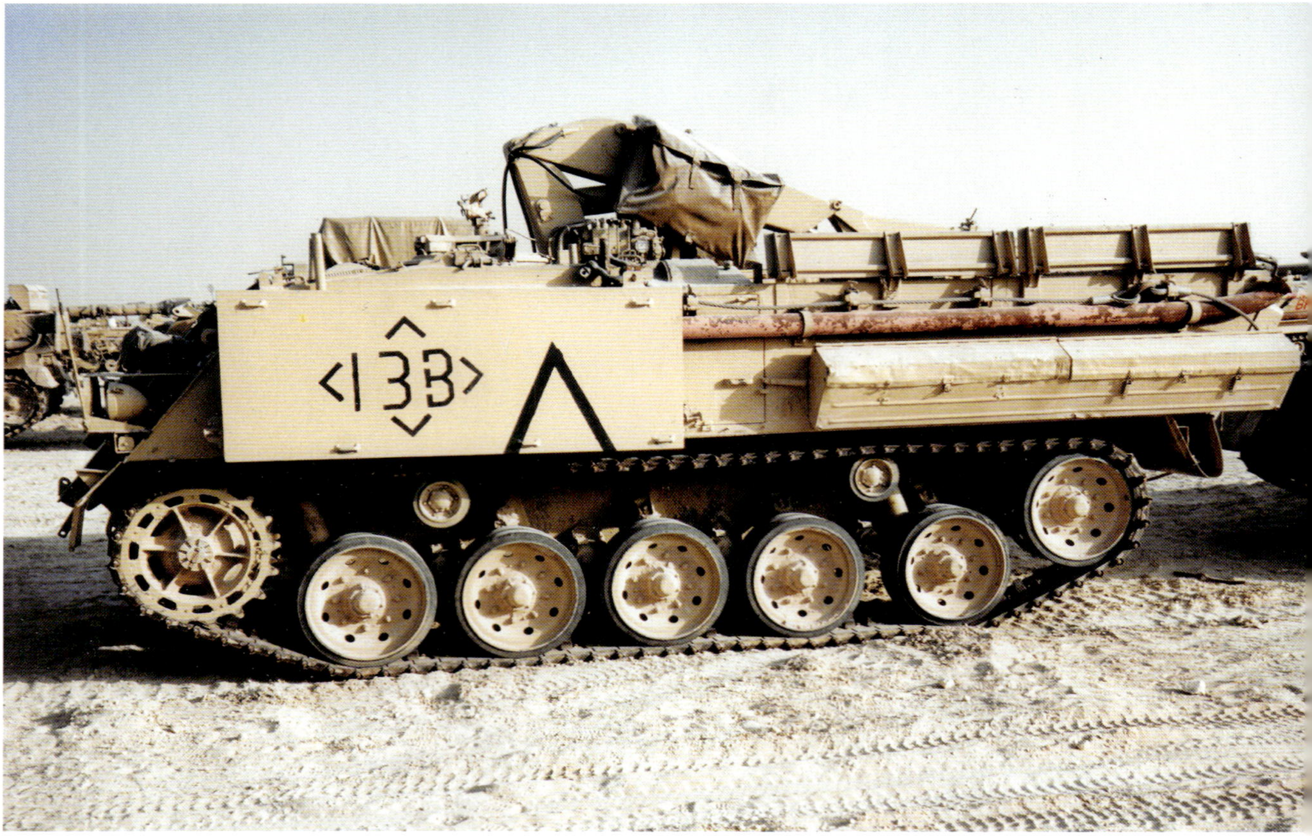
13B

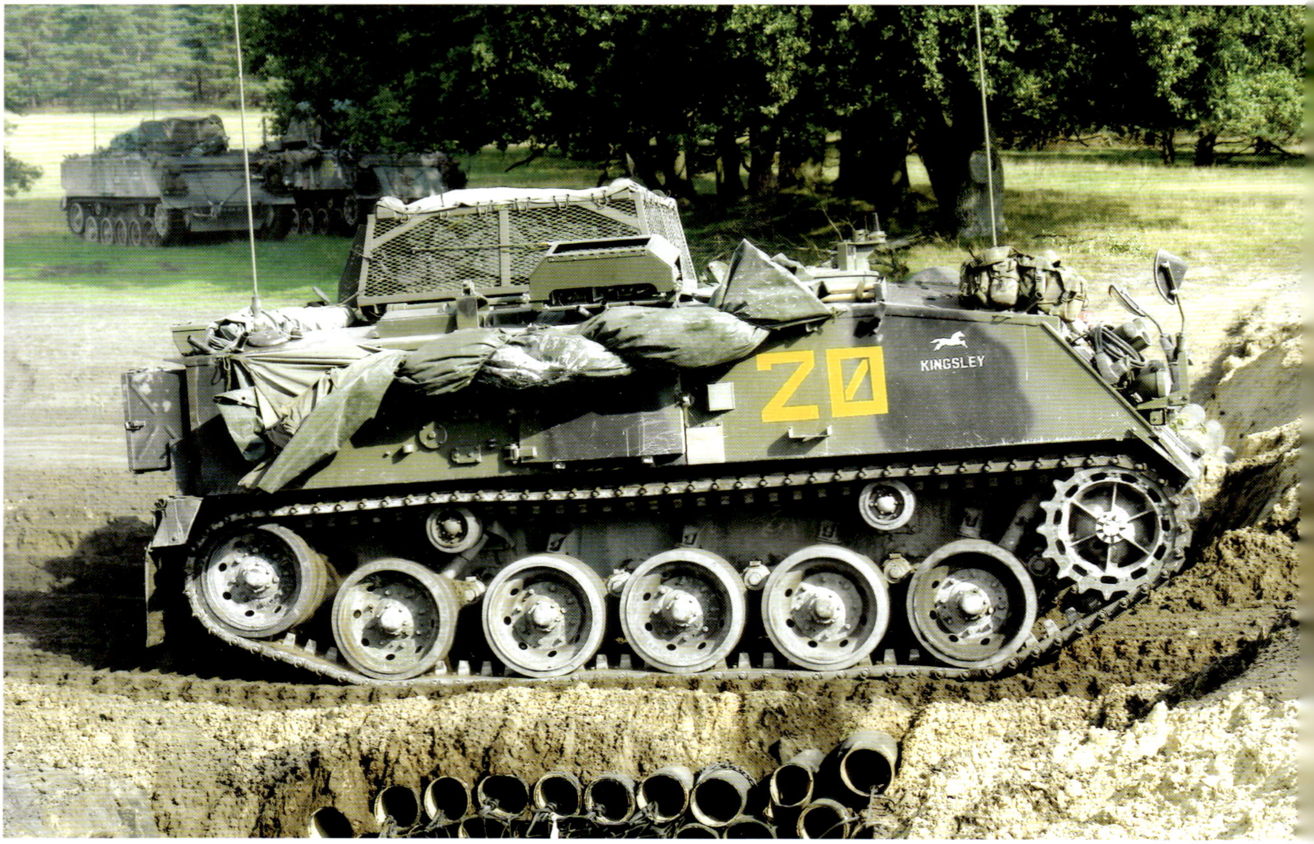
Z0
KINGSLEY

(**Opposite, above**) FV434 after the second Gulf War. It has been roughly up-armoured by the use of a redundant bazooka plate probably from a Chieftain AVRE; it will provide some protection to the crew area. Also notice the coalition inverted black V.

(**Opposite, below**) FV432 crew practising crossing obstacles. Note this vehicle has unusually still got its rear wing and rubber mud flap intact. It has crossed a pipe fascine which is used to fill gaps in ditches or trenches. Also they are doing this closed down which is no fun, and is something they will have to do a lot of in BATUS or for real.

(**Above**) This vehicle has set up with the penthouse erected at the rear for more operating space, and the ubiquitous 9 × 9 tent alongside to give the crew more comfort when sleeping and eating. It also keeps them out of the way of work in the penthouse.

FV432 with the Clansman 8 metre mast fully erected. The advantage of using it mounted to the vehicle like this is the speed at which it can be erected and the use of less guy ropes.

A gathering of FV432 on Salisbury Plain. The sand coloured camouflage is similar to that used at BATUS but is used by the land warfare centre for its vehicles.

FV436 Cymbeline in action in Bosnia. The radar is mounted over the mortar hatches; notice the covered generator and, due to the fact that this is a fairly static location, the sheet the crew have secured over the driver's and commander's hatches to keep the rain out.

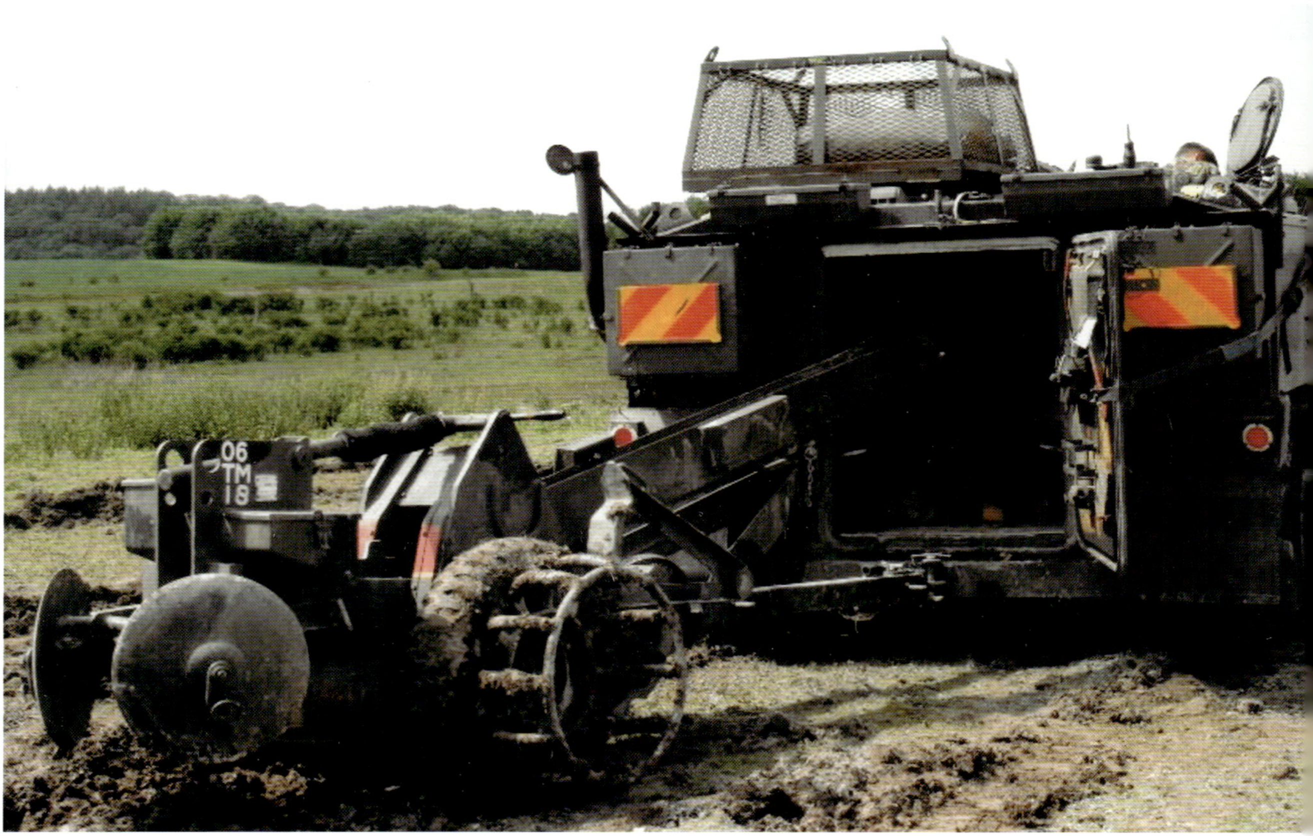
06
TM
18

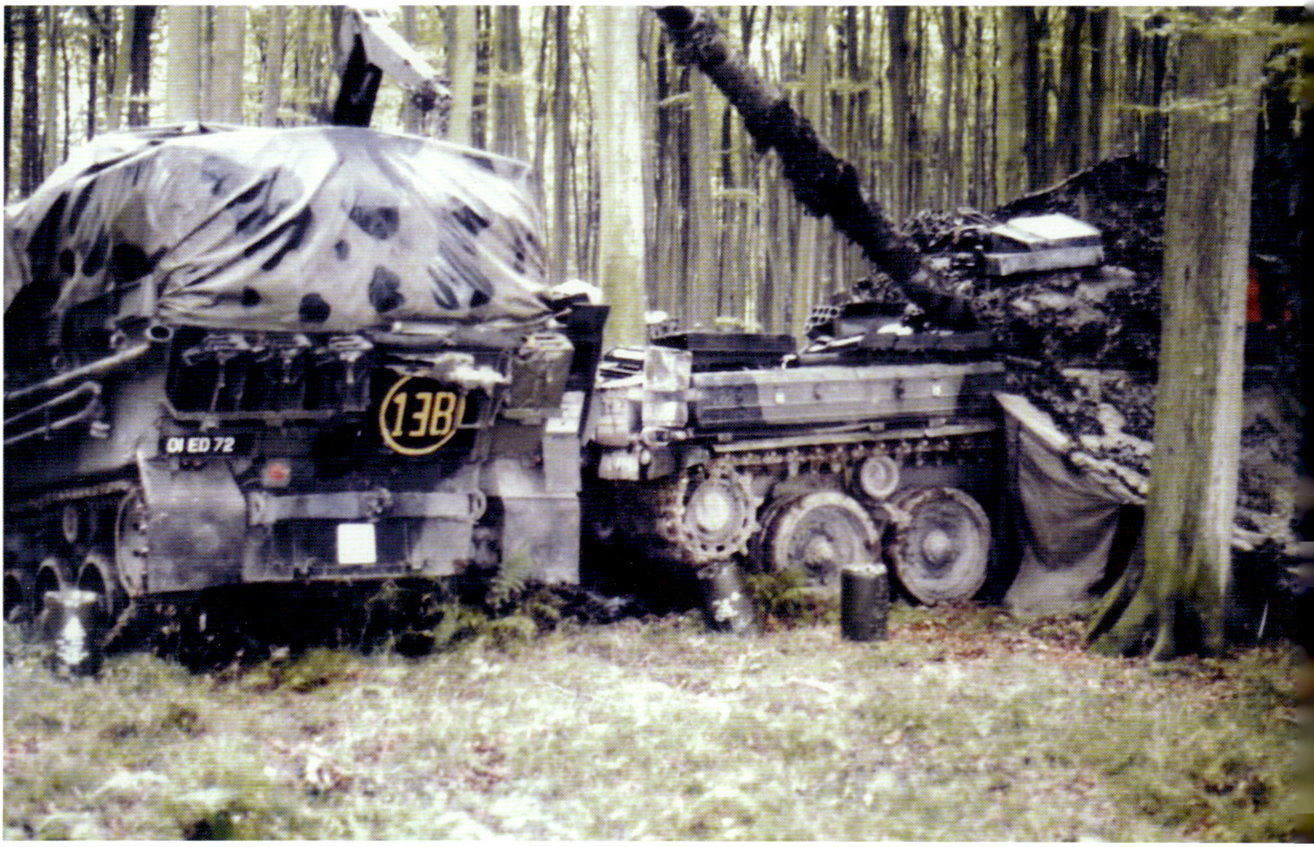
13B
01 ED 72

(**Opposite, above**) The FV432 towing the bar mine layer. This machine is fed bar mines that are stowed inside the FV432, and fed into its loading system by crewmen located at the back door. It will open the ground, lay the mine and then cover it. Using this equipment a large minefield can be quickly laid.

(**Above**) A mortar locating section in Bosnia. The Cymbeline vehicle is carrying barbed or razor wire on its glacis plate, between them is the standard Clansman 8 metre mast erected to improve communications, the vehicle on the right has even managed to erect a decent sun shade. These radar-equipped vehicles were used to detect incoming artillery and mortar fire so the SFOR forces could determine who had fired at whom.

(**Opposite, below**) The FV434 doing what it does best and what was sadly an all too familiar picture of Chieftain in its service days. This tank looks like it will be having a power pack lift and the air cleaner can be seen lying on the turret top. The crew shelter has been erected and it can be seen why they were a desirable item to 'obtain'. The CVR(T) were even better as they had a fitted groundsheet.

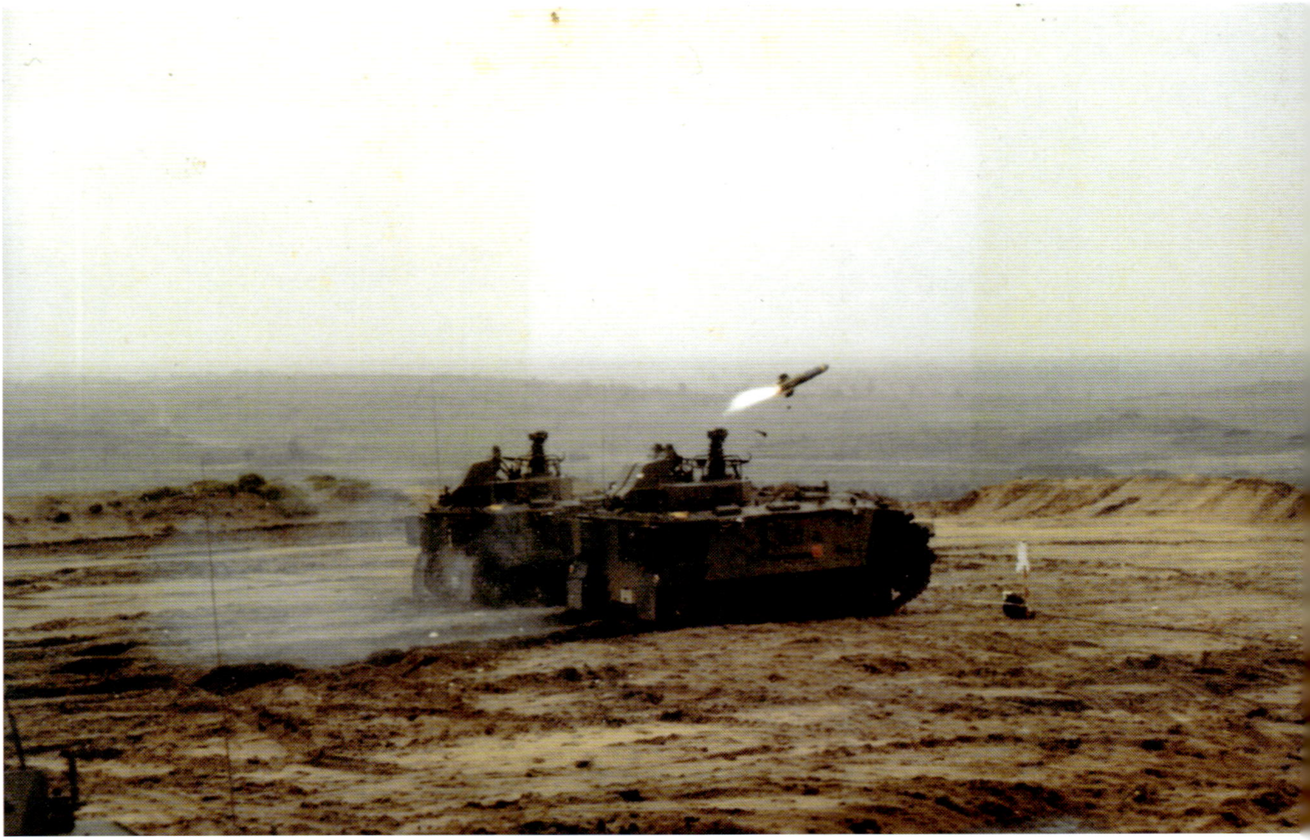

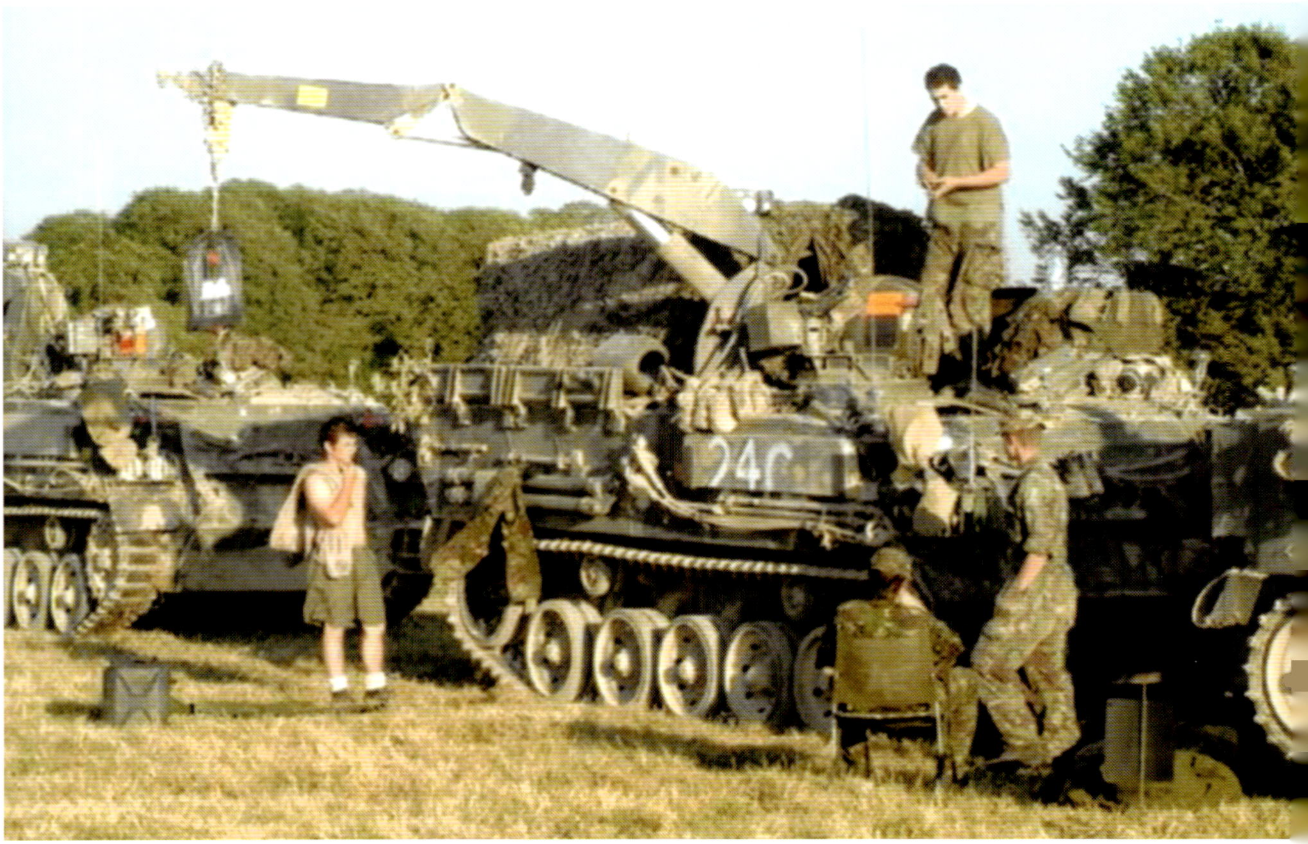

(**Opposite, above**) FV438 Swingfire launching its missile. The Swingfire missile had an effective range of 4,000 metres and originally was issued to the RAC, then transferred to the RA, and finally back to the RAC. It gave the RAC a long range anti-tank killer and they were particularly skilled in its use.

(**Opposite, below**) All the comforts of home. The jib on this FV434 is suspending a field shower with one crewman looking about ready for a wash. No shower curtains in the field, obviously a very non-tactical leaguer.

(**Above**) A well dust-coated FV432. An ideal for those who love to model military vehicles looking worse for wear: the layers of dust and mud splashes and the vast accumulation of personal equipment crammed into the basket.

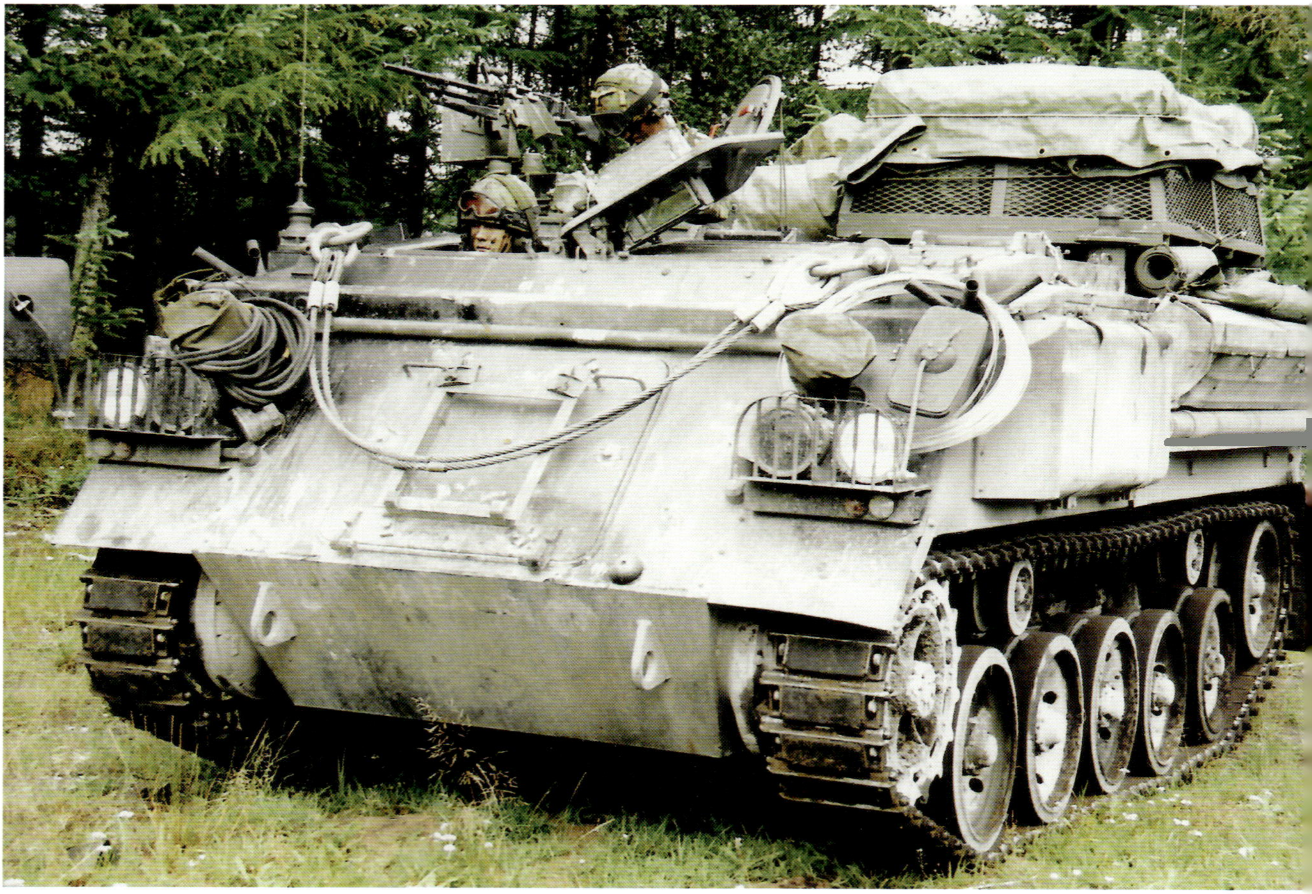

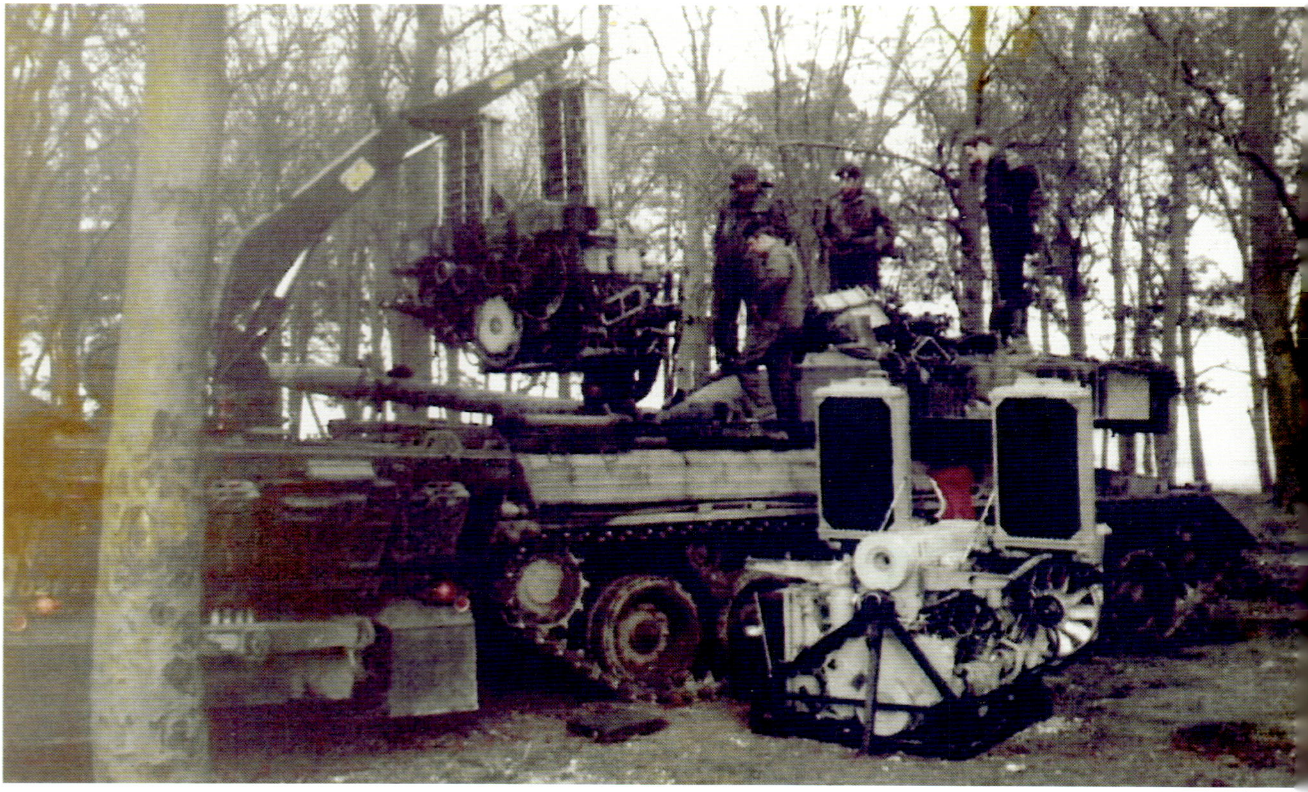

(**Opposite, above**) Each crew has their own favourite way of stowing items around their vehicle. On this one we can see the inter-vehicle slave lead wrapped around the right smoke discharger bank, the tow rope draped across the vehicle front, a roll of wire wrapped around the left smoke discharger bank, and a plastic cover secured with an elastic bungee cord over the basket.

(**Above**) This unusually camouflaged FV434 is from the Berlin Squadron and it is wearing the paint scheme devised by the late Trooper 'Henry' Wilks of the 4th/7th Royal Dragoon Guards. It was felt that the black and green camouflage was of little use in the built up environment of Berlin so a competition was held to invent a new version and this is it. Although when the Berlin Squadron came to use the Soltau training area their camouflage then looked out of place.

(**Opposite, below**) FV434 carrying out a pack lift on a dead Chieftain. The new pack is on the ground and old oil-covered one is just being removed.

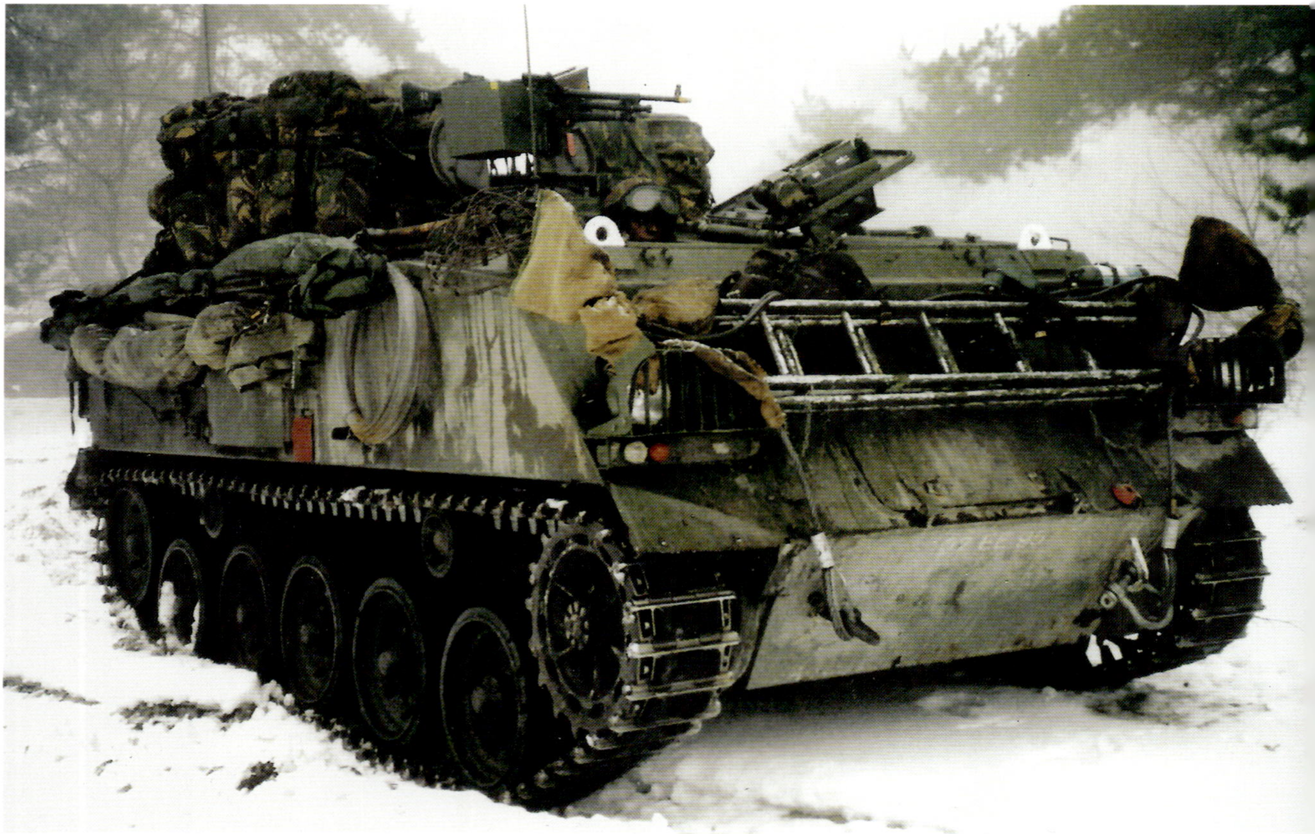

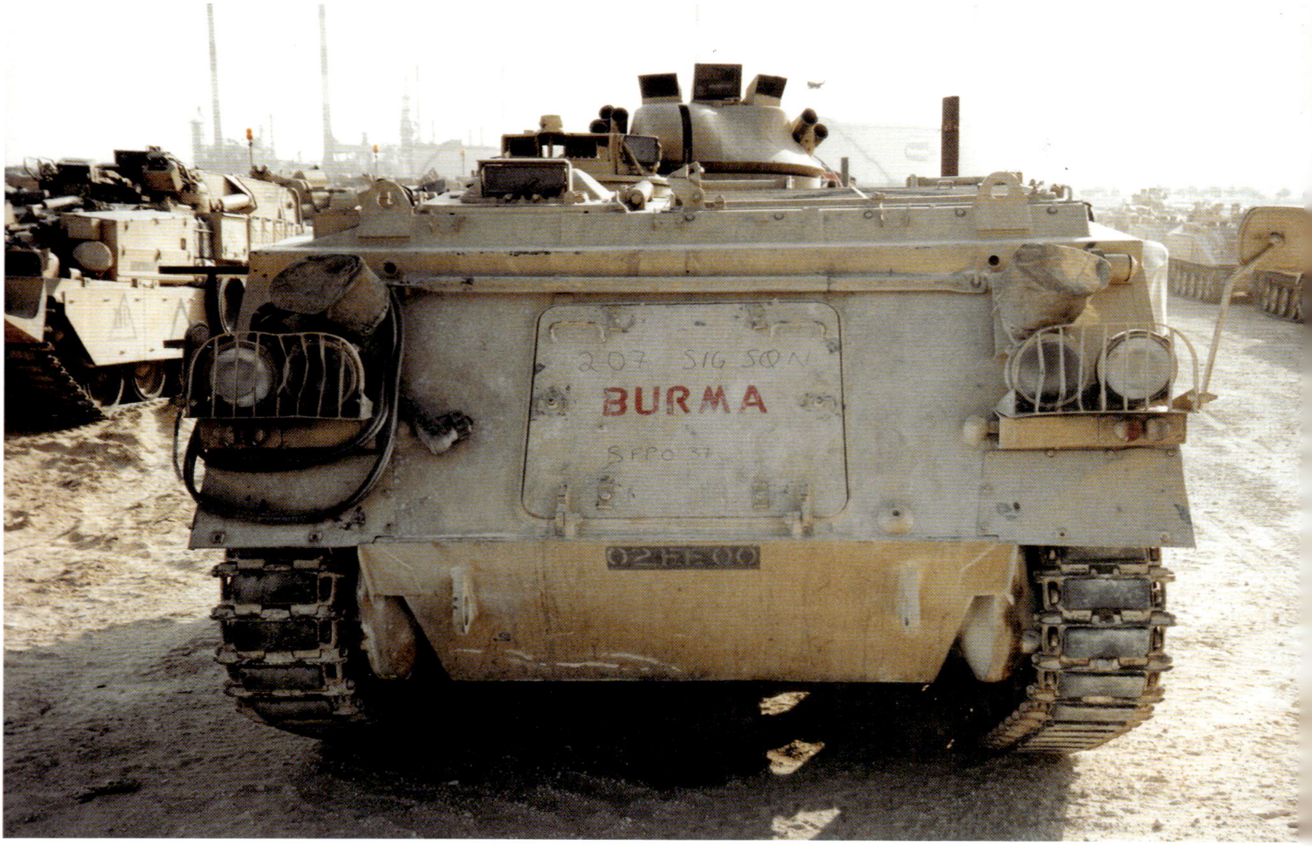

207 SIG SQN
BURMA

(**Opposite, above**) Everything but the kitchen sink would sum up this well laden FV432. Quite possibly could be assault engineers by the presence of the ladders on the glacis, but then again it might just be a useful item that has been obtained. Notice the crews webbing located around the basket, this will be to give more room in the inside.

(**Above**) A better view of the Berlin camouflage scheme. It also shows the drop down workbench complete with a vice located at the rear of the vehicle. Notice the wooden beam on the side below the commander, used for many tasks, including pushing a dead vehicle with the beam between them.

(**Opposite, below**) A peak engineering turret equipped FV432 at the end of the Gulf War. This is the period when the vehicles were de-kitting ready to be shipped back home. Notice the Chieftain ARRV to the left.

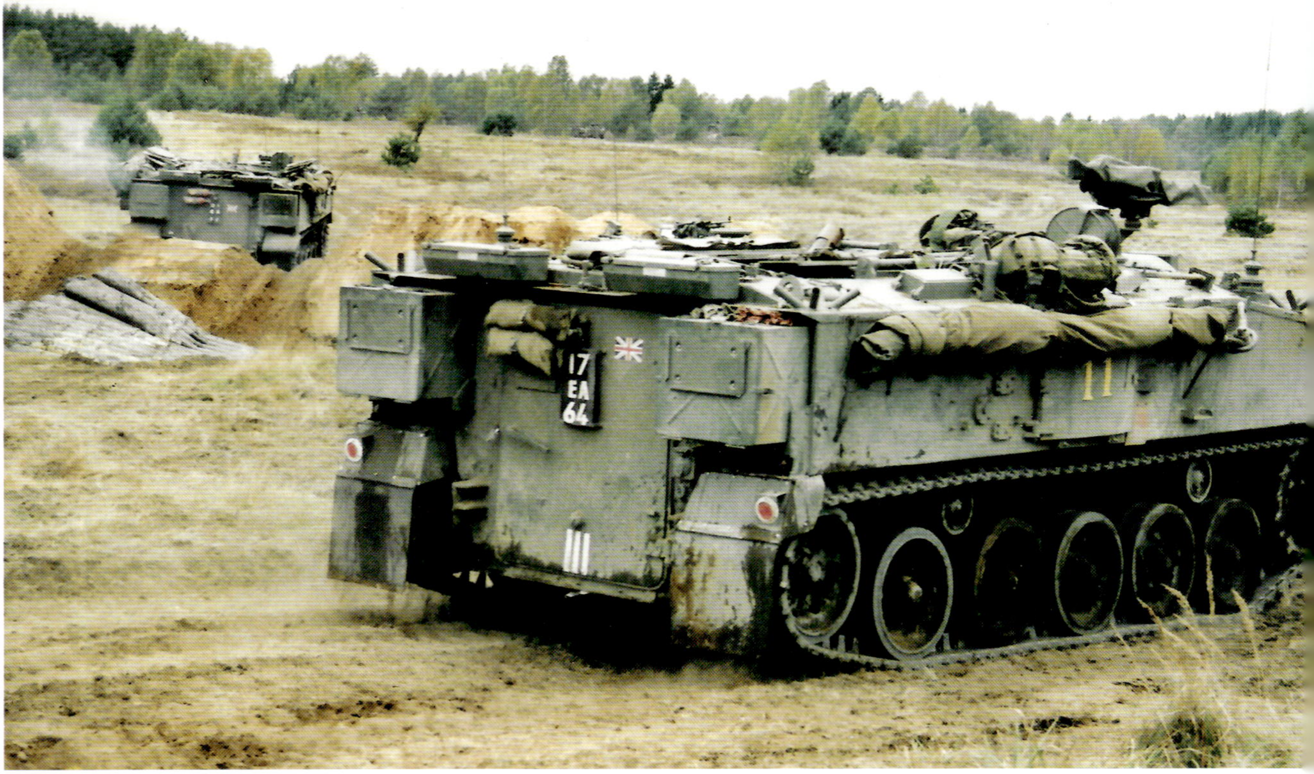
17
EA
64

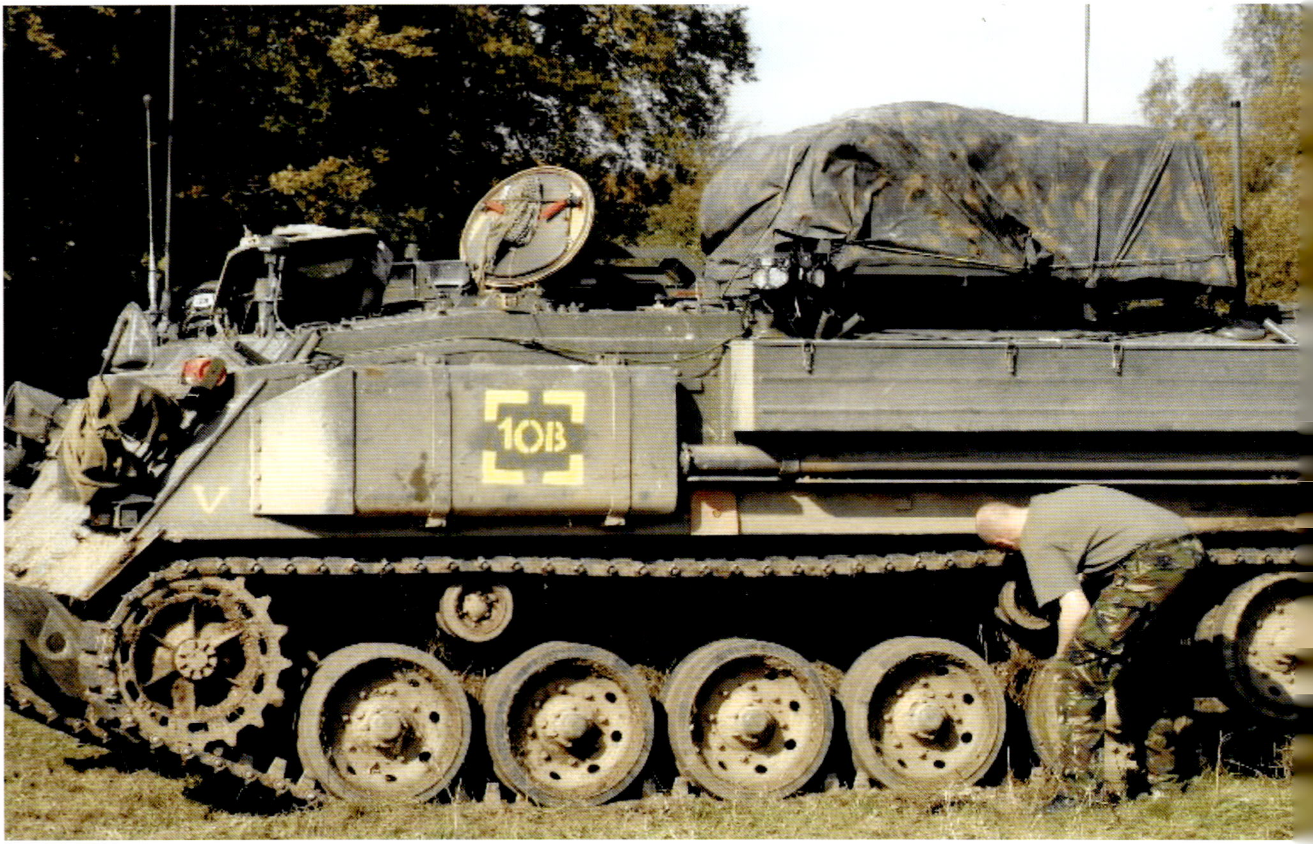
10B

(**Opposite, above**) Two FV432s practising assaulting across an obstacle. One has just crossed the obstacle by driving over the pipe fascine, while the second is giving mortar cover; the muzzle of the mortar can just be seen through the hatches.

(**Opposite, below**) The never-ending checks and maintenance on the vehicle. During halts the driver will take a walk around and check for any damage, leaks and tightness of the track, also the nightmare of wire wrapped around the suspension; if it is not cut away it can lead to a thrown track.

(**Above**) Although in a combat zone, this commander feels safe to be opened up and out of the cupola. Apart from the overall sand camouflage, the big feature is the IR recognition boards either side and on the glacis plate. These were fitted to enable vehicles using night-vision equipment to be able to identify coalition vehicles easily and to hopefully prevent blue on blue.

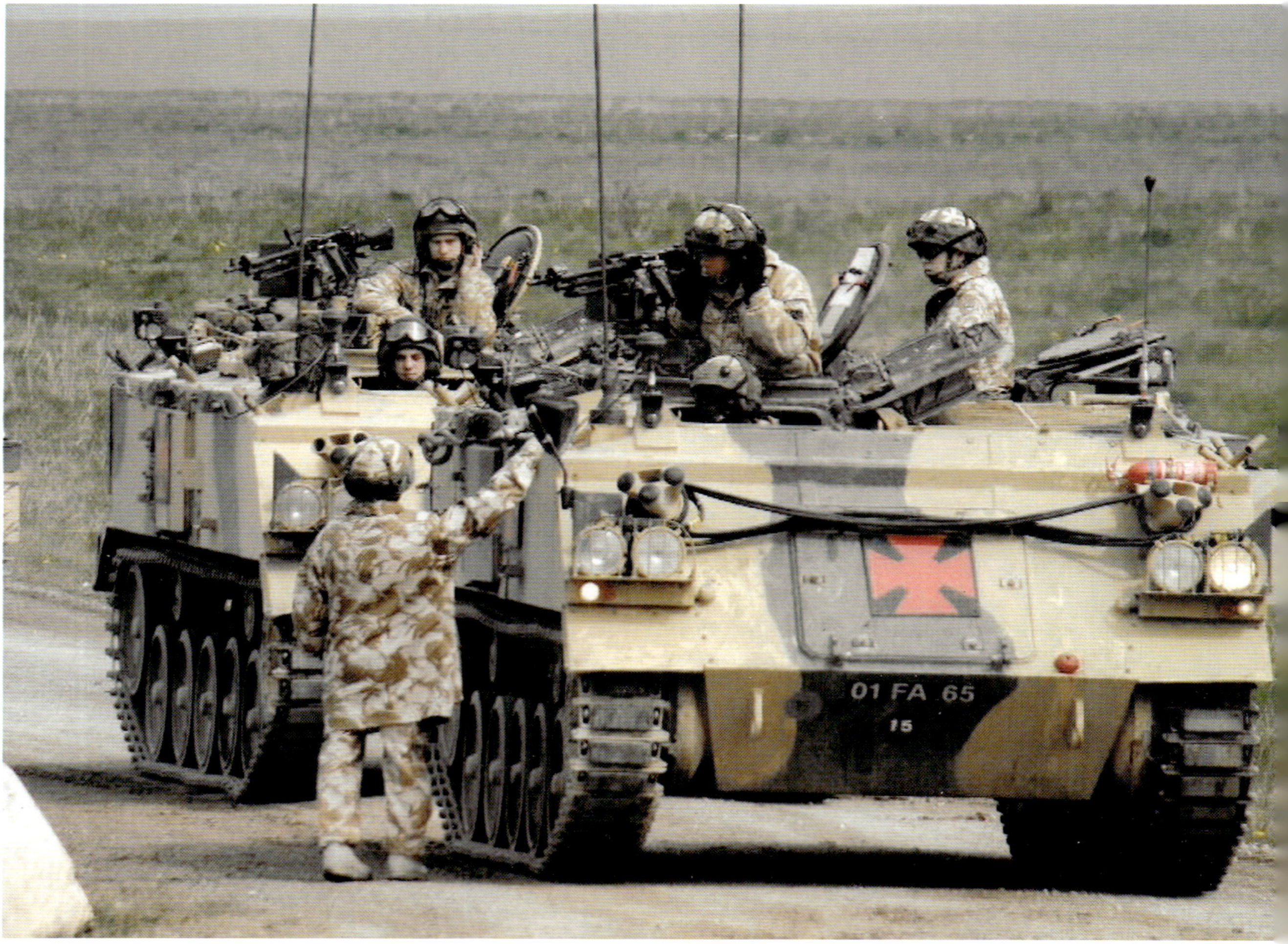
01 FA 65
15

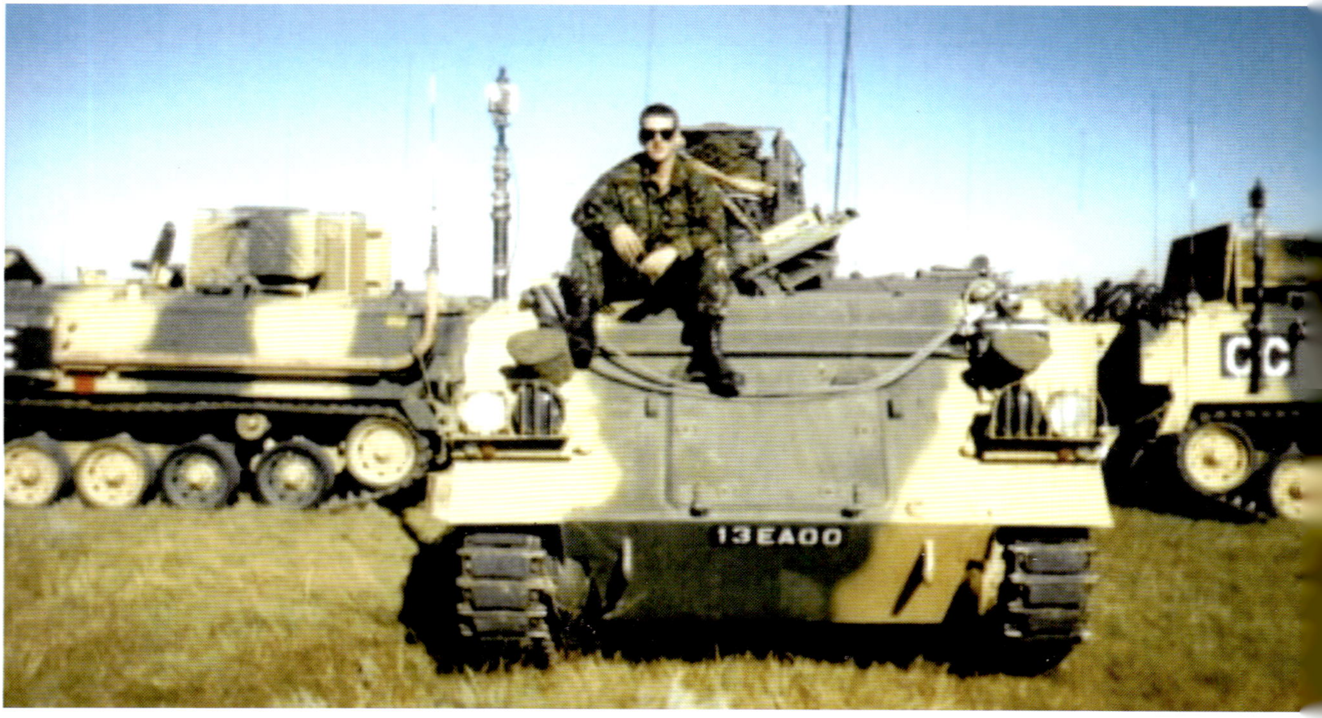
13EA00
CC

(**Opposite, above**) Vehicles from the land warfare centre in their BATUS-type camouflage. Notice the driver is wearing the Clansman bone dome helmet while all the rest are wearing the standard infantry helmet, also the use of the first desert camouflage uniforms.

(**Opposite, below**) Four FV432s (the fourth is hidden behind the centre tank) of the Royal Dragoon Guards forming the RHQ complex at BATUS. The four vehicles are comprised of the command vehicles, the intelligence vehicle, and the fourth is usually the artillery vehicle. Once in position, all the masts and penthouses will be erected.

(**Above**) Bulldog sporting all the latest upgrades to help it survive. Front and side add-on armour, the pole sticking up with a table on the top is colloquially known as 'the bird table', it provides protection against IEDs. The commander has a simple clear bulletproof shield around part of the cupola.

Amazing what you see in the motorway services; this armoured FV434 was parked there so good chance to take close look. Note the use of bar and plate armour, the carriers for the Chobham add-on armour are empty as a security precaution.

A close up of one version of the armoured cupola fitted to FV432. As can be seen it addresses the problem of the commander being exposed by standing up. Below the driver's sight can be seen one of the cameras used when operating closed down; to its left is part of the IED protection equipment.

It's a tough life in the Army! But why be uncomfortable when you don't have to, this crew certainly seem to be enjoying the break, camp bed and sun umbrella, obviously a non-combat zone.

Chapter Four

Variants

It had long been a part of the original design criteria for the new APC that its chassis could be used for a variety of differing roles and since its introduction into service in the 1960s the hull of FV432 has been used in many different configurations. Some of these were the predicted ones and some were not so predictable. In this chapter I hope to list all the known variants and to explain how they have been allocated their various designations.

FV431

FV431 was designed to meet the requirements of Military Objective WO 57/vehs/ A/5969 GS (W) 9 Light tracked load carrier. The British Army had until this period made do with its conventional soft skin trucks for moving its logistical requirements around the battlefield and in fact still does to this day. Convoys of slow moving trucks are always a prime target for the enemy, also if the army is advancing then the trucks need to be able to keep pace with the forces but will always have a problem at water obstacles, and so the requirement for a swimming armoured high mobility load carrier was issued. This was contained within WOP 26 which gave the general requirements, the major of which was that it must be part of the FV432 family and therefore utilise the same components as the FV432.

The resulting vehicle resembled the FV432 from the nose back to a point behind the vehicle commander's cupola. From there the shape changed radically with a raised roof section added. This had a flat top with sloping sides. The sides of the vehicle had been made to hinge upwards for access to the load, which solved the problem, found with FV432 of limited access to the load. The vehicle was powered by the K60 engine and the exhaust ran alongside the vehicle and it was fitted with the early armoured type silencer which was a box-shaped fitting rather than the later unarmoured version. There are few military design requirements that, once produced, comply with all the original requirements and FV431 was no exception. The original specification had called for an armoured body, the prototype was produced with the front half of the vehicle which housed the crew and engine and transmission having the same level of armour protection as the basic APC, while the rear cargo area was left unarmoured. Why this was so is hard to ascertain but I suspect that with the weight of the vehicle, plus carrying a 3.5 ton load, and a requirement to swim it was found that some armour had to go and the load space was the area most obvious.

The vehicle was crewed by a commander and driver who were housed in the same locations and had access to the same equipment as the APC. Provision was made for the carriage of a third crewman who probably would have been used to help load/unload the vehicle. If the third crewman was carried, major modifications had to be made to the vehicle. These included removing all the radios from the pannier to the right of the driver and any batteries fitted there as well, and the fitting of a reclining seat for the third crewman in their place. Not a very easy task in view of the lack of space within the crew area and one that would have been unpopular, I suspect. It would not have been much fun for the third crewman as he had no sighting equipment and only could get in and out of his location once the commander vacated the cupola.

The FV431 was equipped like the FV432 to swim by means of a floatation screen which was fitted around the forward crew area as opposed to the whole vehicle, as on the FV432. The reason that it required a smaller screen was that additional buoyancy had been designed into it, apart from that the system was the same as for all the FV430 family. When in water the vehicle was propelled and steered by its tracks. It was to be armed with a 7.62mm LMG or 7.62 general purpose machine gun the GPMG which was just coming into service.

The vehicle was designed to carry two standard NATO pallets (40 × 48 inches) on the centre line while ammunition of all natures would be stored under the side panels which gave good access to them. One phase included the trial of loading and unloading under various conditions: five RMP soldiers commanded by a lieutenant corporal were selected to be the trial guinea pigs. The trial involved the soldiers loading and unloading both FV431 and 432 under different conditions and with different types of stores and equipment. The results at the end of the trial showed that the FV431 was easy to load while the FV432 proved difficult. While carrying ammunition the FV431 could handle up to eight types of munitions and they could all be accessed easily due to the large opening side panels compared to the fixed sides of the FV432. The FV431 could accept two standard NATO pallets but the FV432 could not, the FV432 however could carry its load under armour whilst the load area of the FV431 was unarmoured. The FV432 was also more tiring to work on than the FV431. The end result was that FV432 could be used to carry stores and it was recommended that it was not used for ammunition, while the FV431 was fully recommended to be the load carrier for the British Army. On the face of it the vehicle seemed to have come out of the trial well, amongst other things the crew were impressed with the engine although they did find many bolts working loose.

The manufacturer was GKN Sankey who was working on the FV432 and expected the 431 to go into service as a result of the trial report. However in one of those typical decisions from the MoD it was decided that the FV431 would not be the preferred choice and instead the contract went to ALVIS and their High Mobility Load Carrier Stalwart, based on their successful Saladin and Saracen chassis. The reasons why this decision was made are still hidden away and such documents that are available were only released in 1992.

There were four, possibly six prototypes built; identified vehicles are in the registration range 06 EB 01 to 06 EB 04. There is no indication as to their ultimate fate, apart from one on Salisbury plain slowly rotting away.

FV432 SCAT

This strangely named version was a short trial to try and improve the AA capability of vehicles. It is not known if it was just to gather information or was a serious proposition. Following the military's love of mnemonics, SCAT stands for 'Should Not Cost a Tenner'. This referred to the cost of material used in its construction. SCAT was a twin 7.62mm GPMG mount that fitted straight into the existing pintle mount on the commander's cupola. The amount of firepower it could throw skywards was tremendous and exceedingly impressive.

SCAT consisted of two GPMGs mounted side by side with about the width of an ammunition box between them, both guns fed from the left and the empty case and links were allowed to free fall as there was no empties bag to catch them. The mounting was very crude and simple but very effective. The guns were fitted into a simple cradle either side which was joined and supported by equilibrator tubes from a Chieftain tank's commander GPMG mounting, the sight was a simple ring sight made in the workshop and resembling the ones seen in all good war films. Each weapon had its butt and pistol grip fitted as if in the ground role.

FV432 WOMBAT

Wombat was one of the family of 120mm recoilless anti-tank weapons used by the British Army. They basically were all very similar, they were a lightweight weapon made of magnesium to help keep the weight down. It was equipped with a M8 .5-inch spotting rifle which was used by the crew to try and obtain an accurate range before firing the 120mm. The weapon had a muzzle velocity of 463m/s and fired a 12.8kg HESH round to a range of about 1,100m and, with a good crew, a rate of fire of 4 rounds a minute could be achieved.

The weapon mount for the FV432 consisted of a pedestal, which was located on the power pack partition sill and was used to support the front end of the barrel when the gun was in the lowered position. Ammunition was carried in racks constructed from angle iron welded to form three tiers with each tier holding four rounds, the rack itself being bolted to the left pannier sill. The rounds rest within the rack on wooden cradles and are held in place by rubber sleeved clamping bars.

A gun crutch supports the Wombat carriage by the axle and takes the weight from the wheels for transportation. The crutch consists of side members connected at the forward end by another angle iron member. The axle supports are pivoted on the base of the frame and are also sprung loaded against limit stops; this maintains them at the correct height to receive the carriage axle. When Wombat is stowed in the vehicle the axle contacts and swings the supports forward and raises the Wombat. Two more lengths of angle iron form guide rails which have their rear ends curved in to form a lead in to the wheels as they move up the ramp to enter the vehicle. The rails are secured to the main floor plate in the rear part of the crutch and will guide the wheels until they engage the side members of the crutch frame. To enable the Wombat to be raised from ground level into the rear of the vehicle a loading ramp is used, which is actually two long ramps that consist of two track guides. These are joined at the rear by a tubular cross-member which is fitted with ball joins where it joins the ramps. This will allow the guide ends to rest firmly on the ground no matter how uneven it is. The ramps have a pin projecting from the forward end, which will engage inside the vehicle doorway when the ramps are used in the loading position. Two short ramps are also supplied and these are used to form a runway for the gun to move up or down when being placed in or removed from the mount.

In the centre of the floor is the platform, which is designed to give the crew a firm, level, raised floor to work from. It is made of wood and sections are hinged to allow for ease of loading or unloading the vehicle.

The depression stop is a curved tubular rail, which is supported by two posts that are bolted to pads which have been welded to the roof plate of the vehicle. The right hand portion of the rail is raised above the level of the rail and provides the right traverse stop. To secure the barrel when the vehicle is moving, a strap made of nylon webbing is fitted on the plate between the inlet and outlet louvres. The strap is fitted with a tensioning device and buckle.

The pannier sill is converted into a locker by the addition of a set of sliding doors to allow access to the stowage area on the sill. A two round ready rack is provided and this is again made from angle iron which forms an upright frame fitted with two padded circular recesses that hold the base of the round while two hinged metal straps secure the upper portion of the round. With all this angle iron in the vehicle it was obvious that some fitting would either have to go or be modified, the main items being the crew seats. In place of the rear left seat a single seat is now provided; this can be placed in an upright stowed position. A double seat is also provided and this is fitted on the left side flush with the power pack covers. Underneath the seat are located two batteries and, to allow access to them, the seat can be tipped forward.

Due to the back blast the rear stowage bins are provided with covers to protect them, the covers are hinged to allow the crew to have access to the stowage bins. To actually move the gun from being in action in a dismounted ground role to mounting it in the vehicle ready for action was a series of thirty drills. After all that all the crew would need in typical army fashion is for an officer to come round and say, 'We don't need that gun fitted into that vehicle now.' Funny though, it is only twelve stages to dismount the gun for ground use.

FV432 AMBULANCE

The conversion to the ambulance role uses fittings common to all marks of FV432, and again involves a lot of removing and bolting in of components. Originally the conversion meant the removal of the ventilation batteries that were located on the floor next to the power pack panels. These now are fitted on the left forward part of the hull pannier. Several variations can be achieved using the conversion kit and it is up to the user to decide which setup to use. In the full ambulance mode the vehicle can accommodate four patients on stretchers, however if only two stretchers are fitted then several sitting patients can be carried. This was the normal set up for a Regimental equipped vehicle whilst the RAMC would have gone for a full setup.

To convert to the full ambulance role all the crew seats have to be removed and a set of carrier brackets installed using the bolts and holes from the seat fittings. The carrier brackets are hinged to the vehicle's lower side by hinge pin brackets. Mounted on the carrier frame brackets are guide channels with a sliding insert. This guide channel is pivoted at the hinged end of the carrier frame bracket, which helps when loading the stretchers on the carrier. To retain the other two stretchers that will be carried on the floor, two pedestal brackets are bolted to the forward end of the personnel compartment floor. When the lower stretchers are employed one handle is fitted into the pedestal bracket and the other end is secured by a webbing strap that is threaded through the floor plate and around the stretcher handle.

To load the carrier frames with a stretcher, the carrier is first swung out so it is at an angle to the rear door to simplify the loading of the stretcher, the sliding bracket is then pulled out to its full extent and the stretcher placed on it. The sliding insert and the stretcher now sitting in it are pushed fully home into the carrier and then the locking pins are placed through the carrier and in doing so they also fit through the legs of the stretcher, thus retaining it in the carrier.

For each sitting injured, a full seat harness is supplied to ensure that they are comfortably and safely secured during the transportation to a dressing station. The ambulance is normally crewed by the driver and the commander who is also either an RAMC medical orderly or a Regimental medic. Treatment is limited to not much more than first aid and the aim of the ambulance is to clear the area and transport the casualties in reasonable safety and comfort to where they can be examined by a doctor. Under the rules of the Geneva Convention the crew are only allowed to bear side arms for personal protection and to protect the injured in their care, so no MG is carried and no other sorts of weapons apart from those of the casualties may be carried on the vehicle. The ambulance must also carry distinctive white squares on the front, side, back and top with large red crosses to indicate that they are ambulances and should not be engaged.

FV432 CARL GUSTAV

It seems to be a characteristic of the British Army to add bits and pieces to in-service vehicles ad hoc. Some of this is down to costing and some to a need to have certain equipment available. One such move was the fitting of the Carl Gustav to the FV432. Normally the weapon would be carried as part of the section equipment but the provision of a fitting kit allowed it to be fired from the mortar hatch, although this was meant to be in an emergency only. This raises the question why bother with a fitting kit in the first place?

To fit the Carl Gustav, the inner mortar hatches are placed in the open position and secured. A mounting tube is transversely mounted above the centre of the hatch, onto the mounting tube a mounting sleeve and gun pivot are fitted. These position the gun in the centre of the hatch and allow the gunner freedom of traverse; a padded bracket and web strap is provided to secure the gun when not in use. To use the gun the gunner and number two will carry out their normal drills, however the gunner will stand straddling the seats in the personnel compartment. This really is not a very good employment of either the FV432 or the Carl Gustav and was rarely used.

FV432 with 81mm MORTAR

One of the requirements for any force attacking or defending is that of firepower; this is usually best provided by artillery, but this is not always possible. For many years now mortars have provided a simple and effective way of supplying at least some of this firepower. Mobility has always been a problem and although the 81mm mortar is man portable it is still a heavy load. The solution was to provide a suitable vehicle that could carry the weapon, crew and a good supply of bombs. While soft skin vehicles such as a Land Rover could manage this task, they really provide no protection for the crew. The decision was taken to convert FV432 to carry the 81mm mortar; the installation can be used in all vehicles and marks except Mk 1/1 vehicles 02 EA 01 to 02 EA 54. This is because the necessary modifications to the floor plate were not embodied during construction. When the vehicle is configured in the mortar role the back door can not be used for entry or exit as stowage for mortar bombs runs across the back of the vehicle.

The mortar mount consists of a base plate onto which a turntable is mounted, and diagonally mounted across the turntable is a fabrication, on one end of which is supported the mortar breech plug and the other end has an extendable strut which supports the mortar barrel. Located on the base plate is a central tower and this forms the support for the azimuth scale. This scale which is calibrated in the military measurement of millimetres rather than degrees, this can be set for alignment with the vehicle heading. On top of the tower is a circular level indicator, which has circular rings graduated to indicate 5 and 10 degree angles of tilt.

An extendable strut is trunnion-mounted to a link, which is pivoted to the fabrication. When the link is in its outward position it supports the mortar barrel in the low angle range and when it is thrown over to the inward position it supports the barrel in the high angle range. Using these two positions gives the weapon an elevation range of 40–80 degrees.

The mortar is secured in the mount in exactly the same manner as if it was in use in the ground role. The turntable can be rotated 6,400mm (360 degrees) by rotating a handle on the throwover link mounting, locking of the turntable is achieved by means of a lever located on the opposite side of the traverse handle. During vehicle moves the mortar can be lowered into the well of the turntable to reduce height and it will also allow the mortar hatches to be closed to give the crew some protection against the elements.

To carry the required bombs for the mortar, bomb racks have been installed around the personnel compartment. The bomb racks are designed to accept twin bomb containers (these are moulded plastic tubes joined together and hold one bomb in each tube). The rear rack holds thirty-six containers stowed in three tiers and the rack located on the right pannier holds twenty-four in two tiers plus an extra five containers can be stowed on top and retained in their guides by clamping bars. Two further containers can be hung from clips located on the inside face of the rear door. The FV432 mortar carrier conversion allows for transportation of the weapon and its ammunition plus the crew under armour, enabling it to be ready to provide fire at very short moment's notice.

FV432 with Peak Engineering 7.62mm GPMG turret

As we have already seen, the firing of the commander's MG is quite a risky business especially if it is being used to give supporting fire during an attack. These problems had been well discussed within the infantry circles and after various trials had taken place it was decided to fit a percentage of infantry FV432 with a GPMG turret that would give the firer armoured protection. The complete installation kit comprises of the turret, which is mounted on an adaptor plate that fits over the mortar hatches, and all associated wiring and communication leads. Secured to the adaptor plate is a bearing ring, this gives added height to the mantlet trunnions and protection to the turret ring. With the turret in place the vehicle height is changed to 2.53m; over the gunner's sight guard and over the open gunner's hatch it is 2.64m; also when the turret is fitted the commander's MG is not issued.

Around the bearing ring is a depression rail, which is in four sections. The rail completely encircles the ring and provides a track for the gun depression stop plunger attached to the turret. Located behind the turret is an elliptical escape hatch, which is hinged to the rear, to assist in opening the hatch a spring type equilibrator is fitted.

The turret is aluminium armour forging that is ballistically sloped with a domed hatch, a cast in aperture slot is provided through which the barrel of the GPMG moves in elevation and depression. A sight periscope and two vision periscopes are also provided for the gunner. Two periscopes face forward while a third is located in the gunner's hatch, giving him some rear vision. Mounted on either side of the turret are two banks of four smoke dischargers that can fire any of the standard issue smoke grenades as used by AFVs. Traverse of the turret is achieved by the gunner turning a manually operated traverse gear which drives a spur gear that engages in the turret ring. The gunner is provided with a folding saddle type seat with a footrest that is attached to the turret and revolves with it. The seat also has a seat belt for the gunner and located either side of him are two ready ammunition boxes, each holding one standard box of 7.62mm ammunition. A single ammunition feed box carrier is mounted on the turret sill adjacent to the gun mounting and a spent case bag is attached by its metal frame to a plate on the right of the mount. To ensure that the spent links and cases fall into the bag a spent case chute runs from beneath the cradle into the bag.

The gunner's hatch is padded for his protection and is hinged to the rear with its weight counterbalanced by a disc spring type equilibrator. The hatch can be secured in either the closed or fully open positions. The gunner has an extension handle from the cradle with a pistol grip that has a trigger fitted to it. This handle is also used to elevate and depress the gun. Linkage from the trigger is attached to the firing mechanism on the cradle that bears against the trigger fitted onto the gun. To prevent the gunner inadvertently firing the weapon in too low a depression and having rounds strike the vehicle, a depression rail is fitted. This allows the gun to be depressed only until it contacts the follower and the profile has been designed to allow the gun to be used with the driver's and commander's hatches in the closed position.

FV432 with ZB 298 Ground Surveillance Radar

The ZB 298 is a man portable ground surveillance radar that was issued to RAC units for use by their reconnaissance troops (not often) and to the artillery. It could be man packed or vehicle mounted in Ferret, CVR (T) Spartan or in the FV432. When in use the radar had a range of 10,000m. It was replaced in service by a system known as MSTARS.

The ZB 298 could be fitted to a FV432 with, as always, various modifications to the basic vehicle. The installation involves some modifications to the mortar hatch covers, which are then locked in the closed position, and the removal of the left front personnel seat, the left front aerial base and some of the stowage facilities. The ZB 298 was a system that one never seemed to see in action, it was one of these pieces of equipment that you knew were there but never saw and many of them probably spent their service life languishing within the stores.

FV432/30 RARDEN TURRET

As we have seen in several instances, one of the shortcomings of the FV432 is its lack of firepower other than the 7.62mm GPMG. This had been realised by the WO/MoD and in November 1966, MVEE were requested to carry out feasibility studies on mounting the 30mm RARDEN armed turret from CVR (W) Fox onto the hull of a standard FV432. A report issued by MVEE in March 1967 listed some costing as well as stating that the idea was a valid one. In February 1968 GSR 3165 was issued to authorise the fitting of Fox turrets onto FV432. On the strength of this, three prototype kits were manufactured and fitted to vehicles. One vehicle went to MVEE for automotive and firing trials and the other two to the users ITDU. These were a Mk 1 and Mk 2. Other trials that were carried out included the effect of the top weight of the turret affecting the flotation of the vehicle. These were carried out at: the MVEE wading pit to ascertain the entry and exit criteria; Horsea Island, Portsmouth for speed trials; and Instow in Devon for stability tests. There were no adverse affects on the flotation of the vehicle although with the weight of the turret there was less safety margin on steep entry and exit slope.

The system was put out to competitive tender on 15 August 1969 with the second stage tender issued in April 1970, with production due in February 1972 with twenty-five units built a month with completion date of November 1973. In the event it seems that only thirteen to twenty conversions were ever made, as the vehicle was not popular with the infantry. This was one of the concerns that GSR 3165 had raised, stating that 'the vehicle must not become specialist and the turret must be capable of being transferred between vehicles within the unit by the REME LAD'. It was found this could be done in 1.5 hours.

The infantry did not appear to like the vehicle as it tied up an APC for what was seen as a specialist role. What they had required was a vehicle with the capability of FV432/30 but the crew capacity of an APC; this would come later with Warrior. However each user unit manned them as they saw fit.

In the end the vehicle was issued to the Berlin Brigade only while the rest of the infantry waited for the introduction of Warrior. Most FV432/30 ended their days serving as 'vismods' with the demo battalion based in Warminster and at the time of writing has only recently been replaced with Warrior. In this role various modifications were added, such as a mock up Sagger ATGW mount over the 30mm to represent a BMP.

The turret for the FV432/30 is identical to that fitted to the CVR (W) Fox and is made from aluminium armour giving protection against small arms and shell bursts. It has full 360-degree rotation, 40-degree elevation and 14-degree depression. The turret mounts the L21 RARDEN cannon, which can fire a variety of rounds including HE APDS APSE and practise. It has an effective range of 2,000m but could fire further if the crew could see the fall of shot. There are ninety-nine rounds carried and they are loaded in clips of three, with the gun having the capability of single shot or automatic, although only six rounds maximum can be loaded into the gun. It has a rate of fire of 90 rpm. The secondary armament is a co-axial mounted 7.62 GPMG. Either side of the turret are two sets of four smoke grenade dischargers.

The commander and gunner are both provided with various sights, with the gunner having both day and image intensified night sight. The gunner's day sight is the Sight Periscopic No. 52 Mk 1; using this sight the gunner can lay the gun for both line and elevation. It is of the binocular type in that the gunner views through twin eyepieces, he is also able to use the sight for general viewing through a unity window, and the eyepieces have a magnification of ×10 while the unity window is ×1. Looking through the eyepieces the gunner will have the aiming graticule pattern visible within his right eyepiece, this can be illuminated if required, and a heater system is also provided for the eyepieces. The sight systems are provide with laser filters to help protect the gunner's eyes due to the common use of laser range finders on the battlefield. A wiper/wash system is provided to ensure that the outside of the sight head can be kept clean.

The gunner is also equipped with the Sight Periscope II L2A1 for night firing. This is an opto/electrical instrument with either magnification of ×1.6 or ×5.8. The sight itself is a very large unit and the front part projects through the mantlet and is covered with an armoured cowl with a door that can be opened from under armour but has to be closed from outside. A heater and washer are provided to keep the lens clear of mud etc. The sight is hinged in the centre to allow the front section to move in elevation and depression. Use of the sight for observation is very tiring and to make best use of it crew rotation is needed. That apart, when it was introduced it was a quantum leap forward as the Chieftain still used IR and a white light searchlight.

The commander is equipped with the Sight Periscopic AV No. 68 Mk 1. Unlike the gunner's sight it is not mounted direct to the turret roof but into sight mount No. 45 Mk 1, this gives the commander independent traverse of the sight up to 60 degrees. This means that if the gunner is engaging a target the commander could, if he is confident that the gunner is having no problems, unlock his sight and within the 60-degree arc look for new targets. The remainder of the sight follows the pattern of the gunner's with illuminated graticule and ×10 eyepieces and ×1 window. It also is provided with laser filters and blackout system. The commander also has seven periscopes, AV No. 43 Mk 3, located around his cupola; these are of ×1 magnification and are provide to give the commander a degree of all-round vision. The gunner is also provided with two of the same sights either side or forward of his hatch.

The commander and gunner both have their own hatches for entry and exit from the turret with the commander's on the left and the gunner's to the right. The gunner's hatch is flat but the commander's is domed to give him that bit more movement when closed down. The APC role commander's cupola is replaced with a simple hatch, as there is no requirement for a separate cupola. Both the commander's and gunner's seats and backrests are identical in construction and layout with height adjustment (four positions) and they can be used with the backrest that converts to a seat when using it in the fully opened up position. The footrests are spring loaded in the vertical plane and will require downward pressure to hold it down.

A turret traverse lock is fitted to the turret sill and is used to relieve shocks on the traverse gears whilst the vehicle is in motion. The trunnion-mounted mantlet provides the facility for the main and co-axial weapons to be moved in the vertical plane by means of the elevating gear. The mantlet provides the mount for the 30mm gun, the machine gun and the gunner's night sight. The left mantlet trunnion has an extend shaft which is fitted with two linkage arms that are connected to an equilibrator trimmer assembly. This is two powerful flat type springs which balance the force created by the weapon being breech heavy. Mounted on the left, complete with its firing solenoid gear, is the MG cradle. Leading from the cradle is a spent link and case chute that leads to the canvas bag attached to the main ammunition rack by screw type hose clamps.

FV432 Fitted with Winch and Earth Anchor

This was another conversion that could be fitted to most versions of FV432 except Mk 1/1 vehicles 02 EA 01 to 02 EA 54 as securing brackets and welded pads were not fitted during the production of those vehicles. The aim of this conversion was to try and give the REME more recovery capability without having to resort to a heavy ARV. It also was going to be a support element at river crossings where it would be able to winch out any FV432 type vehicle that was floundering or had trouble in making the crossing. The fact that the winch vehicle may also have had problems in crossing as well seems to have escaped the designers. In the end the conversion was not popular and was never widely brought into service.

The mechanically driven winch is mounted above a two-speed gearbox, which is driven from the transverse gearbox of the vehicle power pack by a universal joint and hydraulically operated clutch. Two levers control the operation of the winch; one is used for gear ratio selection and the other for direction of travel of the rope. A freewheel brake is mounted in the rope gear train, this controls the paying out of the rope when it is being drawn out under a load rather than pulled by hand. The winch rope itself is 230m (750ft) long and is connected to a pilot rope 15m (50ft) long, this painted red and the first 15m of the winch rope main is painted yellow.

The most noticeable visible change to the vehicle is to the rear door. This is a foreshortened version of the standard door with the following changes: an extra observation block fitted to the right side of the door, the convoy light mounting has been raised, and the mounting bracket for the boiling vessel tray has been modified to accommodate the convoy light housing. The door strut is a much bulkier item than the original one and the winch itself takes up a large amount of the normal space in the vehicle.

The earth anchor blade, which is lowered prior to winching operations, is used to prevent the winching vehicle being dragged towards the casualty vehicle. The earth anchor itself is a curved aluminium blade which is fitted with a coarse toothed digging edge, which can be replaced if damaged, is fitted on to two hinged and tapered posts that are fitted to one either side of the rear door. A rope is threaded through a lug on the blade and the ends secured with quick release pins to the posts to prevent the blade becoming detached when the vehicle moves forward. When not in use the blade is dismounted and stored in the vehicle for transportation.

A tow bar is provided as part of the equipment and when fitted it acts as anchorage for a recovery snatch block that would be used when carrying out a two or three part pull. When not in use it is also stowed inside the vehicle. The tow bar stowage frame is mounted on the left pannier sill and provides facilities to stow the hollebone (these are two large round arms linked at one end with eyebolts at the other that, when assembled, form an A-frame for towing), drawbar and hand lanterns. Stowage is also provided on the left sill for a man portable welding kit and jerrycans. With a full complement of REME crew and all their personnel equipment the inside the vehicle was very cramped. One of the main complaints was that the winch forever seemed to have a permanent oil leak, which meant that the operator was always slipping and sliding around in it. The vehicle performed well enough and, if asked, those who used it will say that it did its job but for the above reasons was not particularly popular. In the end the FV434 seemed to manage most jobs apart from seriously bogged vehicles and it was felt that there was not a requirement for the conversion and with the phasing out of flotation equipment it was not employed.

FV432 with MILAN

Milan was a man portable ATGW system for use by the infantry. Milan was usually broken down into several components for man packing but if it could be carried in a vehicle so much the better as more missiles could be carried, along with any spares that might be required, and the crew remained fresher and therefore more efficient.

FV432 was converted to carry Milan and its missiles and night sight. This conversion can be employed on all marks of FV432, when so modified the vehicle can carry two firing posts complete with tripods, two Milan infra-red adapters (MIRA) and twenty missiles in their launch tubes. Conversion involved fitting special stowage to hold the various items, and a simple adaptor could be located over the mortar hatch to allow the launcher to be fitted and fired from the vehicle.

FV432 with Bar Mine Layer and Ranger

While this equipment is mostly seen being towed by an FV432 it is more an employment of the FV432 than a full conversion, as all the crew have to do to carry the mines is raise the crew seats. This equipment can be towed behind a conventional FV432 and very little modification is required to the vehicle except for a tow bar to pull the minelayer.

Once the lane has been decided then the FV432 towing the bar mine layer travels along the route, as it does so the bar mines are fed from the back of the FV432 into the mine layer manually. The layer has two plough-type wheels which cut the ground and allow the mine to lay in it at the correct height. As the layer passes over the mine the earth is turned back over it to conceal the mine. Up to 600 bar mines can be laid in one hour by a three-man crew. Also mounted on top of the vehicle could be the Thorn EMI Ranger scatterable mine layer, this consists of seventy-two tubes each containing eighteen anti-personnel mines. When fired, the mines were projected in a random pattern to a distance of 100m. The mine contains 10gm of PDX explosive and will cause serious injury or death to anyone detonating one. Since the signing of various agreements on the use of anti-personnel mines the UK no longer uses this system, although the bar mine anti-tank system is still used.

FV432 BATES

BATES was a battlefield artillery engagement system which has been designed to centralise the command and control of artillery, with all fire missions being routed through a central control cell and then passed on to the appropriate fire units. Access to the system was available down to the level of artillery FOOs (Forward Observation Officers) who will have their own digital entry devices. BATES eventually replaced FACE (Forward Artillery Computing Equipment).

Artillery intelligence entered in the system such as NBC reporting is available for commanders and their staff through the WAVELL interface and much of the routine and logistic tasks are processed by the equipment, thus freeing the staff for other tasks. BATES went out of service in 2005.

FV432 FACE

This is another specialised Royal Artillery version and acronym, field artillery computer equipment, and again is carried in specialised FV432 or Land Rover. It provides the forward observation officer data based on survey information, meteorological information and the variables of the weapons being used. It was to be replaced with BATES.

FV432 Sound Ranging

Sound ranging is a method employed by the Royal Artillery to locate enemy artillery quickly and accurately and to plot the source of the sound, thus allowing counter bombardment to be launched. The system consists of specialised microphones that are extended on top of masts, linked into the host FV432. When a weapon is fired the microphones detect the pressure waves and by using several vehicles set up in a pattern, these signals can be triangulated to pinpoint the firing point. Sound ranging can locate an enemy position within 50m at 10km, although longer ranges are normal.

FV432 Cymbeline

This was the mortar locating radar used by the Royal Artillery which now has been phased out, to be replaced by a new system. It is mounted onto a standard FV432 on top of the mortar hatches, internally the seating has to be rearranged, an operators table is provided and also a davit and hoist to help with removal or changing of the units in the field. There is a self-levelling unit incorporated in the system to ensure that the radar is as level as possible when operating. For transport the radar is folded down and is protected by a mesh cage, when in use it is fully unfolded and the cage removed. The system works by detecting the flight of an incoming mortar round at two points of its trajectory as it passes through the radar beams. Rapid computing then enables the grid reference of the enemy base plate to be identified and engaged by artillery. An 81mm mortar bomb can be detected at about 10km while a 120mm bomb can be detected at 14km, although these are only general ranges as the actual distance is determined by many factors.

FV432 Mine Plough

While we have looked at methods of laying mines by the Royal Engineers, they also have to clear minefields as well. To date there is no really 100 per cent efficient method of clearing mines mechanically and still the best way is for a soldier armed with a mine prodder to slowly move through a suspected area probing for mines. This is slow and very dangerous. Many mechanical methods have been tried but they all have one failing in that they cannot guarantee to be 100 per cent effective. They can be quicker and in a fast moving battle it is sometimes accepted that some vehicles will still hit mines when crossing a minefield that has been mechanically cleared.

The FV432 has been used in several experiments to provide a suitable mine clearance system. It has been fitted with a full width mine plough which works by the vehicle moving forward and the plough turning over and disrupting any buried mines. Often this will detonate the mines and damage to both the plough and vehicle is unavoidable. This system was sent to the Gulf for the first Gulf war and was also seen at several equipment demonstrations, but was not accepted into service.

As we have seen the FV432 is not the most heavily armoured vehicle and the driver is very close to any source of explosion. A solution was to equip one vehicle with the plough but to have it remotely controlled from a second vehicle. Therefore if a major explosion happened to wreck the ploughing vehicle then there would be no human casualties. This system was also used in the first Gulf War, but when being controlled remotely the blade was more like a bulldozer blade than the track width ploughs on the driven variant.

FV432 Flail
A flail mine clearance system is very simple with the flail being a drum with weighted chains fitted to it driven by either a power take-off from the vehicle or a separate engine. It usually extends some distance from the vehicle by being mounted on arms; this helps protect the vehicle from and blast damage. This system, mounted onto an FV432, was trialled but not accepted, although a flail vehicle was in use with the British Army which was known as Aardvark; it is a combination of wheels and tracks and can be operated by a driver or remote control.

FV432 REME Turret
When the FV432 was in Aden in the mid-sixties the lack of protection for the commander when using the MG was apparent even then. One local variation that was designed by the REME was to fit a Saracen or Ferret turret to the commander's position. This gave him full armour protection to fire the fitted .30 Browning machine gun from under armour. This was a stopgap in the hope that a better idea would be designed, which as we have seen was in the shape of the 16 cupola. In the end, like the 16 cupola, it was not brought into service. As can be seen in the photograph it changes the profile of the FV432 considerably.

FV433 Abbot self-propelled gun
This is the first of the major variants based on the chassis and components of the FV430 series; to give it its full title it is gun self-propelled 105mm Field Gun Abbot FV433. So what do we get for that long title? The vehicle is, as its names states, a self-propelled gun (often called by the misinformed media a tank) that uses many of the FV432 components, but on a completely different hull and also mounting a turret.

In the late 1950s was a requirement to replace the Royal Artillery's ageing fleet of weapons. Several new projects had been formulated such as the FV3802 Centurion. These had come to nothing, leaving the gunners using essential towed field pieces such as the 25-pounder and 5.5 gun. Some American full tracked self-propelled 155mm M44 were still in service, but these needed replacing very soon.

The decision was taken to design and build a new SP gun and to ease the logistics it was decided to utilise the running gear of the new FV430 series of vehicles, giving commonality of parts. The new vehicle was to have a turret that could be traversed a full 360 degrees, provide the crew and equipment with armour protection, be capable of carrying a good onboard load of ready ammunition. Vickers was designated as the design parents for the new vehicle and by 1961 they had completed the first prototype of what was now called Abbot. Eleven other prototypes soon followed, with the first six being powered by the Rolls-Royce B81 petrol engine as used in the Mk 1 FV432. The Rolls-Royce K60 powered the remaining six. These first twelve vehicles differed from what would be the production vehicles in a number of ways. On the prototype models the flotation screen, instead of lying flat on top of the hull, sloped from the rear of the vehicle to the front. They also only had twin headlights instead of the four that were later fitted; they also had the exhaust pipe exiting from the left hand side of the hull above the flotation screen. During rebuild of these prototypes all these features were removed and the vehicles configured to production standards.

After the usual round of trial and testing the production order was given to Vickers and from 1964 to 1967 the Abbot was in production for the British Army. One variant of the Abbot was known as the value engineered Abbot and this was produced to help sell the vehicle to countries that wished to purchase the vehicle but either for cost reasons or for training did not want all the facilities of the British standard Abbot. The version that came to be known as the Value Engineered Abbot or VE Abbot had the following changes to it:

No rubber pads on the tracks.
No flotation screen.
Dial sight replaced by one German sight as fitted to German M109.
Turret traverse and elevation are all by hand.
No MG pintle on cupola.
Limited external stowage.
No power rammer for loading.
No fire wire warning system.
No smoke dischargers.
Split hatches for the loader.
No interior padding.
K60 engine only develops 213bhp.
No NBC system.
Only one set of batteries.

All of the above could of course be retrofitted if required by the customer as well as any extra upgrade items that might be required. The VE Abbot could also not be used in the anti-tank role but again if required it could be equipped with HESH and a simple sight. Of the original twelve prototypes at least three have ended up on the ranges at Otterburn in Northumberland as hard targets.

The British Army bought 146 Abbots and the Army used these worldwide. They also took twenty VE Abbots who spent their working life in BATUS, Canada where they probably became the hardest working Abbots of the whole fleet.

Description

The vehicle's lower hull resembles that of FV432 with the same type of suspension and road wheels, top rollers and track adjuster system. The engine used is the same K60 as found in FV432 but the power packs are not interchangeable due to the different layout adopted in the Abbot. Individual parts can be changed however. The transmission and steering box are the same as for the FV432. In its original form a flotation screen was fitted around the top of the hull, this was removed in later life once the requirement for swimming had been dispensed with. The driver is located on the front right of the vehicle with access through twin hatches. He is provided with a day sight for closed down driving and this can be interchanged with a night driving sight. The driver's compartment is considerably more cramped than that of the FV432 and the driver can find that his thighs touch the compartment sides, such is the narrow width. The instruments and switches are similar to the FV432 but they are laid out in a different manner and some of them are very difficult to see, although in time you get used to their location and it is almost location by touch.

Access to the fighting compartment is either via the commander's or loader's hatches or from an armoured door at the rear of the vehicle. When in action this door will serve for the supply of ammunition that has been prepared and stowed outside the vehicle. Within the door is a spring-loaded, hinged flap that is used to dispose of empty brass cases when operating in the closed down mode. Under an armoured cover is a pressure relief flap valve. This is designed to open at a set pressure of three inches standard water gauge when using the NBC system so the vehicle does not become over-pressurised. If it did it may cause the various seals to blow and allow NBC agents into the vehicle.

The fighting compartment is the enclosed portion of the vehicle beneath the turret. It houses the detachment with the exception of the driver who is located in the hull. The fighting compartment also contains all the necessary equipment for the efficient fighting of the vehicle like gun, sights mounting and radios. Air purification and filtering equipment operated by an electrically driven fan is fitted on the outside of the turret, this draws air through a particulate filter. The air is then routed through trunking and is then discharged through diffusers located at convenient points around the turret. Air for the driver is vented into ducts and then through the rotary base junction to the cab, the diffusers can be rotated to give the best position for each individual crewmember. There are seats provide for the No. 1, layer and loader.

The turret is fabricated from steel armour plates of varying thickness, these however are only to protect it from shell bursts and small arms. It does not give it the same protection as an MBT. The turret rotates a full 360° mounted on bearings set into the race ring. The turret is equipped with a cupola vision AFV No. 14 Mk 1. This is for use by the commander and it is capable of being traversed through 360-degrees by hand and locked in to any position required by means of locking levers. The hatch over the loader's position is a single-piece octagonal plate. The weight of this is balanced by the means of a laminated torsion bar and the hatch can be retained in either the vertical or fully open position by means of spring-loaded plunger inside the turret engaging in a recess in the hatch hinge pin.

Armament

The Abbot is equipped with a QF 105mm L13A1 gun, which consists of a body and a breech mechanism, and these are further broken down into a barrel assembly, fume extractor, muzzle brake and breech ring assembly. The barrel is of a monobloc construction and it is forged from high tensile steel. Internally it is shaped at the rear end to form the chamber (this is where the projectile and propellant are loaded). This portion has smooth walls while the section forward of the chamber is rifled. At approximately halfway along the barrel, machined seating has been formed to accept the fume extractor The fume extractor is located on the machined seating and consists of a fabricated metal casing with each end bored to fit onto the seating. It is recessed to accept 'O' type sealing rings. After a round has been fired and the shell has travelled along the gun bore to a point beyond the fume extractor ports, propellant gases flow through the ports and build up a pressure within the fume extractor. The gases under pressure are stored in the fume extractor until the pressure in the bore drops below that in the fume extractor, after which the gases pass back through the inclined ports, and out through the muzzle of the gun. The sucking action created in the wake of the gases ejected from the fume extractor ports causes the residual gases in the breech end of the bore to be expelled from the muzzle.

The breech mechanism is of the semi-automatic type and consists principally of the breech block, electric firing needle assembly, actuating shaft leaf spring, breech block actuating cranks, extractor levers and the lever breech mechanism (LBM). The point of the needle will come into contact with the base of the round and when the firing switch is pressed allow electric current to flow, causing the primer in the base of the round to ignite. This in turn will ignite the propellant and drive the projectile along the bore.

Due to the long fire mission that the guns are called on to deliver, the crew would soon become exhausted by the sheer amount of ammunition that they would be required to load into the gun. So to assist the loader, a power rammer is fitted to carry out part of the loading drills.

To complete the firing circuit the appropriate firing button is pressed, once the gun has fired recoil takes place, during the run out phase the breech block will be opened ready for the next round to be loaded. The lowering of the block imparts a slow powerful rearward movement to the extractor levers to unseat the empty cartridge case followed by a sharp kick to the extractors which will eject the spent case. All this takes place very rapidly and is over in split seconds. To control recoil twin hydraulic buffers are fitted

The elevation gear that is provided on the Abbot is hand operated only, as no power system is deemed necessary. It is of the rack and pinion type of gearbox with the assembly bolted to the right gun support bracket with the elevating rack being bolted to the cradle. The elevating hand wheel contains the trigger switch and wiring for the completion of the firing circuit.

To use this system is simplicity itself: the layer rotates the handle anti-clockwise and the gun will elevate, and in clockwise direction it will depress.

The turret traverse system is servo operated from the turret batteries and provides for traverse at varying speeds in either direction. In an emergency or when the engine is not running, a manual hand operated system can be used. The hand traverse assembly is a two-speed gearbox which has an output shaft that connects it to the main gearbox.

Sighting equipment

The Abbot has two separate sighting systems, one for the laying of indirect fire and the other for direct fire. The system consists basically of a dial sight for indirect laying, a dial sight mount incorporating a tangent elevation (TE) and angle of sight assembly, and a telescope for direct fire. Although not an anti-tank weapon the Abbot is equipped with Sight telescopic AFV No. 29 Mk 1 and HESH ammunition to enable it to be used in the anti-tank role. The telescope is for direct fire and has a magnification of × 1. Three No. 32 Mk 1 periscopes are fitted side by side in the cupola to give the commander a wide field of view when closed down, with the centre periscope being able to be tilted in the vertical plane to give more observation.

Ammunition

The range of ammunition will include high explosive, which can be set to burst on impact or for air burst, white phosphorus smoke, which once the phosphorus is exposed to the air will create an instant white smoke screen or a base ejection smoke round. To enable the crews to practise live firing while attempting to reduce costs, practise HESH rounds have been developed. These basically employ the same case as a service round but have the explosive filling replaced with an inert substance, often concrete, that will give the same weight as a service round. This will mean that the round will follow the same trajectory as a live one, thus providing the crew with the required experience. One further round used was the illuminating round; this was used to light up the battlefield and was of great use to Chieftain Tanks before thermal imaging became the norm.

The 105mm gun uses a system of variable charges to obtain specific ranges. Which charge to use will be passed to the guns by the command post. Charges not required will be removed by the No. 4 and shown to the No. 1. All natures of cartridges used by the system use the same size brass case that is made of drawn brass. It has a hole in the base to accept an electric primer and the mouth of the case has four indentations to accept a plastic lid or the holder for increment No. 5 of the normal cartridge incorporated in the Mk 2 system.

All the ammunition used has markings on them that denote when they were filled, the type of explosive, who filled it and the batch number. This is used to trace any problems if there are incidents with ammunition in use anywhere in the world.

FV434 Fitters

The FV434 is the other major variation to the FV430 family and it was developed to provide the REME detachments with the user units with a repair vehicle and also with limited recovery facilities, although these are limited to towing a vehicle by the use of hollebone bars. Winching was to be provided by the FV432 equipped with a winch that we have already looked at. Now if a vehicle is bogged down it will be helped by one of the Warrior recovery variant or a Challenger recovery vehicle.

The report WO 32/18899 FV434 which had remained closed until 1996 has a letter dated 1960 in which a strongly worded comment makes reference to doubts expressed about the viability of the REME requiring the FV434. Acceptance of the FV434 was at a meeting held at FVRDE on 10 June 1965. The vehicle came about due to doubts in policy of spare tanks held in reserve and repair by workshops many miles behind the lines raised in August 1960. The author of the letter raised hackles with comments about global war lasting hours not days which was contrary to everything that NATO was saying. This elicited a swift reply from the current DRAC. A requirement for 304 FV434 was found to replace the in-service half track fitters vehicle. On 29 November DCIGS requested a presentation on the concept of FV434. The Presentation took place 18 January 1961; it was shown that the vehicle would use components of the FV432, making it one of a family of vehicles using a common chassis a 2.5 ton payload and adequate protection for the crew. It was agreed that a winch was desirable but that it would be fitted into a 432 rather than 434. The crane must be capable of lifting the power pack of main battle tanks. First design drawings show the floatation screen slopes down to the rear of the vehicle and not all around as on production vehicles.

Immunity from Russian 12.7 AP at 200m is required for frontal protection. In June 1963 the name Trident is being used for the vehicle. Trial planning was well under way and a lot seems to be in line with work on the FV431 load carrier. Consignment notes for March 1964 show trial vehicles issued to Tech group REME, School of Artillery Larkhill, 1st Battalion Royal Irish Fusiliers, 17/21st and 6 infantry brigade workshops.

On 24 September 1964 a demonstration at ROF Leeds showed that the current layout for 434 was not enough to allow it to carry the L60 power pack. As capacity of load area was the second most important requirement it looked as if it would have to be modified and the vehicle designated not fit for service until this was done. However no firm decisions were to be taken until the trial reports were received. A wooden mockup of the new layout of the cargo bay was ready on 1 February 1965.

The BAOR trial summary stated the overall vehicle was well received, although its inability to neutral turn, insufficient space in the fitters' section and travel sickness when closed down were noted. These were the major complaints as a result of the troop trial. Comments on lack of stowage and restricted cargo bay and poor access to vehicle are also mentioned, as all access has to be from top of vehicle. The fitting of a HIAB crane was liked but it was criticised for its tendency to creep in use.

The FV434 is based on the Mk 2 hull and from the commander's cupola forward it is identical. However to the left and slightly to the rear of the commander's cupola is a square crew hatch, which is officially used by the radio/crane operator but is useful to allow a couple of crew members from the dead vehicle into the FV434, although this produces some very cramped conditions. The rear part of the vehicle has been modified extensively in that where the personnel compartment used to be is now a large open well; this space is used to carry the spare assemblies required. There is also stowage for the oils and lubricants that will be required during a major assembly change. The rear of the vehicle has stowage and a drop down workbench fitted with an engineer's vice. Extensive equipment is carried on the vehicle to aid the fitters when attending a casualty. The FV434 is fitted with a HIAB hydraulically operated crane that has a lifting capacity of 1,250kg at 3.96m reach to 3,050kg at 2.26m reach. The hydraulic shock absorbers have the facility to be locked when the crane is in use to improve stability.

Once the design of the FV434 had been settled it then went through the trials system to make sure that it would be up to what it was required to do. At FVRDE in October/November 1963 trials using FV434 prototypes P1 and P2 were put through their paces to prove just that. An impressive array of 'casualties' awaited them: a Mk 7 Centurion, Mk 2 Conqueror P1 and P2 FV432 Mk 1 B81 versions, and a P6, the prototype K60-powered FV432. The trial involved changing and replacing just about every major component that you could think of. Each trial had various problems introduced that might be encountered by the crews in the field. There was, at this time, still the requirement for the vehicles to be able to swim so P1, fitted with a production power pack, carried out full saltwater trials at Hornsea Island. A water speed of 4mph was achieved although the nose down attitude that the vehicle adopted because of the crane caused some water resistance.

During its time at the RAC centre at Bovington in Dorset, P2 loaded a Chieftain MBT L60 power pack into its load carrying area and then drove back to FVRDE at Chobham in Surrey. This road run showed that a special carrying frame on which to place major assemblies when being carried in the load area was required, due to the L60 wooden crate starting to break up. There being no set way to carry assemblies at that time they were simply placed in the load area in their wooden transit crates and tied down.

Interestingly the WO equipment policy statement issued on 26 January 1968 on accepting the FV434 in service gave it a working life of fifteen years from its introduction in 1967. However, at the time of writing (2018), it is still in service and soldiering on.

FV435 Wavell

Although this variant is based on a conventional FV432 hull it has a separate designation due to the nature of the equipment fitted into it. Converting the vehicle to the FV435 role is a workshop job. This vehicle is one of those that can cause confusion in following the FV number sequence of the FV430 series. Wavell variants can be converted from the standard FV432; they then will become FV435, however some vehicles have erroneously been known as FV438 Wavell. This is because some defunct FV438s had the missile equipment removed and converted in carriers for Wavell; they should however be known as FV435.

Wavell is a battlefield automatic data processing computer system designed to accept information from all the available intelligence agencies and from this information produce a hard copy or display it on a VDU. This information can then be used to aid commanders and their staff in interpreting intelligence to enable them to make their plans for future operations. Wavell is located at corps headquarters and down to brigade level and they are all linked into the Ptarmigan secure communications network.

FV436 Green Archer/Command/438

This vehicle has a crew of three and as with the FV434 the front part of the vehicle is the same as an ordinary FV432. From behind the commander's hatch the vehicle has a flat load area onto which the EMI radar is located. The radar had its own self-contained generator system but was a much heavier system than Cymbeline, which replaced it. The designation of FV436 then was allocated to specialist built command post vehicles.

These contain all the equipment to convert the vehicle into an office, containing map boards, tables, central seating, document stowage and extra strip lighting. This will also include in many cases extra radios and batteries. The map boards are made from plywood edged with aluminium strips for strength. They are located in runners in front of the left and right pannier stowage. The boards are designed to slide to enable items stowed behind them to be reached more easily. Four fluorescent lights are fitted to give better vision over the normal lighting system. All the lights are connected to a blackout system on the rear door that, if the door is opened, all light will go out and not come on again till the rear door is secured.

To give the staff a solid writing surface, four tables are provided, two either side, with the two on the right hand side being narrower than the left to enable them to clear the backrest of the bench seat. The tables can be folded up when not required. Seating is provided by a tubular frame supporting seat pads and a backrest, and the whole assembly is bolted to the centre of the floor. Apart from carrying all the extra radio equipment such as 8m masts, the vehicle also carries a portable shelter. This can be erected and attached to the rear of the vehicle to give more working space. Most crews have built extra stowage using anything that comes to hand, ranging from old army steel lockers to purpose built baskets welded from dexion mesh. The framework for the shelter is stowed on the left hand side of the vehicle. As can be imagined this is not something that can be set up and taken down in a matter of minutes. To supply the power needed to run the command post, without the need for the main engine to be run for long periods, the dedicated FV436 armoured command post has two generators mounted on the roof in lightly armoured boxes. These help to distinguish between the simple user conversion to a command post by fitting the benches and map board that are available for this role. To confuse the numbering issue even more the FV438 Swingfire as we shall see had a fixed turret over the area of the mortar hatches.

FV437 Pathfinder

This was an experimental version of the FV432 that was designed with the aim of aiding vehicles that had been involved in swimming across water obstacles to be able to make their exit at difficult withdrawal points. This was required as, although entry points could be made as good as possible, during operations it was obvious that the exit point could not be prepared and some vehicles would have difficulty in exiting the obstacle and may even founder.

To enable it to carry out these tasks it was equipped with a capstan winch but, unlike the winch conversion that we have already seen, the winch rope exited from the front of the vehicle. It stands to reason that this vehicle would encounter the same problems as the vehicles it was designed to support, so to enable it to perform its allocated tasks it was provided with hydro-jet propulsion instead of using its tracks to power itself when swimming. This is a system that was also used in the Stalwart; in effect it is a propeller working in a shroud that sucks water in one end and propels it out of the other, creating a similar effect to a jet engine. Steering is usually effected by blocking the exit end of the shroud; this forces the water back along the shroud and allows it to exit in slots cut in the side, thus giving rearward motion or steering. To assist the vehicle in leaving steep banks a rocket propelled earth anchor was mounted onto the roof. When the vehicle approached the bank the earth anchor would be fired and by using a winch attached to the anchor line and the power of its own tracks the vehicle would haul itself out of the water. The crew would then position the vehicle near the exit and deploy the winch rope ready to hook up to any vehicle that was struggling. While it was an excellent idea it was not proceeded with.

FV438 Swingfire anti-tank guided missile launcher

This conversion was produced to give armour protection to the BAE Swingfire anti-tank guided missile, the British Army's main ATGW system. The British had been slow to accept the value of the missile in the early days and its development was slowed down by the critics who doubted that the shaped charge warhead that is employed on the missiles would be effective at all.

Swingfire had a much larger warhead than previous British missiles, with a diameter of about 150mm; its flight speed is 185m/s out to a range of 4,000m. When you watch these missiles in flight the flight speed seems so slow that you feel if you were in the vehicle being attacked then it would be easy to avoid action. The truth is different, as even if you could see the missile in flight the operator would be able to track you, although at the extreme ranges the reaction times for the missile to respond are greater.

The Swingfire had many advantages over earlier missiles and one of these was the fact that an automatic programme generator built into the missiles ground control equipment meant that the missile was brought into the operator's line of sight far earlier than previously. This means it has the ability to engage at shorter ranges, 150m for Swingfire. Although the capability for short-range engagements was there, it was not the preferred use of the system. It had been designed for the long-range engagement of the massed Soviet armour it was expected that BAOR would have to face in the event of a Soviet invasion of then West Germany.

Swingfire can be operated from within the FV438 or by means of a separated sight up to a 100m away. Using the separated sight means that if the vehicle launch position is detected and return fire destroys it, at least the crew will have survived. The disadvantage is that the operator loses the protection of armour and the vehicle, the protection of mobility, until the operator is back on board. Swingfire is a second generation missile guided to the target by means of very fine wires connected to the missile and the operator's control equipment. Movement of the operator's joystick is transmitted down the control wires and converted into signals to vector controls on the missile.

The FV438 is a standard FV432 with the mortar hatches removed and a non-rotatable turret which is located over the mortar hatch area in the hull roof. The turret contains two launcher bins with one missile in each bin. When not in use both bins lie flat, and in this position can be loaded from within the vehicle. When the launcher is required to be elevated for firing an interlock device is engaged that will allow one bin to be elevated and the other to remain flush with the turret. Once the missile has been fired the empty bin is pulled down manually and the interlock will raise the loaded bin. The bins being mounted on torsion springs assists elevation. As the bin is raised an efflux door at the rear of the bin opens automatically. This is to allow the gases from the rocket motor to leave the launcher bin. Fourteen missiles are normally carried with two in the launcher and twelve stowed in three racks in the fighting compartment, holding nine, two and one missiles respectively. The two stowage bins at the rear have been replaced by armoured bins containing the sight, mounting and cables required to operate in the dismounted separated sight role.

Once it has been launched, the missile is programmed to appear in the controller's line of sight; thereafter the controller applies corrections to the flight of the missile onto the target, using the thumb controller on his sighting equipment.

FV438 was originally issued to tank regiments of the RAC where it was often used to provide long range protection out to the flanks. It then was transferred to the Royal Artillery for a period of time before coming home to the RAC where many felt it really belonged. Swingfire finally retired in 2005.

FV439 Royal Signals

Of all the conversions that have been applied to the FV432 and have or are in use, this one is the most secretive of them all. Not so much regarding the vehicle, as it can be seen on exercise anywhere, but more the radio equipment used by the Royal Signal that is fitted inside.

FV439 is another conversion that once it is in this role is not easy to convert back to a basic APC role again. The vehicle can be recognised by the large box structure on the rear right of the roof housing a generator, also there are several masts fitted to the vehicle, one of them being a hydraulically operated one. The vehicle houses components of Wavell and Ptarmigan communications systems, one vehicle is on display with the hydraulic mast in the erected position at the Royal Signal museum at Blandford Forum in Dorset, which is only a short distance from the Tank Museum. These vehicles will stay in service until the very end of the FV430 life span due to the highly important nature of their role, and the simple fact that there is nothing else to carry out that role as of yet.

Falcon

One final vehicle that was developed but never went into service was the Falcon, self-propelled anti-aircraft vehicle. This was a venture to provide mobile AA to the army. Based on the Abbot hull, it had a two-man powered turret mounting twin 30mm Hispano-Suiza stabilised cannon with a rate of fire of 1,300 rounds per minute and an effective range of approximately 3,000m. The British army has never been a big fan of SPAA, and Falcon lacked much. It had a small ammunition supply and there was no radar to track and aim the guns. While it worked in trials it was never taken up. The hull was seen in use at the Vickers site being used as a tug or for carrying loads, and who knows, somewhere tucked away in a dusty factory corner could be the turret.

Driver Training

One final piece of equipment that is hard to place was a driver training system designed to teach new drivers how to handle the vehicle before being allowed onto the open road. The simulator based at the driving and maintenance school at Bovington Camp was built by Link Miles and consisted of a representation of a cab mounted on hydraulic struts that would simulate movement, an instructor's console where the instructor could monitor the trainee and also introduce faults, and a scenic layout where a camera mounted on a boom followed the road or cross-country route and this image was shown to the trainee driver to give the impression that he was actually moving along the projected image. This, it was hoped, would give the learners a better feel for things before being let loose on the open road.

The old meets the new; FV434 joins up with the Warrior REME repair vehicle. (*Author's collection*)

A well posed picture of the FV438 Swingfire version. The control sight can be seen extended on top of the launcher box. (*Author's collection*)

It is hard to believe that these two Chi-Ha tanks are actually replicas made from cut down FV434s. (*Tim Virr*)

This is known as 'half tracking'. It's not ideal but it will enable the vehicle to make it back so proper repairs can be carried out. *(Daniel Novak)*

A shot of the mine plough as fitted to the FV432; not an ideal vehicle to use as a mine clearing vehicle though and the project was dropped. *(Author's collection)*

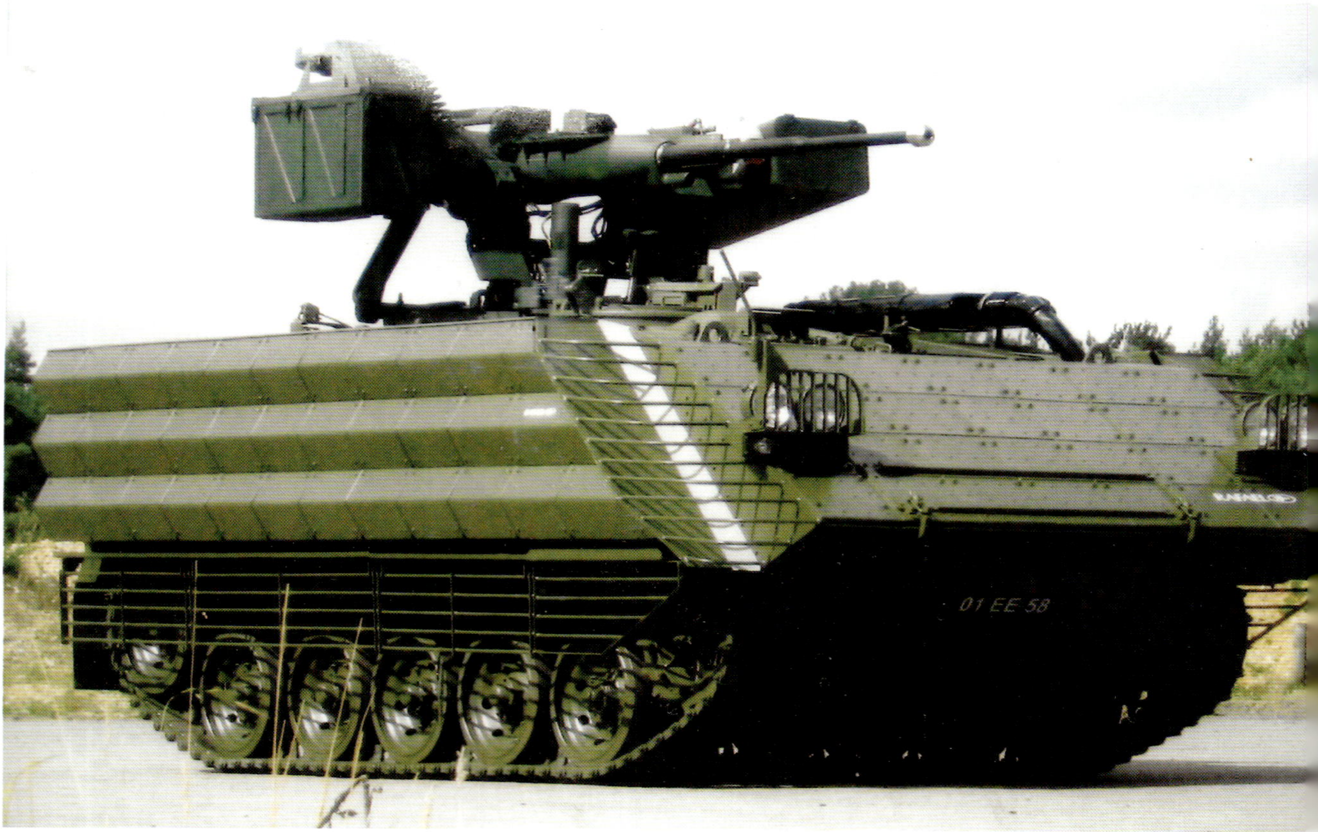
01 EE 58

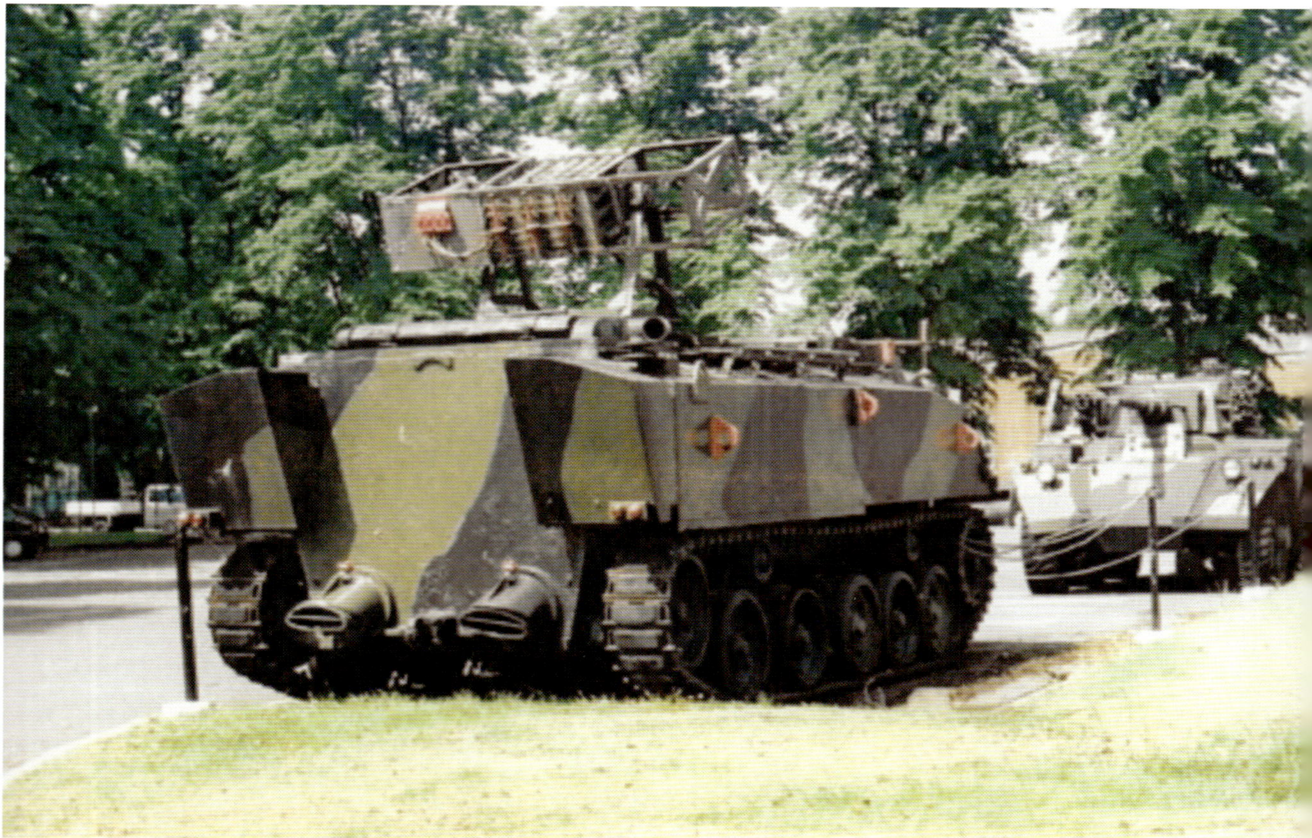

(**Opposite, above**) A stunning upgrade by BAE systems in conjunction with the Israeli Defence Industry. Notice the remote controlled cannon which is 30mm calibre. (*Author's collection*)

(**Above**) A good view of the very substantial base required for mounting the mortar. (*Plain Military*)

(**Opposite, below**) This rear view is of the water jet powered version that was to assist in crossing rivers and to aid casualties. Note the sloping rear with no door and also the outlet for the two water jets. The vehicle has the ranger scatterable mine system fitted to it. (*Author's collection*)

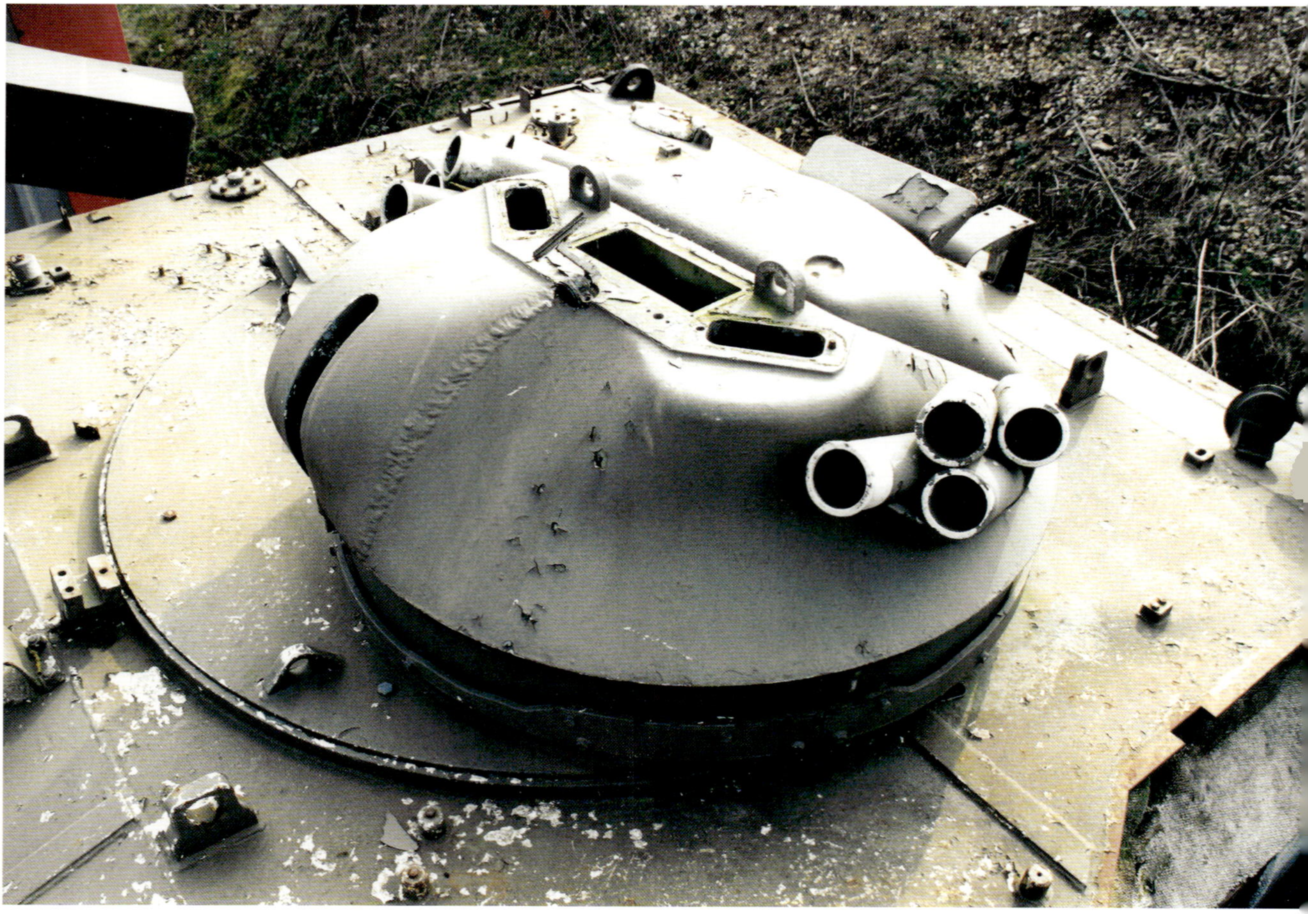

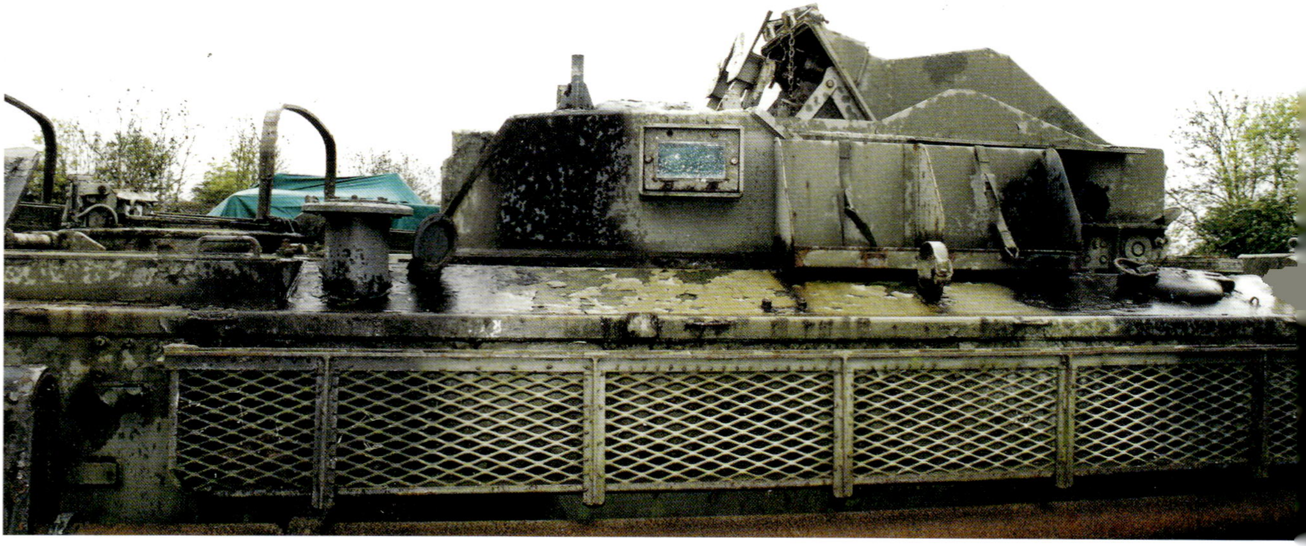

(**Opposite, above**) Showing the size and fitting of the Peak Engineering GPMG turret, the apertures for the three periscopes can clearly be seen on the turret top. *(Rob Griffin)*

(**Opposite, below**) Although now a scrap vehicle, this FV438 side view does show the launcher box and its location on the hull roof. Also note the fixed vision block on the forward edge. *(Rob Griffin)*

(**Above**) Rear view of the SCAMP mine clearing system. It can be seen how wide the actual cleared lane would have been. Note the camera on the boom forward, this would have been used either to assist in driving closed down or when the vehicle was radio controlled and empty. *(Author's collection)*

FV436 Green Archer mortar location radar. This is a comprehensive rework of the basic vehicle and the major changes are quite visible. Compare this to the fitting of the later Cymbeline. *(Tank Museum)*

A good right hand view of the FV436. This shows just how much had to be done to the basic FV4322 to accommodate the radar. *(Tank Museum)*

Left hand view of the FV436. Notice the early light armoured exhaust box and the short exhaust pipe. The vehicle is still fitted with the flotation screen and this can be seen running around the hull top. (*Tank Museum*)

Rear view of an unarmoured FV432 showing the use of bar armour and the armour add on packs. Note the camera mounted over the rear door and the protection given to the commander if using the GPMG. (*Plain Military*)

The FV432 in the mortar role and this is a good shot, for if you look closely you can see the mortar bomb on its way.
(Plain Military)

A very good close up of the remote weapon station, this time fitted with the 7.62 GPMG although the .5 Browning heavy machine gun can be fitted. Notice the thermal camera on the right of the weapon and its ammunition feed, this gun has been fitted with a blank firing adaptor which is the yellow plug at the end of the barrel.
(Plain Military)

(**Above**) Rear view of FV432 in the mine laying role. The mines are fed into the layer by the crewmen sat by the door, the ground is lifted, mine placed in and the ground is covered over again; this allows a small team to lay a large minefield quite easily. (**Below**) A three-quarter view of the mine laying operation. It can be seen that the door is held open with a ratchet-type strap as the simple hook and eye would be too dangerous to both crew and equipment when going cross-country. (*Plain Military*)

Wombat 120mm anti-tank gun fitted to FV432, on top can be seen the .5 spotting rifle. It can be noted how high the mount is when you look at the wheels just in front of the gunner. (*Tank Museum*)

The not very often seen fitting to allow the use of the Carl Gustav launcher from the APC, it really looks like a lot of effort for not much gain. (*Tank Museum*)

A Peak Engineering FV432 in the APC role. It would seem that this was taken after the end of hostilities as it is very bare of all the odds and ends that accumulate on a vehicle in combat. (Dennis Lunn)

FV439 the conversion to the Ptarmigan system. The large generators fill the whole of the roof space, a very tempting target. (Daniel Novak)

The ongoing cleaning that is the result of firing any weapon, and on the day this was shot the mortars had fired a large amount of ammunition. *(Rob Griffin)*

A mixture of ammunition as carried by the Abbot self-propelled gun, from left to right the rounds are smoke, practice HESH and service HESH. (*Author's Collection*)

The trial using rocket assistance to aid exits from a river bank, spectacular but of limited value so the plan was dropped. (*Tank Museum*)

How to make a Japanese WW2 Chi-Ha tank: take one FV434 and cut it up. FV430 vehicles have been modified to represent several Second World War tanks. (*Tim Virr*)

(**Below**) FV432 fitted with the ZB 298 radar. When fitted the mortar hatches cannot be opened; also look at the height increase it creates. (*Tank Museum*)

(**Opposite, above**) FV431, the proposed load carrier that was beaten in trials by Stalwart. The crew of two/three were carried in the front, armoured portion while the load area was unarmoured; the side could be raised giving easy access to the load. One big advantage this had over Stalwart was if the engine failed it was accessible, on Stalwart the whole load would have to be unloaded first. (*Tank Museum*)

(**Opposite, below**) Rear view of Green Archer FV436. The generators used to power the system can be seen below the fold antennae. The top cover of the flotation screen is clearly visible. (*Tank Museum*)

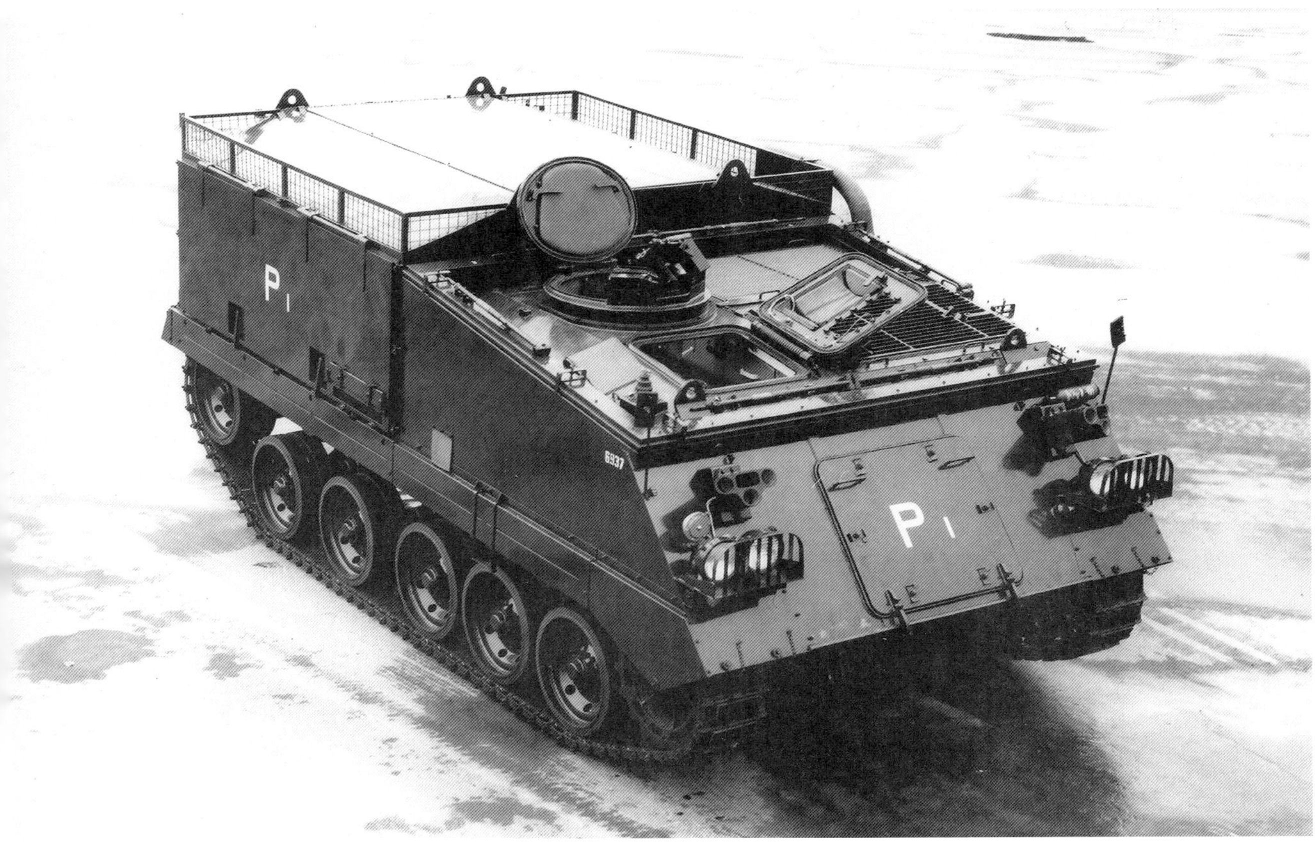
P1
6937
P1

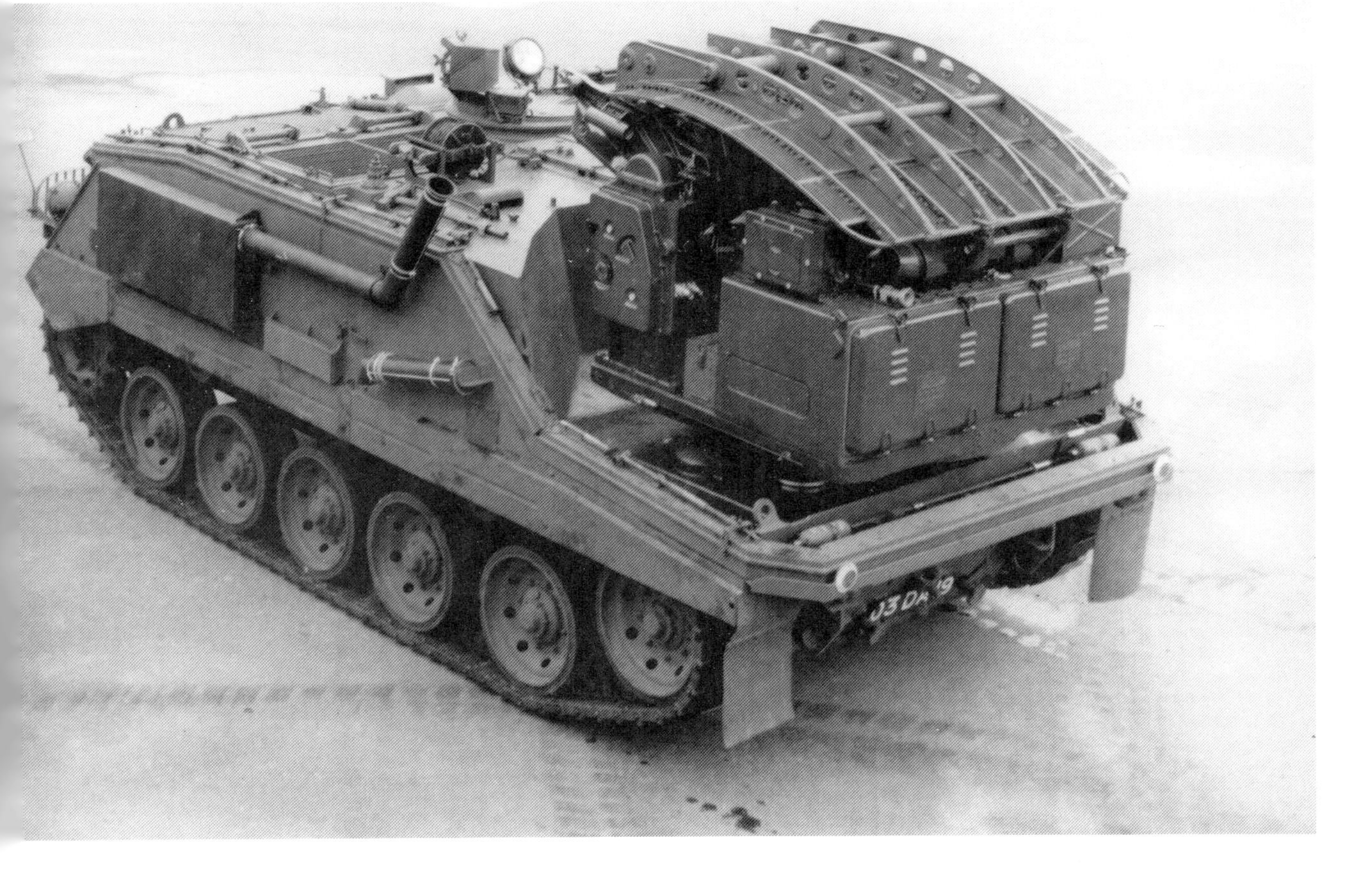

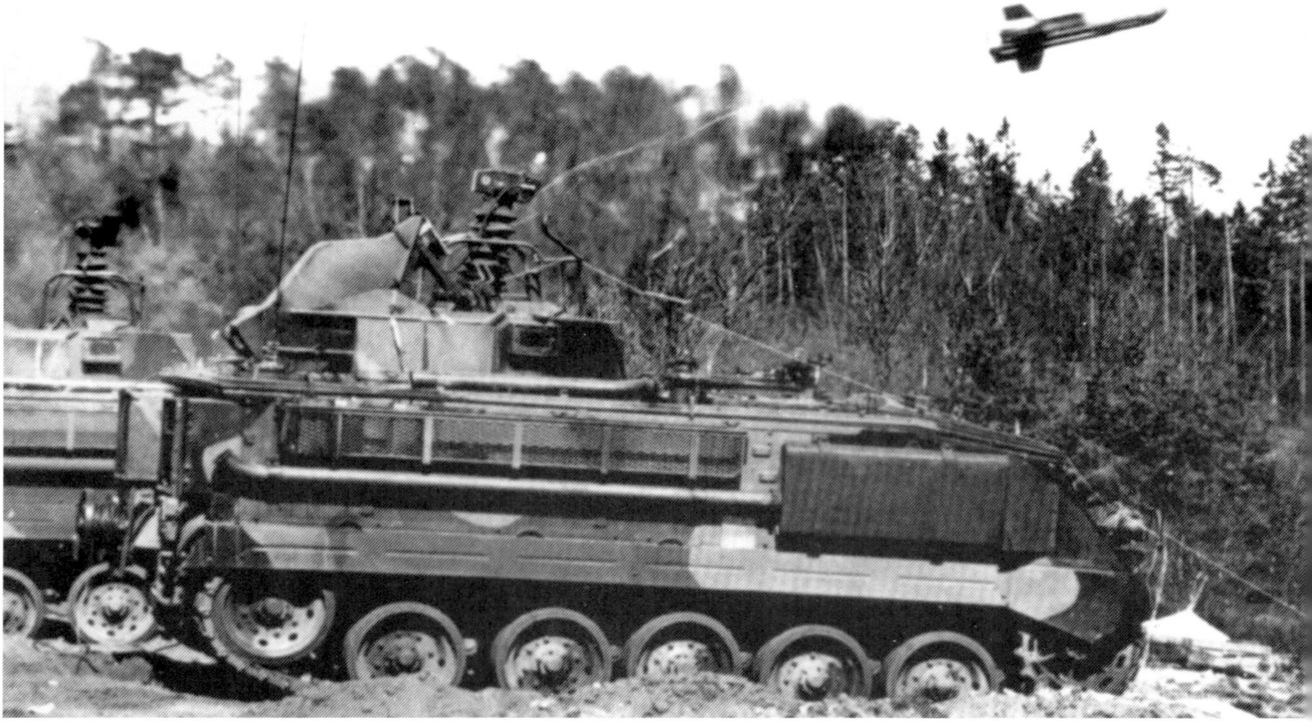

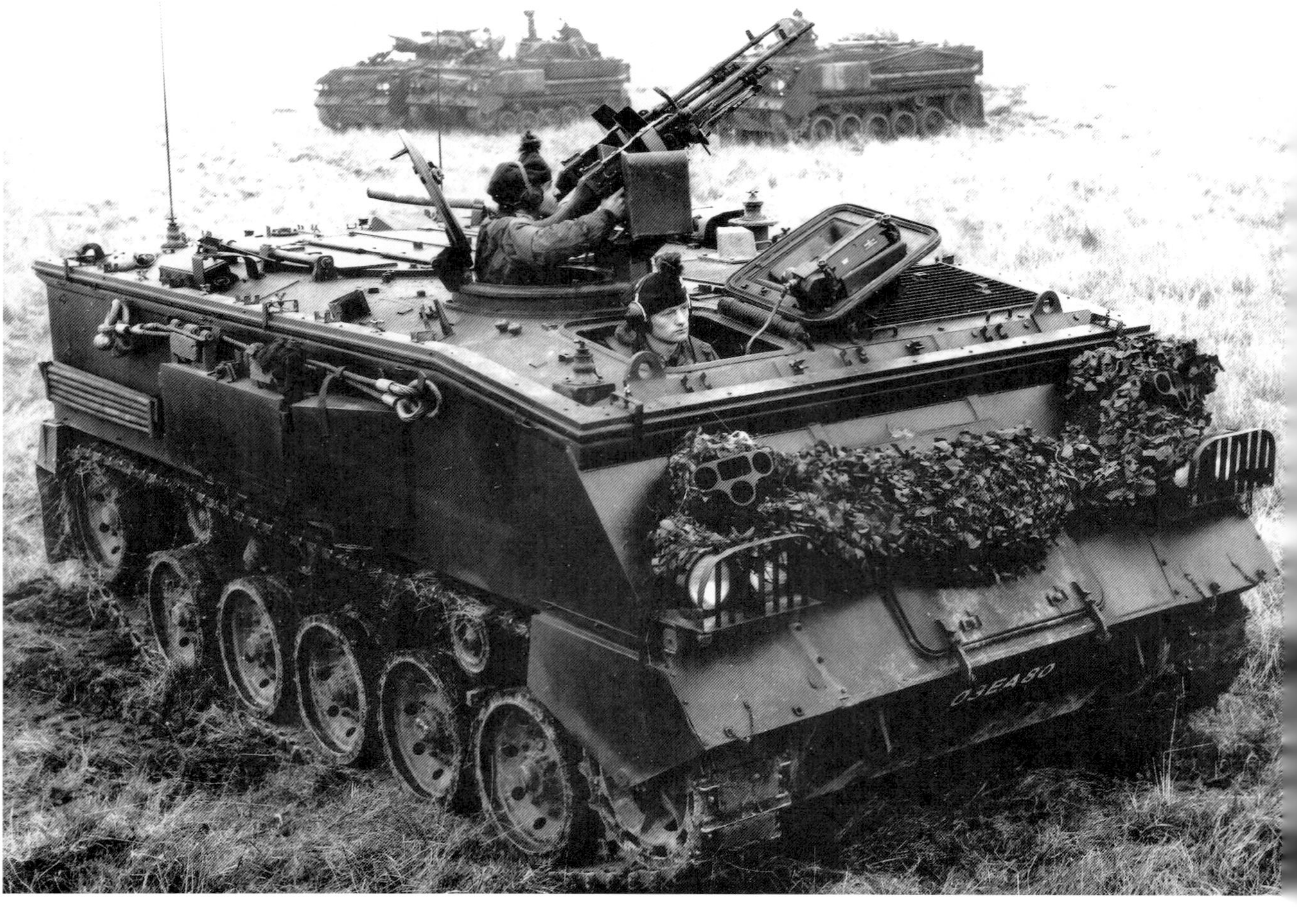
03EA80

(**Opposite, above**) A Swingfire missile leaves the launch box of its host FV438. The control wires can just be seen behind it and also wire from a previous shoot is lying over the vehicle. (*Author's collection*)

(**Opposite, below**) The SCAT mounting with its twin GPMG, a fun conversion but never adapted. This is probably the infantry trials unit, for a FV438 and FV43/30 can be seen in the background. (*Tank Museum*)

(**Above**) The ambulance conversion showing all four stretcher locations. To aid loading, the top two frames can be swung into the centre of the vehicle and extended, the batteries that would have been at the head of the left bottom stretcher will have been moved to the left sponson. (*Tank Museum*)

The driver's area inside a Mk 3 FV432 Bulldog. The biggest change is the introduction of a yoke-style steering wheel. Below that is the screen from the cameras mounted in the front to be used while closed down. Bottom right of the picture can be seen the new (then) Bowman radio system. *(Plain Military)*

The operating screen and control handle for the remote weapons system. *(Plain Military)*

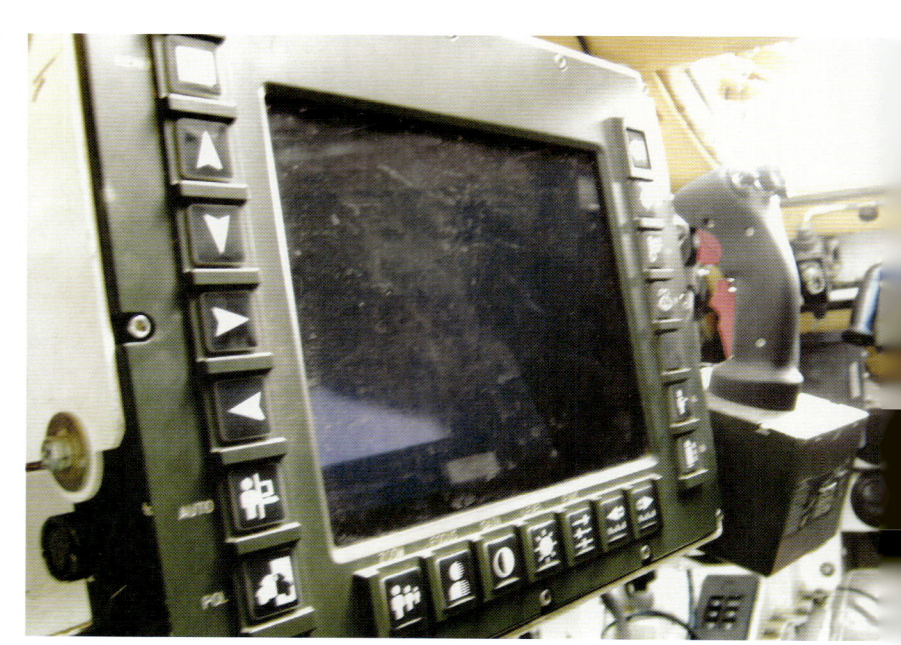

Looking down onto the mortar base plate. This must be very secure otherwise it will cause inaccuracies to creep in which could lead to accidents. (*Plain Military*)

The full width mine pusher system known as SCAMP fitted to FV432. Notice the camera mounted on the long pole in the front of the vehicle. (*Author's Collection*)

The typical barren open area of military ranges. This could be Otterburn or Hohne in Germany; they all look the same. The FV438 has just launched its Swingfire missile and will be able to use it up to its maximum of 4,000 metres. (*Author's collection*)

A rather dusty FV439 Ptarmigan carrier. Notice the large antenna that is located on the left side. Ptarmigan was a battlefield communications system that could be linked to many modules, giving great coverage. (*Plain Military*)

154

Fully bombed-up mortar carrier version. This shows just how much, or how little, space there is once the bomb carriers are fitted to the inside of the FV432. (*Rob Griffin*)

Close up of part of the blade from the SCAMP system. This was taken at the vehicle depot at Ashchurch where the system had been left till someone made a decision on what to do with it. (*Rob Griffin*)

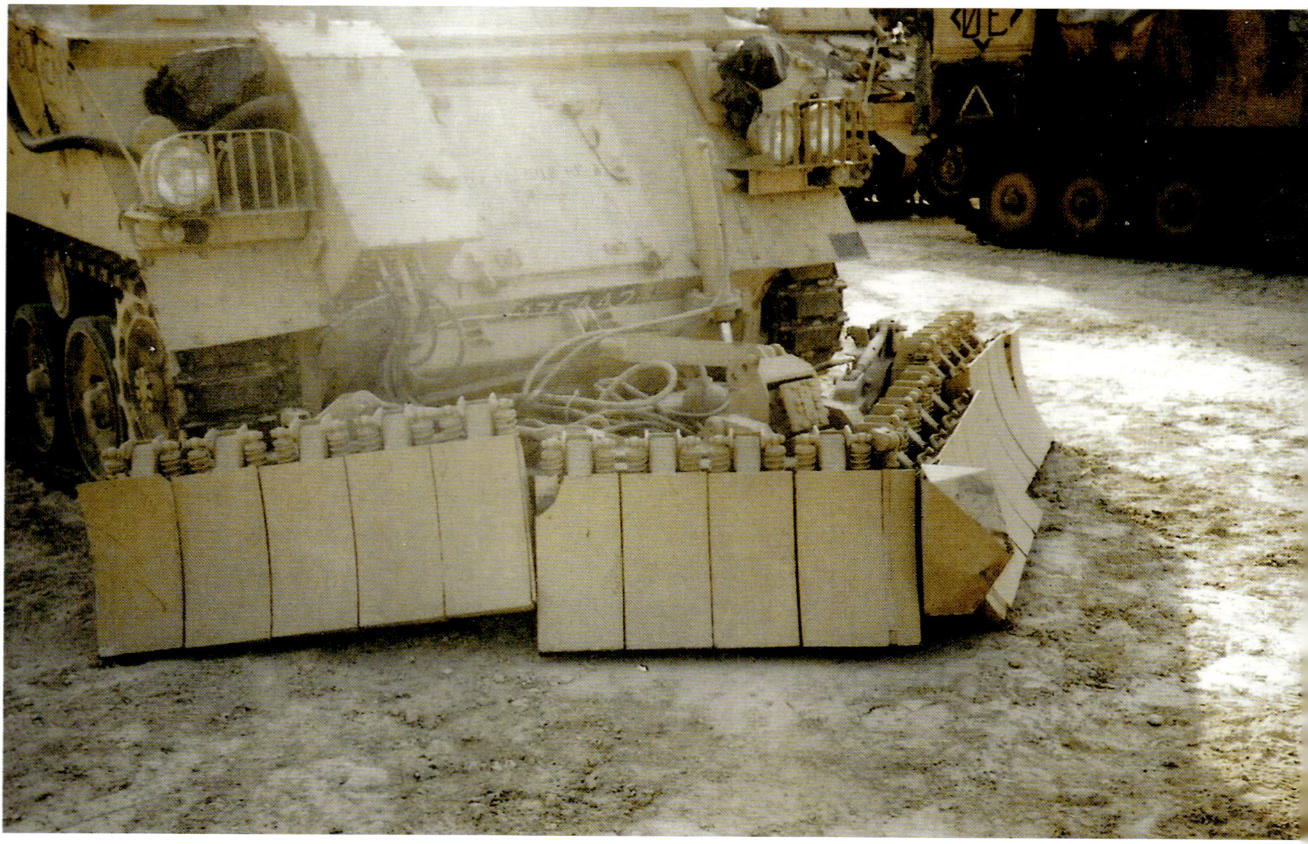

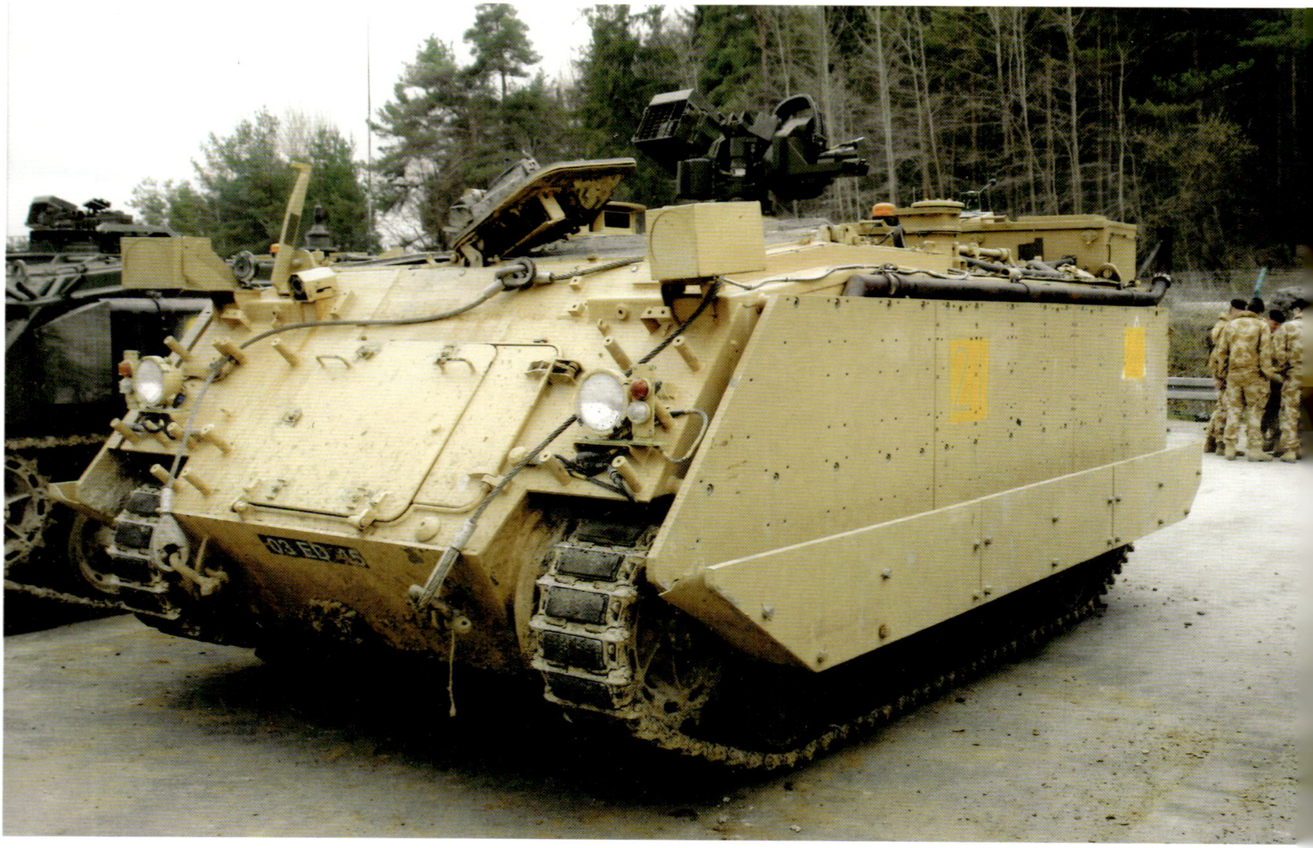
03 ED 45

(**Opposite, above**) Scamp after use in the Gulf War. It can be seen that a lot of hydraulic lines are located on it, possibly not ideal if a mine is set off. *(Dennis Lunn)*

(**Opposite, below**) A partially up-armoured Bulldog. Note the new style of access plate on the glacis, this is now two hatches rather than the original one. It is fitted with the remote weapon station, armoured side panel and the troughs for carrying the Chobham type panels which are not fitted unless it is going into operations. *(Plain Military)*

(**Above**) A cluttered, well lived in mortar carrier. The crews individual 24 hour ration packs can be seen behind the crewman and the obligatory flashing amber light for breakdowns. Located on the left of the mortar tube is its sighting system. *(Daniel Novak)*

FV432 in the process of laying bar mines. It is working hard as can be, judging by the exhaust plume. *(Plain Military)*

A close up of the pipes and fittings to enable FV432 to operate SCAMP mine clearing equipment. This particular vehicle was involved in the Gulf War. *(Dennis Lunn)*

FV433 Abbot self-propelled gun. This vehicle and its 105mm gun was the mainstay of the Royal Artillery for many years in the self-propelled role. *(Author's collection)*

An experimental vehicle to see if an acceptable self-propelled anti-aircraft vehicle could be produced. This was Falcon, mounted on FV433 chassis and fitted with a power turret mounting two 30mm Hispano-Suiza cannons. Not proceeded with due to poor ammo load and no radar. *(Author's collection)*

The bar mine layer. The twin knife edge wheels at the rear are used to cut the ground to allow the mines to be laid. (*Author's collection*)

A rear view of the remote weapon station with the ammo box located on the left and night vision equipment on the right. It is light-years away from the original stand up cupola for the commander. (*Plain Military*)

This shows how the stretcher frames are mounted. If not in use it can be swung up and secured to give more space. (*Rob Griffin*)

Looking very smart in its Berlin camouflage is this FV432/30. Sixteen vehicles were converted to mount spare Fox CVR(W) turrets, designed to give the infantry a bit more punch. In the end it was the infantry who in general did not like it, a fun vehicle to crew though. (*Andreas Kirchoff*)

(**Above**) This shot of the mortar carriers shows the bomb stowage around the side of the compartment. It has that typical lived in look that all military vehicles acquire. *(Rob Griffin)*

(**Opposite, above**) Top view of Bulldog fitted with the remote weapon station showing the changes to the forward end of the mortar hatches and also how the top of additional armour is fitted. *(Plain Military)*

(**Opposite, below**) FV434 in Berlin scheme pictured carrying the infamous Leyland L60 power pack from a Chieftain tank. Next to it is a FV432/30. Berlin is the only area they were fully deployed. *(Andreas Kirchoff)*

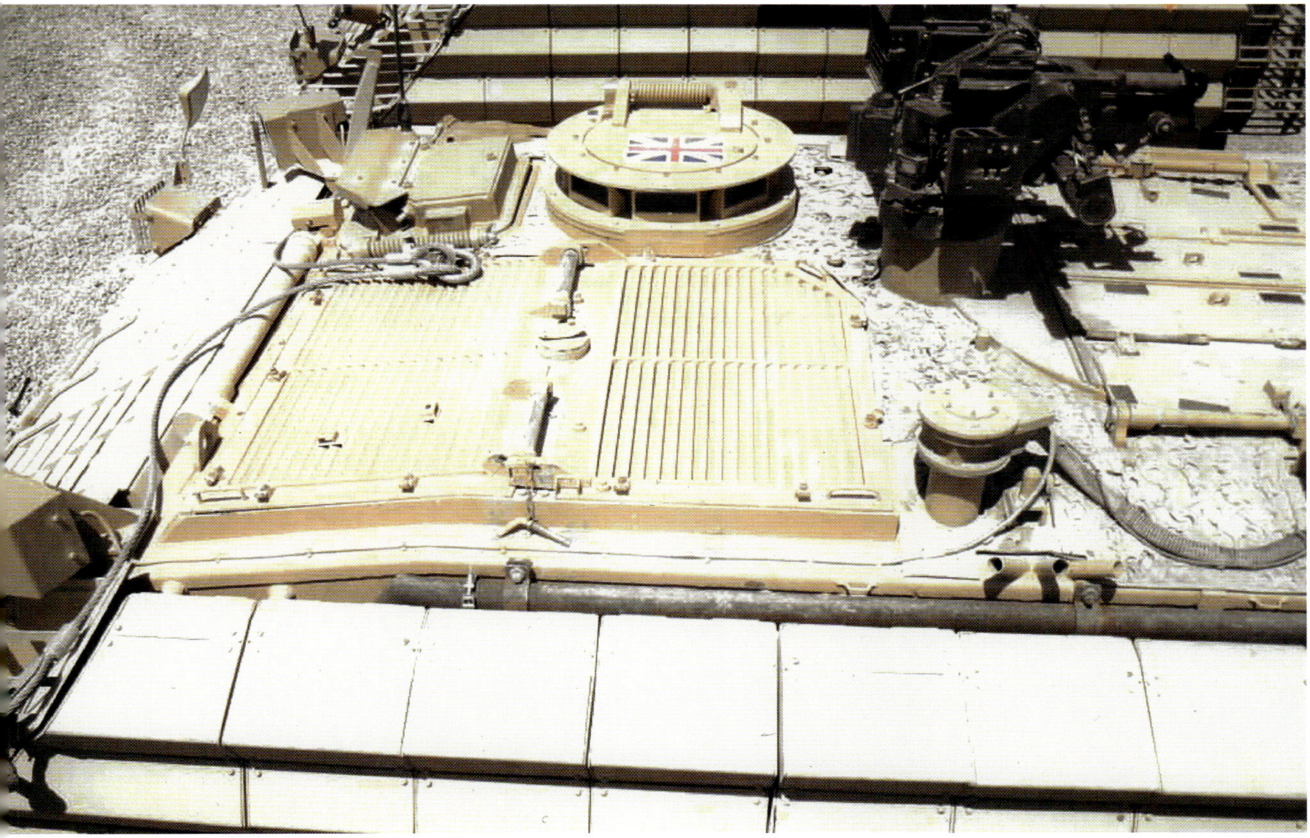

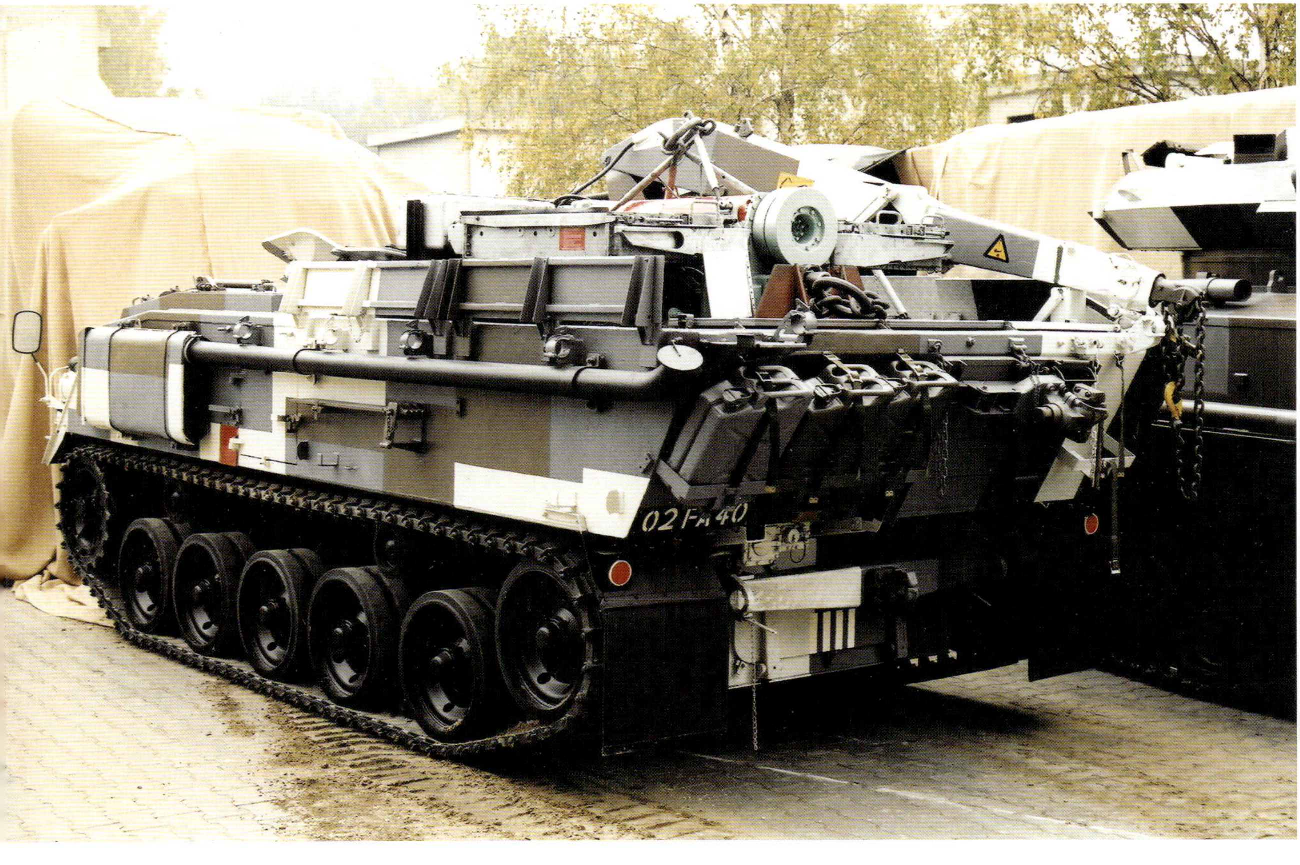
02 FA 40

(**Above**) The improved steering system found on Bulldog; the yoke type wheel and new power pack and gearbox made life a lot easier. To the left is the screen for the forward facing cameras and in the left of the shot can be seen part of the control handle for the remote weapon system. *(Plain Military)*

(**Opposite, above**) FV439 shown here possibly in Bosnia although it still retains its sand camouflage. *(Daniel Novak)*

(**Opposite, below**) Good side view of the Mk 1 vehicle showing the oval access hatch behind the yellow call sign, it is also fitted with a Peak Engineering GPMG turret. *(Rob Griffin)*

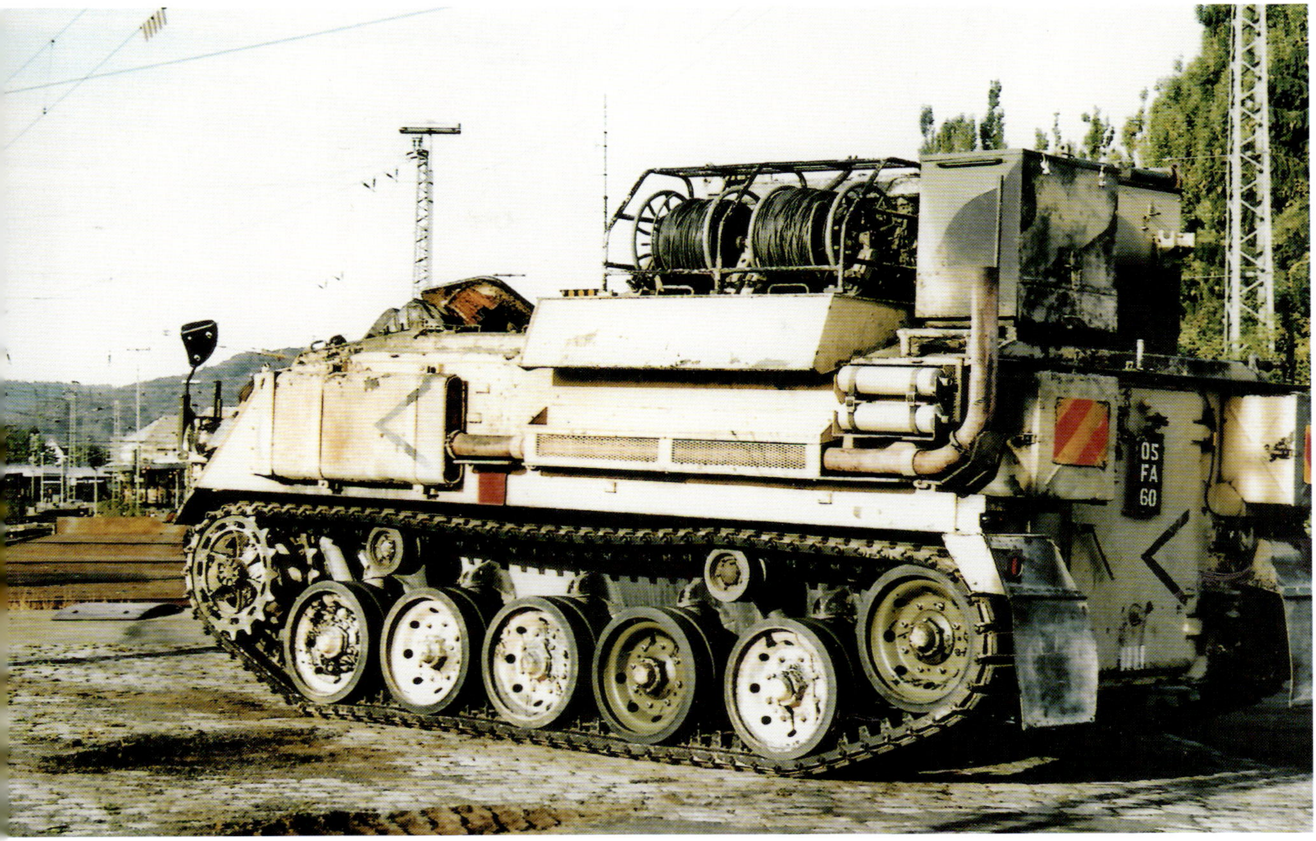
05
FA
60

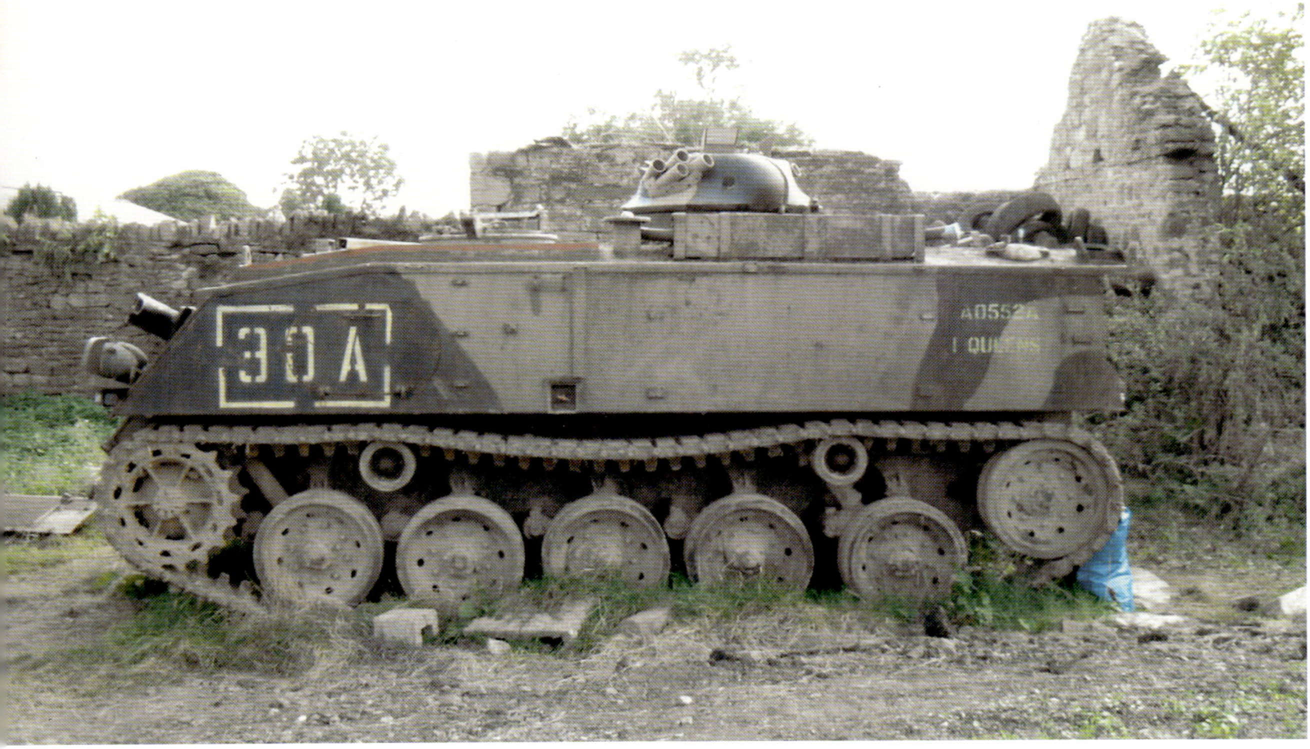
30 A
A0552A
1 QUEENS

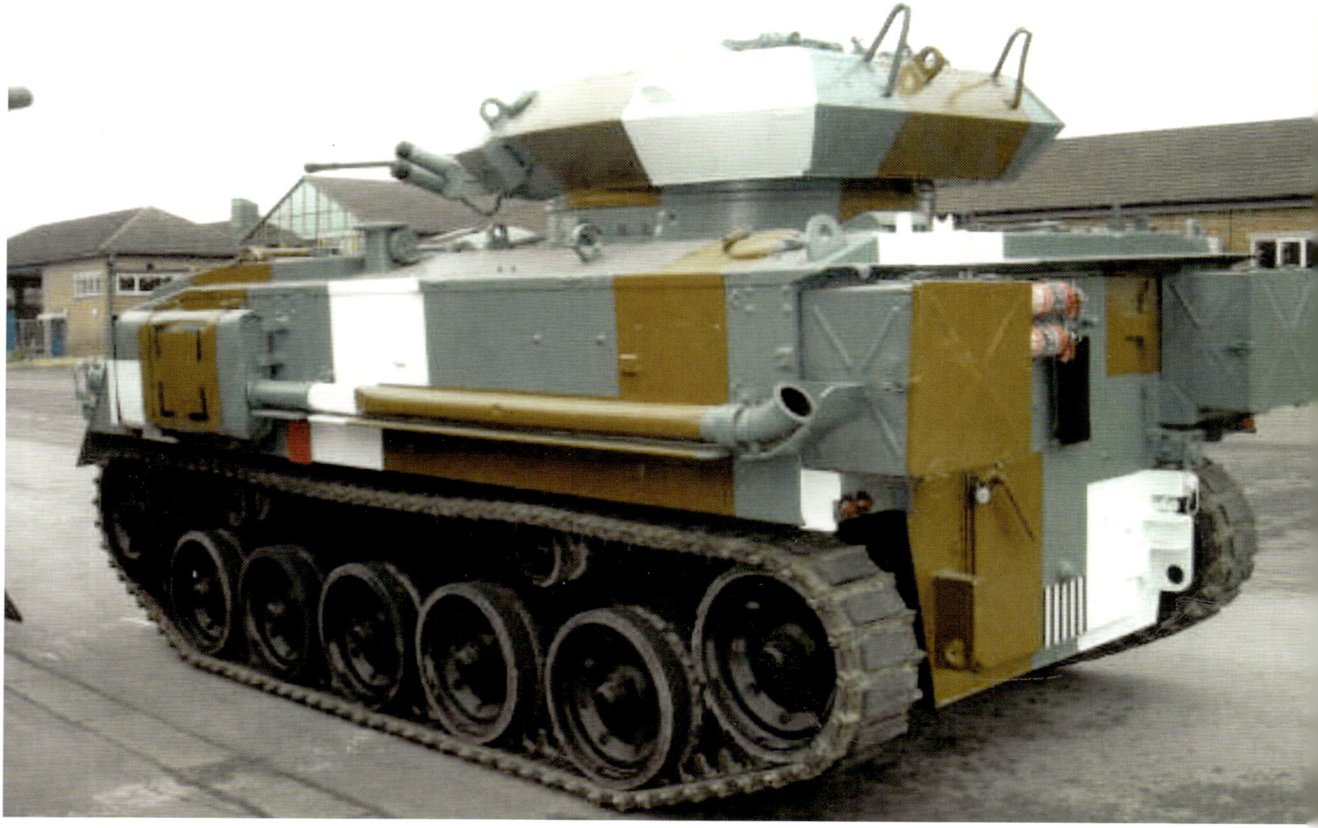

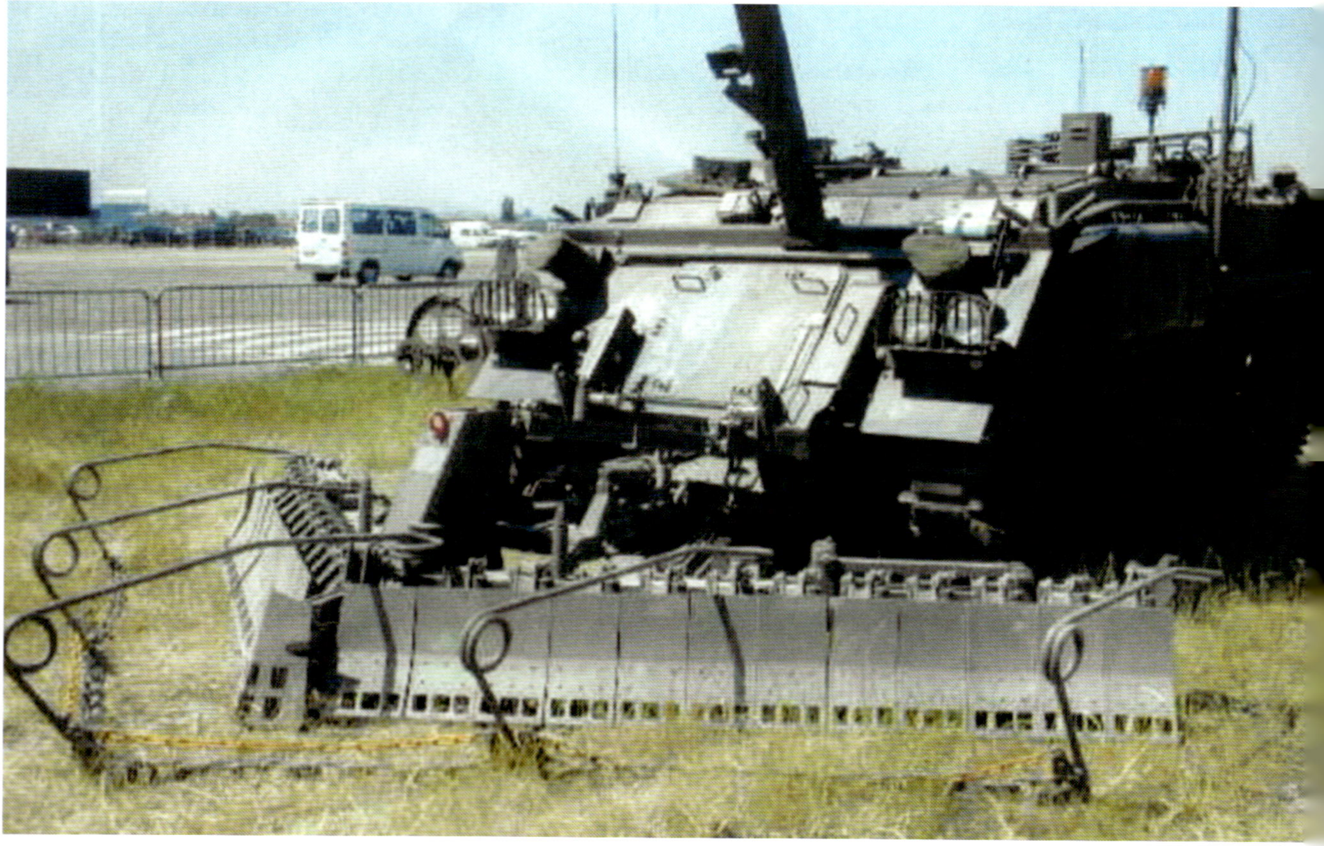

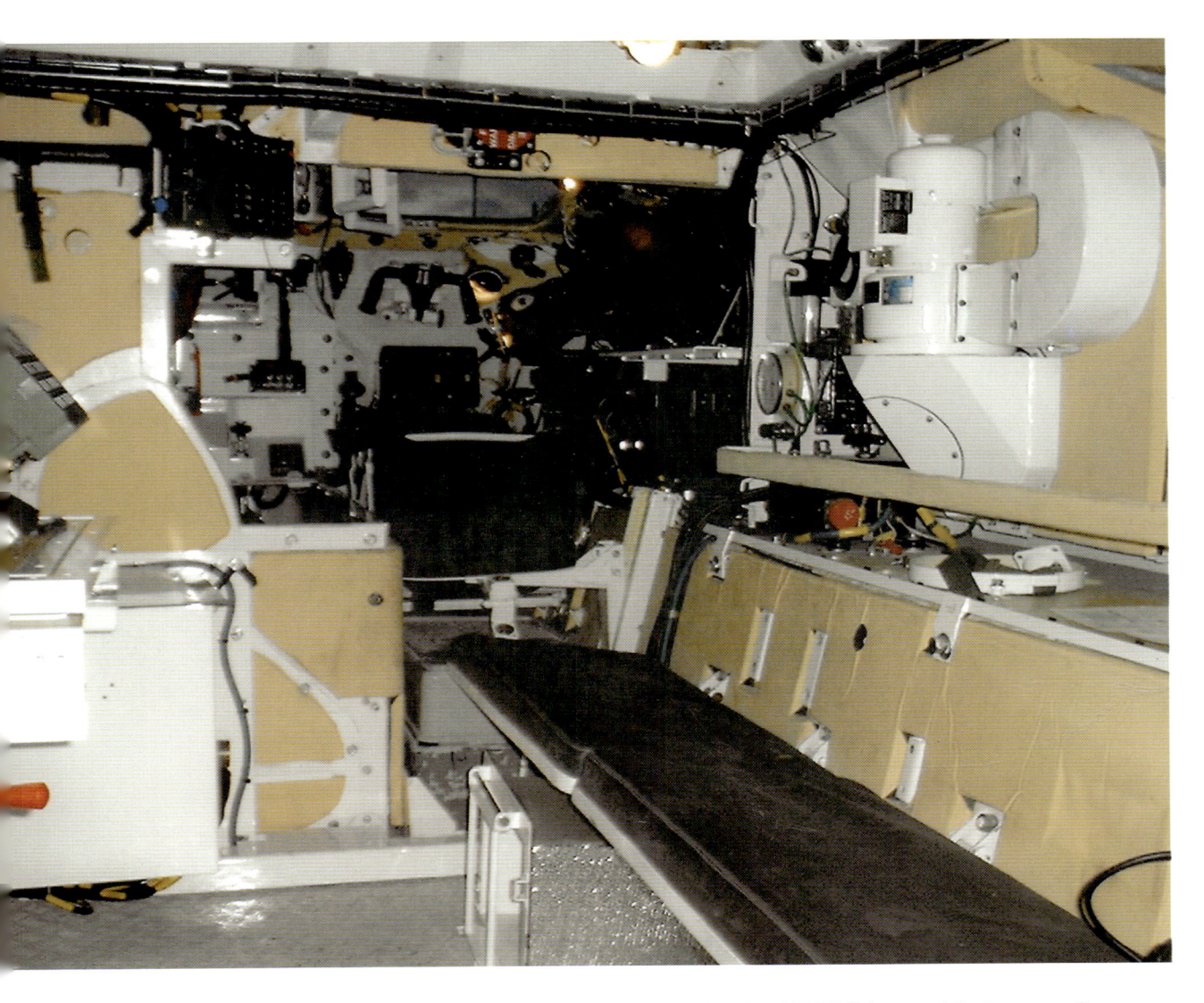

(**Opposite, above**) A three-quarter rear view of the FV432/30, sporting the 4/7 RDG invented Berlin camouflage scheme, there were several variations on colour choice for this scheme. (*Andreas Kirchoff*)

(**Above**) Straight from the factory after rebuild, the mint interior of the Bulldog will not remain like this once it deploys on exercise. (*Plain Military*)

(**Opposite, below**) To ensure that a mine catches its victims, a vertical trigger is often used so if the vehicle was to pass with tracks or wheels either side it, it would hit this tilt switch and detonate. In this shot of SCAMP can be seen, at ground level, the chains designed to catch these tilt switches. (*Armoured Engineer*)

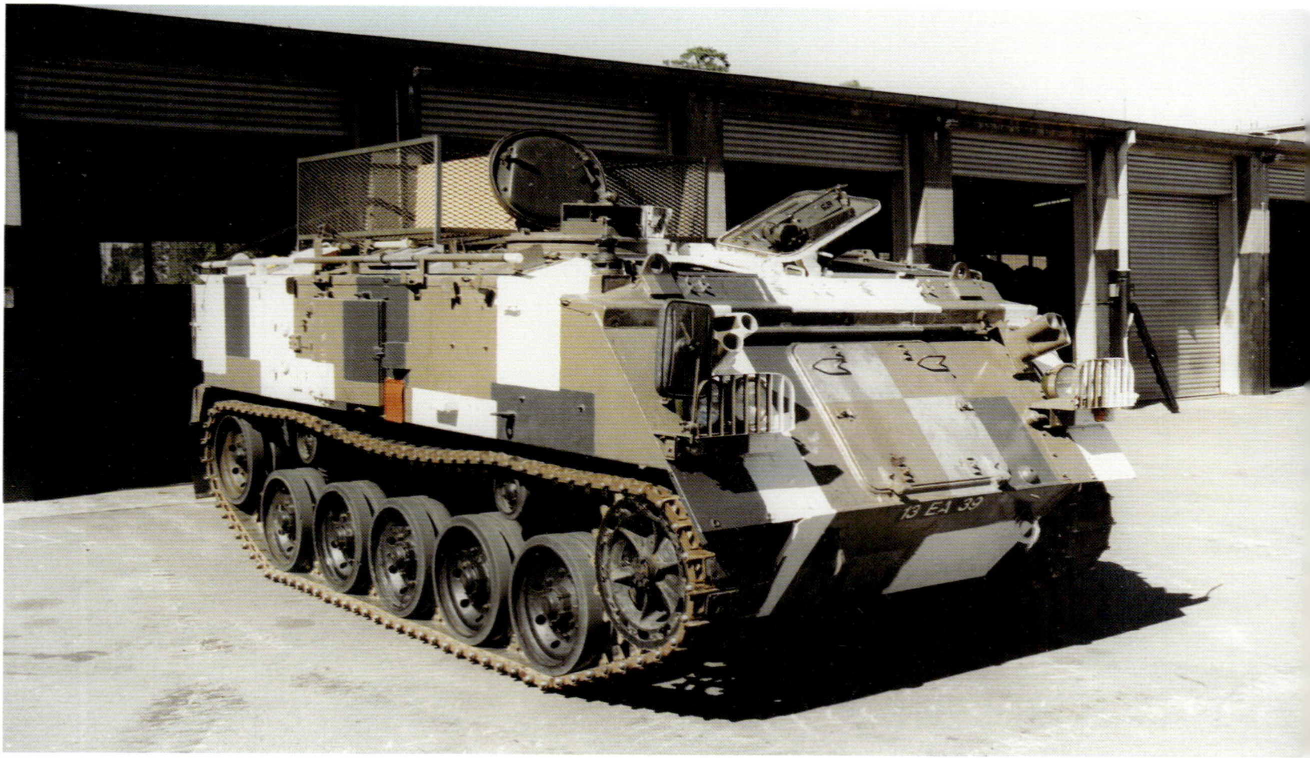
13 EA 39

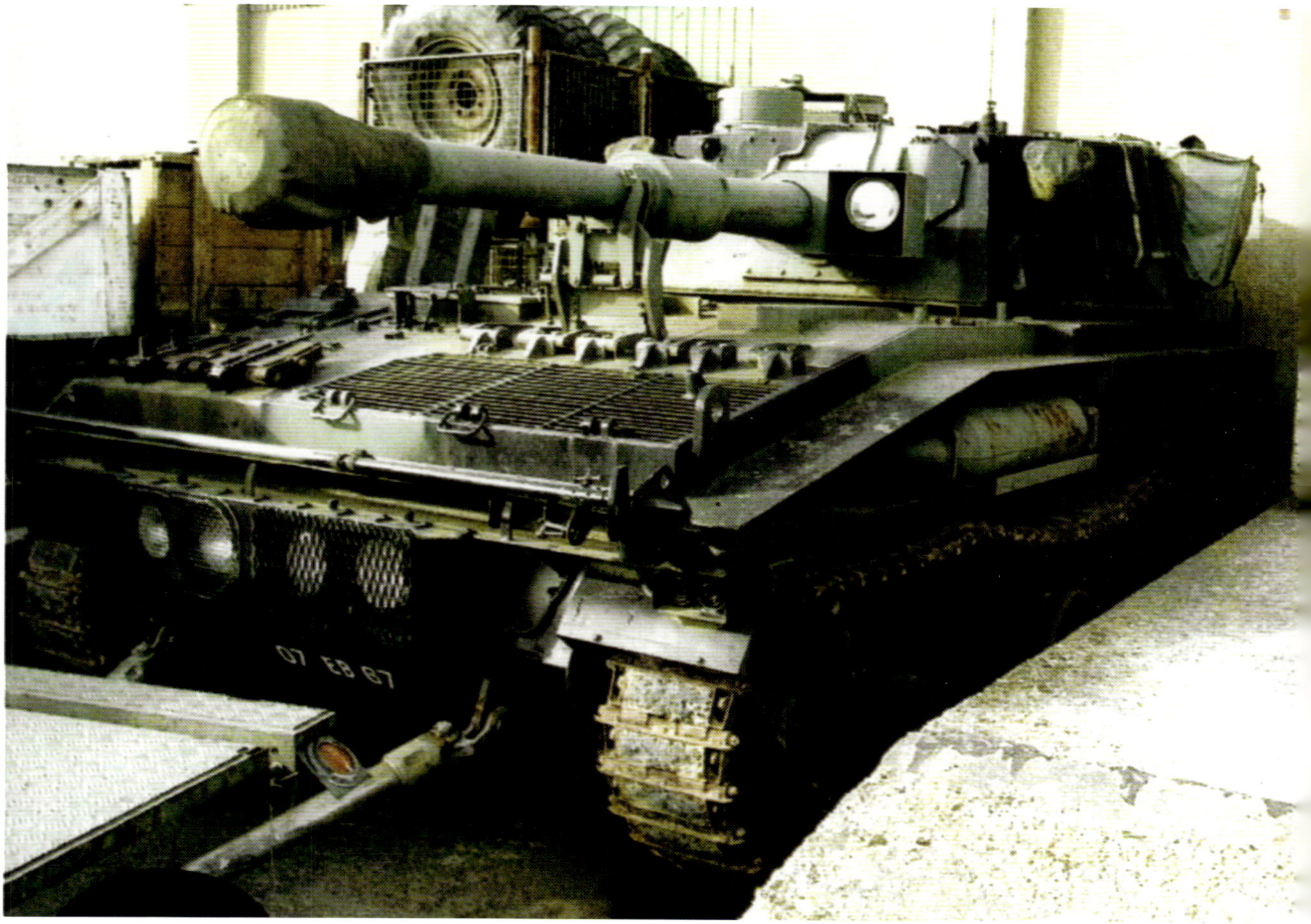
07 EB 67

(**Opposite, above**) Basic FV432 in Berlin colours, it has had the swimming screen removed and a local produced basket is fitted on the roof. Andreas Kirchoff)

(**Opposite, below**) FV433 Abbot looks as if it has broken down and been pushed into the space, as the A-frame bars can be seen connected to the lower glacis plate. *(Rob Griffin)*

(**Above**) No it's not the Germans coming but a reenactment group with a Stug III built on an FV432 chassis, the obvious give away is the road wheel layout. *(Rob Griffin)*

170

(**Opposite, above**) Side on view of the FV432/30. Behind the exhaust extension on the roof the adaptor collar for the fox turret can just be made out. Andrea Kirchoff)

(**Opposite, below**) This view of an early Mk 1 shows the trim vane that was used when swimming. It was mostly left in the stores unless swimming was on the menu as it was awkward to remove to allow access to the front access hatch. (*Author's collection*)

(**Above**) A group of weary looking FV422s located somewhere in Bosnia. This will be during the IFOR/SFOR period as by then the white UN scheme had been removed. (*Author's collection*)

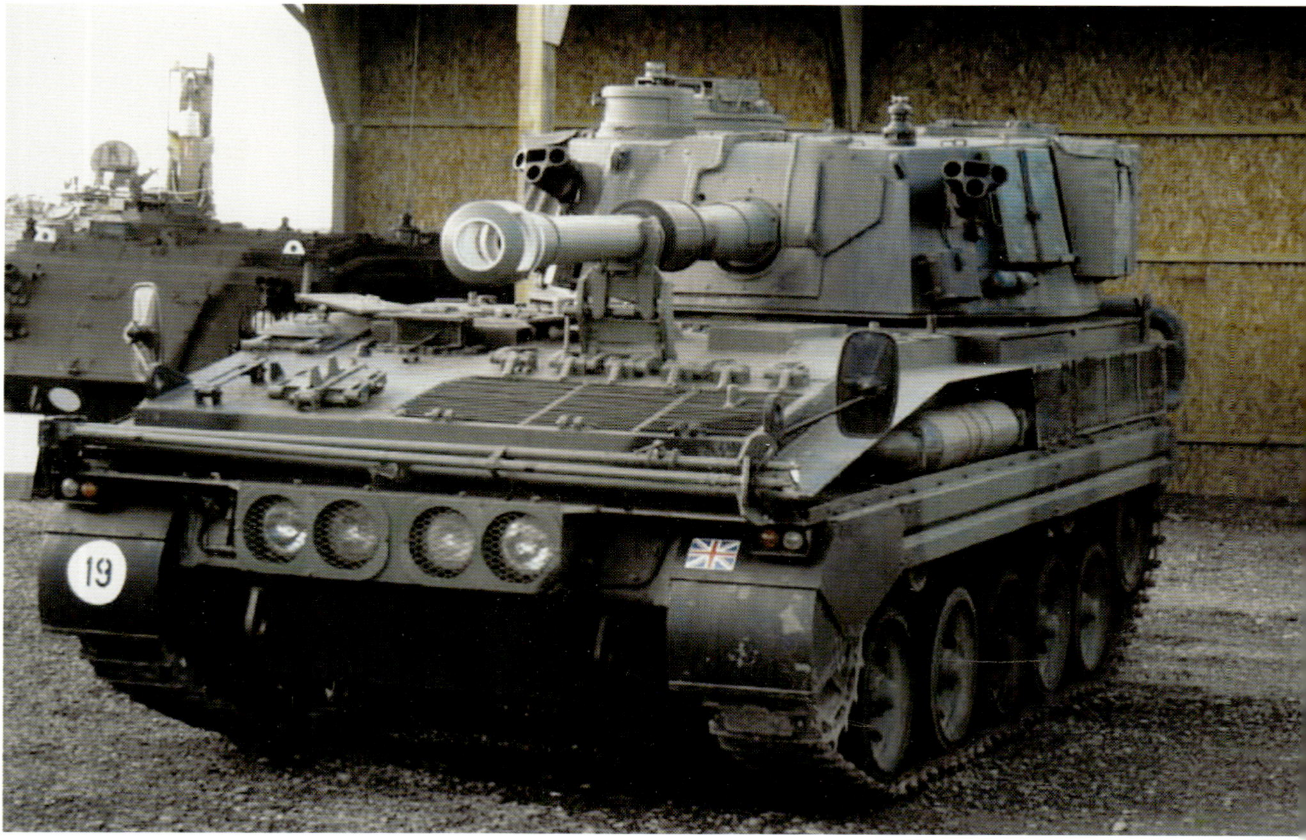
19

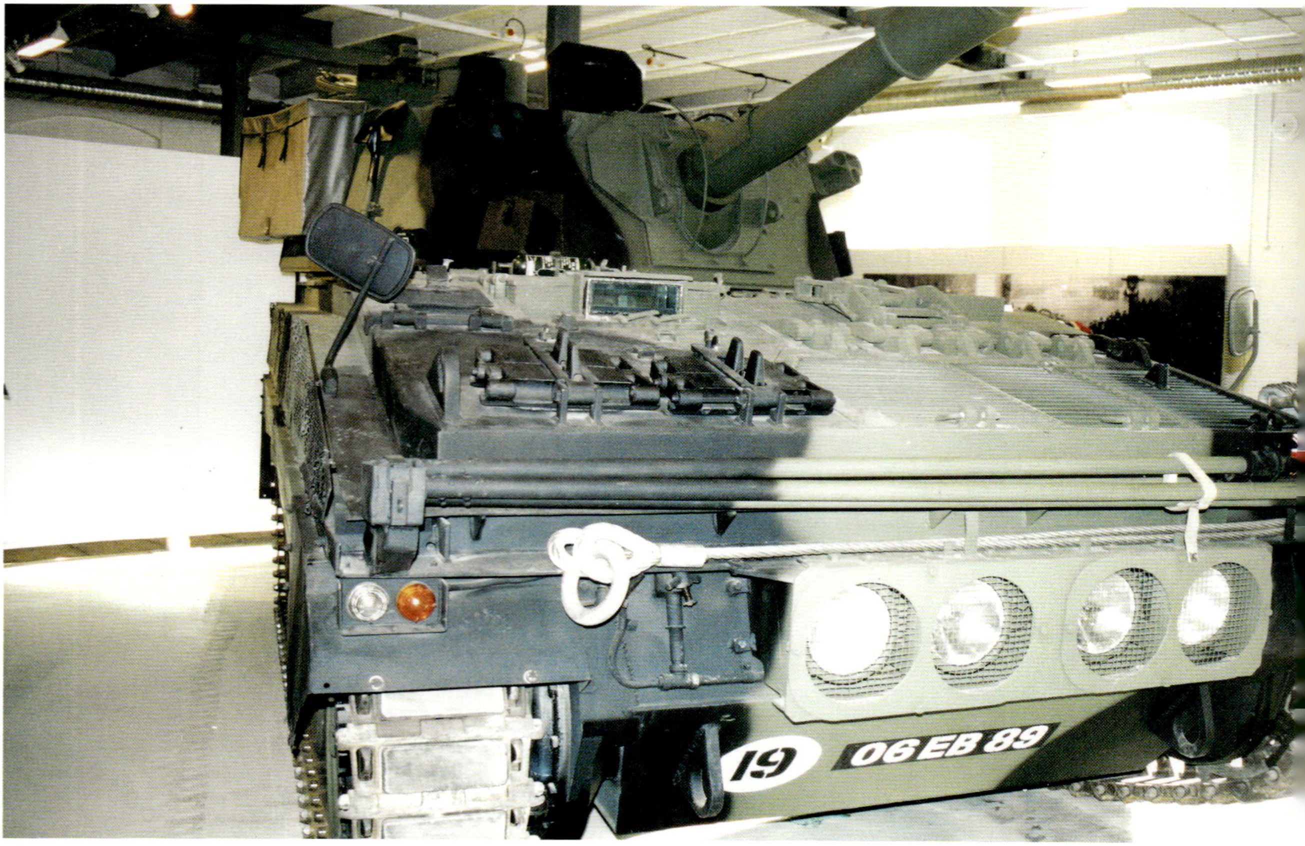
19
06 EB 89

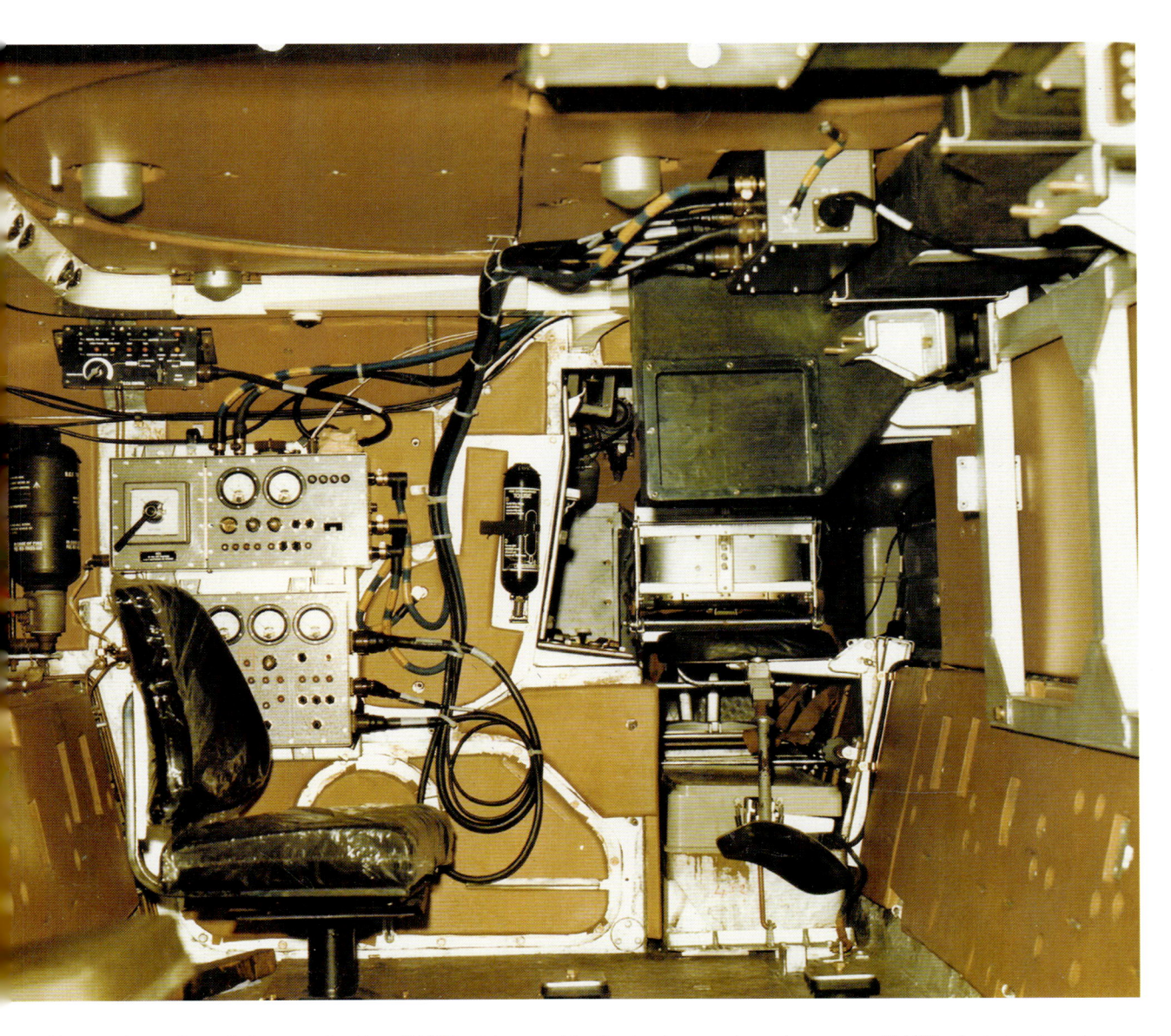

(**Opposite, above**) A smart looking FV433 Abbot and in the background can be seen a FV432. (*Author's collection*)

(**Above**) The inside of a FV435 Wavell communications system. This is an automatic data-processing computer system designed to accept information from all the battlefield intelligence agencies, for security most of the equipment is not fitted in this image but gives an idea of layout. (*Author's collection*)

(**Opposite, below**) A very smart FV433 Abbot. Notice the spare links on the left of the sloping glacis plate and the plastic type stowage bag on the turret die, there was another on the opposite side, not the best idea for stowing kit. (*Rob Griffin*)

A bar mine layer crew taking a pause. The layer is in its operating configuration with the wheels down. As always notice the amount of equipment cluttered around the vehicle. Author's collection)

This Berlin colour scheme FV432 shows the metal tent frame that is fixed to it that can be pulled out to make a penthouse for command post vehicles. *(Andreas Kirchoff)*

A close up of the mast base fitted to FV439. This is in the lowered position. *(Author's collection)*

The twin 30mm Hispano-Suiza cannon fitted to the Falcon anti-aircraft vehicle, it was not a success and only the one was built. *(Author's collection)*

(**Above**) A rotating flail fitted to an FV432 by Aardvark Mine Clearing Ltd; worked but found FV432 not the ideal vehicle. (*Aardvark Mine Clearing Ltd*)

(**Below**) Grainy and possibly one of the only images showing the REME turret fitted to FV432. This was in Aden and the turret came from either a Saracen or Ferret scout car. (*Author's collection*)

(**Opposite, above**) An unusual view of the mortar tube fitted to FV432. This shows how solid a construction the base is. (*Plain Military*)

(**Opposite, below**) FV432 at the former Royal Engineers museum at Chatham. This one is fitted with the Ranger scatterable mine system, a piece of equipment that is not banned. (*Author's collection*)

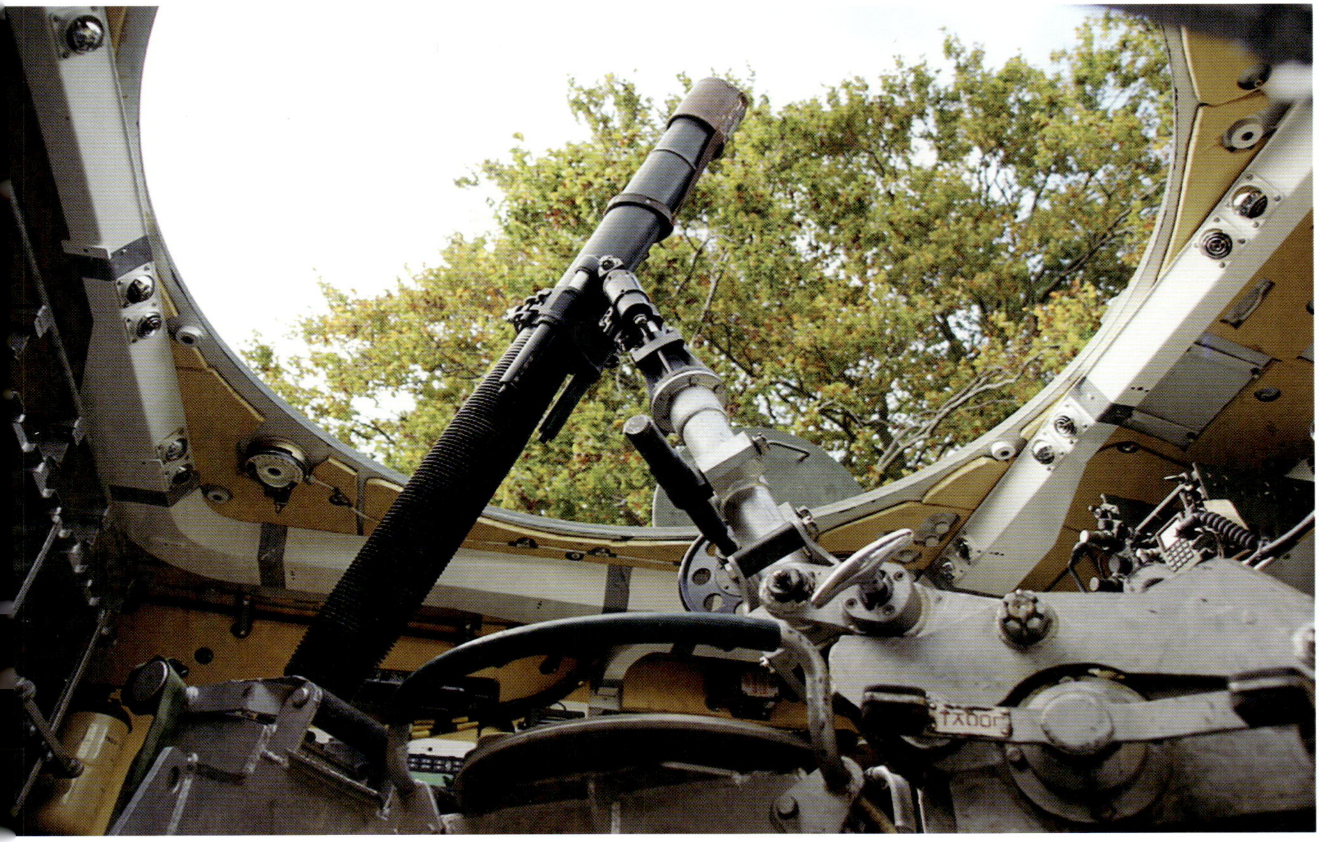

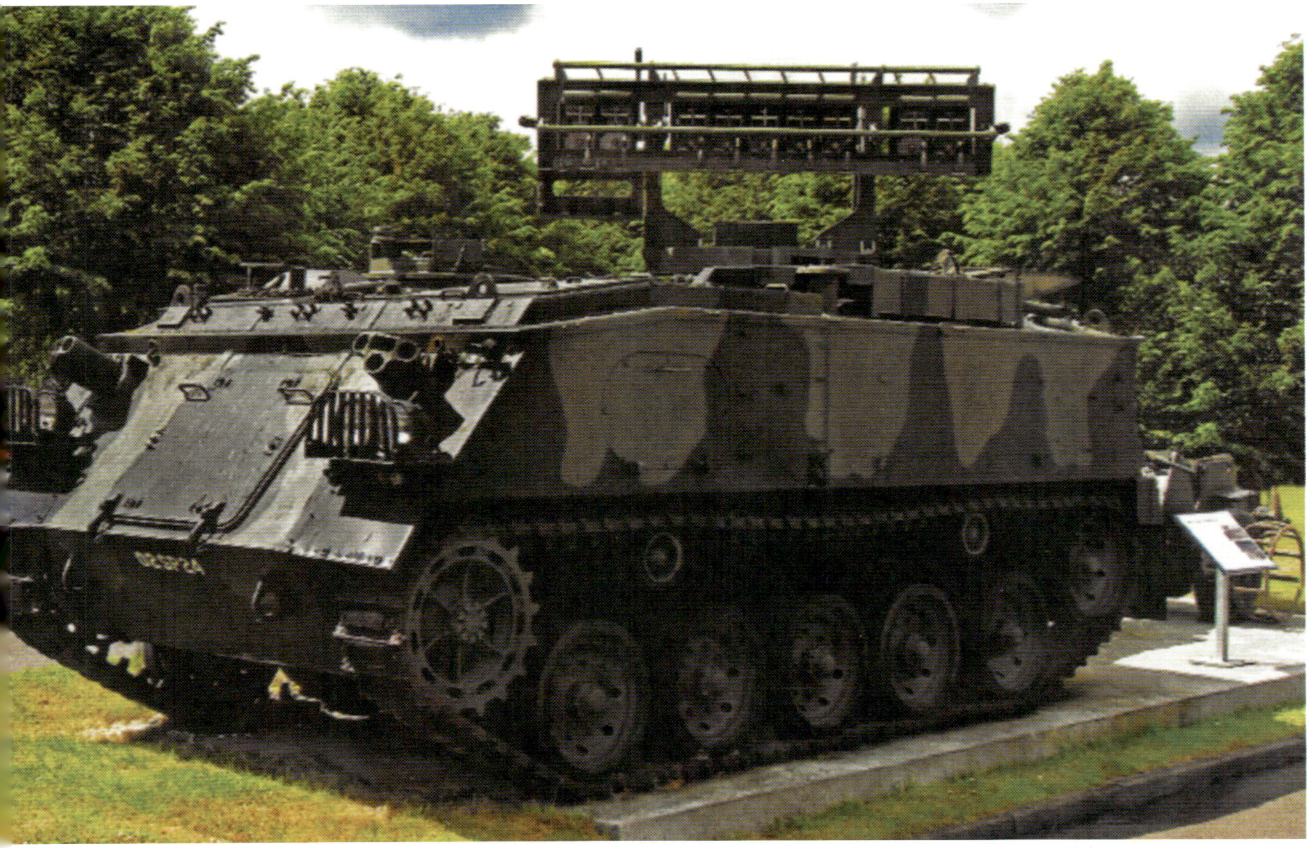

Notice in this image how the rubber mud flaps can be turned up and secured. Also notice the triangular shaped driving mirrors on the front right. The soldier is wearing the one piece DPM camouflage tank suit. (*Plain Military*)

The army felt that it needed another APC so the Stormer was born (seen here on the left of the FV432), based on the CVR(T) chassis. As an APC it was not too brilliant as its section was limited to five men, but it found other roles in life. (*Plain Military*)

Chapter Five

Growing Old Gracefully!

In June 1980 the following statement concerning FV430 series was made in the British Parliament: 'The present armoured personnel carrier for the Army, the FV432 series of vehicles have been in service since the 1960s and will need to be replaced by the mid-1980s. There have been two vehicles considered for this replacement, one is the MCV-80 (Warrior) and the American M2 fighting vehicle, which would be built in the UK under licence. I have chosen after considering all the relevant operational, financial and industrial factors, that the vehicle selected will be the MCV-80 (Warrior). Cost will be £1 billion and full development will commence shortly.' The first production vehicle was delivered to the Army in May 1987 and the first Battalion that was operational using Warrior came online in mid-1988.

Reading the above the reader could be forgiven for assuming that FV430 series were nothing more than range hulks or museum pieces now that Warrior has replaced it. The truth however is slightly different: Warrior is being planned for a major upgrade but the FV430 series, as announced at the Royal College of Military Science recently, is expected to carry on in service, finally retiring in or around 2025 (in 2005 the government announced that both CVR (T) and the FV432 series would soldier on till at least 2025). The reasons for this are varied, but one is the British MoD's search for a new vehicle to fulfil the roles of the CVR (T) series and the FV430 series. This has been down several routes with no success, so in the short term it was felt cheaper to retain them until such time as the new vehicle comes into service.

As we have seen in the chapter on variants, FV430 has or is carrying out many varied roles. It has taken place in operations in the Balkans and two Gulf Wars and has managed to fulfil its tasks well. However a lot of the credit for that must be placed with the hard work in maintaining it by the vehicle crews. This coupled with the long hours and ingenuity put in by those often unsung heroes of the Royal Electrical and Mechanical Engineers (REME) in finding ways of keeping the old warhorse on the road. This obviously places a high load on both men and equipment and sadly some of the vehicles have reached past that sell-by date and have been disposed off. They have ended up in many different and varied situations. The lucky ones have been purchased by the growing band of military vehicle enthusiasts that will take what most would consider a wreck and a few years later the vehicle will look as good as it did on the day it left GKN's factory. Others will be restored to represent a particular vehicle from a set period of time or unit that the new owner served in. Others will have to earn their keep being used by the corporate entertainment industry, unfortunately many of these do not receive the care and maintenance that they need and deserve as their main role is to make money. Some companies are better than others but a few really are grim. These vehicles may well have many modifications to help the owners comply with health and safety regulations; these could include steps welded to the side with large handrails to help customers onto the vehicle. Often the mortar hatches are also removed to prevent them inadvertently coming loose and catching the poor customer a sharp crack on the head.

Some vehicles will spend the rest of their days either as museum exhibits or as gate guards outside various units or museum. Some will find fame as film and TV stars although we might not recognise them as FV430. The hugely successful *Band of Brothers* TV show cut down several FV432 to form the base for German World Second World War vehicles. The same thing happened to several FV434s in Australia that were converted to represent Japanese tanks for a film called *The Great Raid*. The other fate that can befall these retired warriors is that of becoming hard targets on the ranges. Whilst this is indeed a sad end, it is a matter of financial expediency, the Army needs hard targets and they are in short supply, so any cast vehicles will be used for this purpose. The author confesses to feeling nostalgic on finding some of his Chieftains battered to pulp; my thoughts go back to when you sweated blood to keep them on the road or ready for inspection.

This takes care of the vehicles that have been disposed of from active service but how are the remainder kept up to full operational readiness? When they become so unserviceable that they need a major overhaul this cannot be carried out by the unit, as it requires so much specialised equipment that a line unit will not have. In days past, the vehicles would be back-loaded to a base workshop. These were large workshops established in the rear area and manned by REME with civilian help. They would be stripped to a bare chassis and then be sent through a production line to emerge the other end as a virtually new vehicle. These have now disappeared to be replaced by largely civilian-type organisations; this is due to cost and politics under the heading of streamlining. Like it or not these are now part and parcel of the military vehicle maintenance system.

The largest of these that serve the Army is the Army Base Repair Organisation (ABRO) and they provide repair and overhaul services across a broad spectrum of vehicles to many customers including the British Army. This is not an easy task, requiring diversity and adaptability, but now with years of partnership with the British Army, ABRO has developed an excellent level of service to the forces.

ABRO operate from a range of strategically located sites, usually the old base workshops themselves, and an example would be the old 18 Command REME workshops at Bovington, now a major ABRO site. Within these sites the repair facilities can handle a wide range of defence equipment from the simple infantry weapons to major armoured fighting vehicles. In a typical year ABRO can expect to repair at least 36 MBT, 330 infantry fighting vehicles and reconnaissance vehicles, 1,000 trucks of all types, 13,000 electronic items and 10,000 small arms. The process for all equipment is the same, with each piece of equipment receiving an inspection to determine what work will be required for it and also to allow for the ordering of any special stores items that are needed. It is also the opportunity to carry out any major modifications that are due on the equipment. Before leaving the workshops all equipment is rigorously inspected several times before being pronounced fit for service. ABRO also is proud of its response to situations such as the Gulf War in maintaining vehicle flow and repairs to ensure that enough vehicles were fit and ready for deployment. Whilst many would bemoan the passing of the REME workshop it would seem that ABRO have inherited that mantle and are carrying on the tradition of support to the services.

So how does all this affect the life of the FV430 series? Because all the vehicles go through the ABRO system, this will decide if they are to be cast (scrapped or sold) or to go through the re-working process. As already mentioned, the vehicles undergo a full strip down on arrival and this leaves the collection of parts that are around the workshop looking like a very large model construction kit. Certainly not one your wife or girlfriend would like lying around the house and being worked on. Once the vehicle has been stripped and inspected, any parts that can be reused are taken to be worked on, leaving just the bare hull which is mounted onto four special adapters that fit, two on either final drive locations, and two on the idler locations. As can be seen in the photographs these each have a wheel on them allowing the empty hull to be moved around the workshop with relative ease. The hull will be steam cleaned and then shot blasted to remove all dirt and oil traces; it then will be placed into an assembly line where the process of rebuilding will take place. Each stage is carefully monitored and inspected to ensure that the end product is 100 per cent to the required standards of ABRO and the end user. Due to the ever-ongoing need to modify or upgrade equipment, the vehicle that leaves the assembly point may well be quite different to the vehicle that entered it. A major factor in that is the relative ease that the FV430 can be converted from one variant to another, enabling workshops to maintain the requirements of the user when carrying out any rebuilds.

The upgrade that has been mentioned several times during this book was finally announced in November 2005; the contract, worth £80 million, being awarded to BAE Land Systems as the overall design authority who will be responsible for supplying the sub-systems from the original equipment manufacturer to ABRO, who will then carry out the upgrade work at its Bovington site. The first upgraded FV432s were expected to be completed by August 2006 and after that production will rise to twenty units being converted a month. It is estimated that each conversion will take about thirty days worth of work to complete.

The upgrade will give the vehicle a new engine in the shape of a Cummins diesel, developing 250hp, linked to a new Allison X200-4C automatic transmission. Other improvements will be in the electrical system and an improved system for braking and a new cooling system. The driver will see the end of the two steering levers and that will be replaced by a steering yoke similar to that used in Warrior. Proving that the vehicle still has a long life there is even talk of a Super FV432 with enhancements such as additional armour and possibly some sort of remote weapon mounted on the hull roof; one such example trialled is the Rafael remote weapon station which has both 30mm auto-cannon and 7.62mm MG. It is not clear if this project will go ahead although a lot of work has been carried out in this field, in the end it will probably be decided by financial constraints.

What of the vehicles that are no longer required by the army? Those that can be sold on will usually end up in the hands of private dealers for onwards sale to private owners, although it is not unusual for a private owner to buy direct, however this can be fraught with difficulty if you are new to the game. A tale that goes the rounds is of someone who wished to own a FV432 and went to an auction to buy one, thinking that if he put in a bid for each one that was there he must win one of them. Unfortunately the auction house accepted all of his bids and he ended up having to take all six vehicles. This must provide a salutary lesson to all those who wish to go it alone. Most owners will purchase their vehicle from a known dealer or from adverts in the military vehicle magazines. As can be seen from the photographs, the lengths that some owners will go to restore their vehicle is almost as thorough as the work carried out in workshop; the major difference being in the working conditions, few owners have the luxury of a fully equipped building that can be used as a workshop. Therefore they must work in the open, exposed to the elements, but the standard of work that is achieved is truly amazing and it is fair to say that without vehicle groups and enthusiasts like these, many vehicles would simply disappear to the scrap man.

Other vehicles will simply end their days on the ranges being used as hard targets. But before they can do that they will be drained of all oils and fuel to prevent any contamination to the environment, also any parts that are still serviceable will be saved and reused. Some vehicles actually can be of use in helping to save the environment. A few years ago several Saracen wheeled APCs were used to help create an artificial sandbank to combat erosion. The Americans have also used vehicles to create new reefs for coral to grow on as well. Another strange use for old vehicles is the Conqueror tanks that have been dumped along with several other vehicles in a Scottish loch and now divers can dive on the wrecks.

One use for old vehicles is for units to have them as gate guardians. In this role they will be placed on a plinth or some such similar location outside or very near the entrance to a barracks. Quite often the vehicle may be painted to represent some particular vehicle in the unit's history. These vehicles remain in those locations and do not follow a unit around. How much attention is paid to them will reflect in the condition of the vehicles after a few years. Some will be in mint condition while others will sadly start to rust away and generally look very tatty.

Apart from scrapping vehicles one more rather explosive method is used. This is to smelt the vehicles down to pure metal and many of the disposed Chieftains have met this fate, as have FV432 vehicles. The process in its simplest form involves stripping the vehicle to its bare shell then lowering it into a smelting furnace to meet its fiery end. A large metalworks that can be viewed on the left hand side as you drive north on the M6 near Sheffield usually carries this out.

Some, as we have seen, could be used by the film industry to be converted into representations of real vehicles; good examples are the Tiger 1 tanks from *Kelly's Heroes* and *Saving Private Ryan*. These will never be good enough for the purist, but suffice for the general audience.

Many things will dictate when a vehicle is ready to be disposed of; these will include age, mileage, condition of vehicle, and requirement for that type. Some vehicles will be lucky and will just soldier on and on while others seem to have a very short service life before becoming surplus to requirements.

There are many lists and figures thrown around concerning how many vehicles of a particular type were built. It is really a question that is never answered 100 per cent to everyone's satisfaction and there are always the odd ones that escape all official lists; official lists are only as good as the information that is entered on them. On checking the history of an FV432 for an owner, I was told that it was in service in BAOR with the Royal Green Jackets. This was fascinating as I had seen it the week before under private ownership at Duxford. The sergeant at the other end of the phone line was adamant that the vehicle was still in service as that is what it said on his computer screen!

However between those dates many more vehicles will be slowly phased out and those remaining will be converted with the new power pack that we have already mentioned. There is a large batch of vehicles waiting to be put on the disposal list as of writing; this will see the complete withdrawal of all Mk 1 vehicles and a large portion of Mk 2 and 2/1.

A great chance for history to be saved was missed here; the only known hull of FV431 that has survived, if only just, resides on Salisbury Plain. *(Plain Military)*

Slightly luckier is this FV432 enjoying its days in the United States, now used by Five Star providing corporate entertainment, allowing members of the public to drive an APC. *(Michael Levy, Five Star)*

Sad fate has befallen this FV432; it has been used in a fire power demonstration and has just been blown up to simulate driving over a landmine. (*Plain Military*)

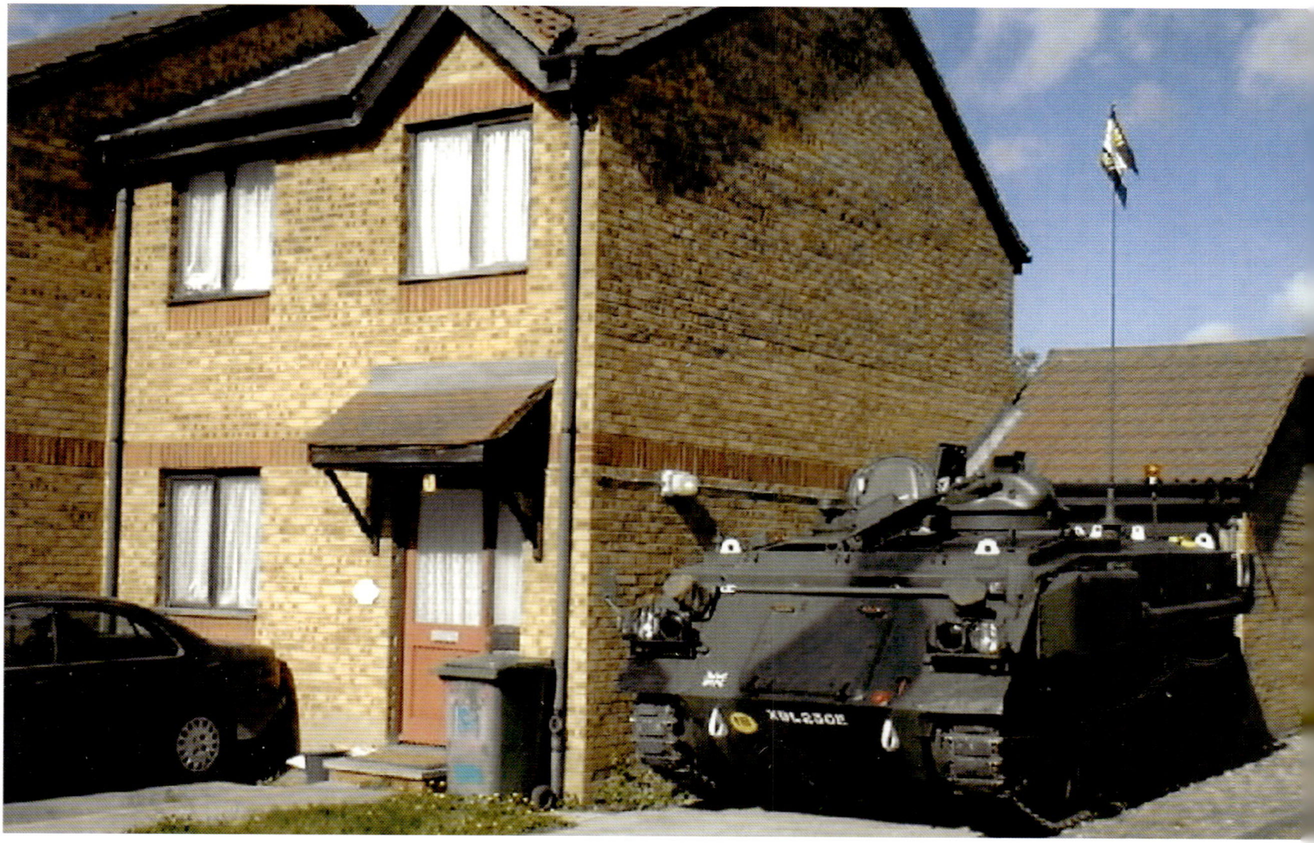

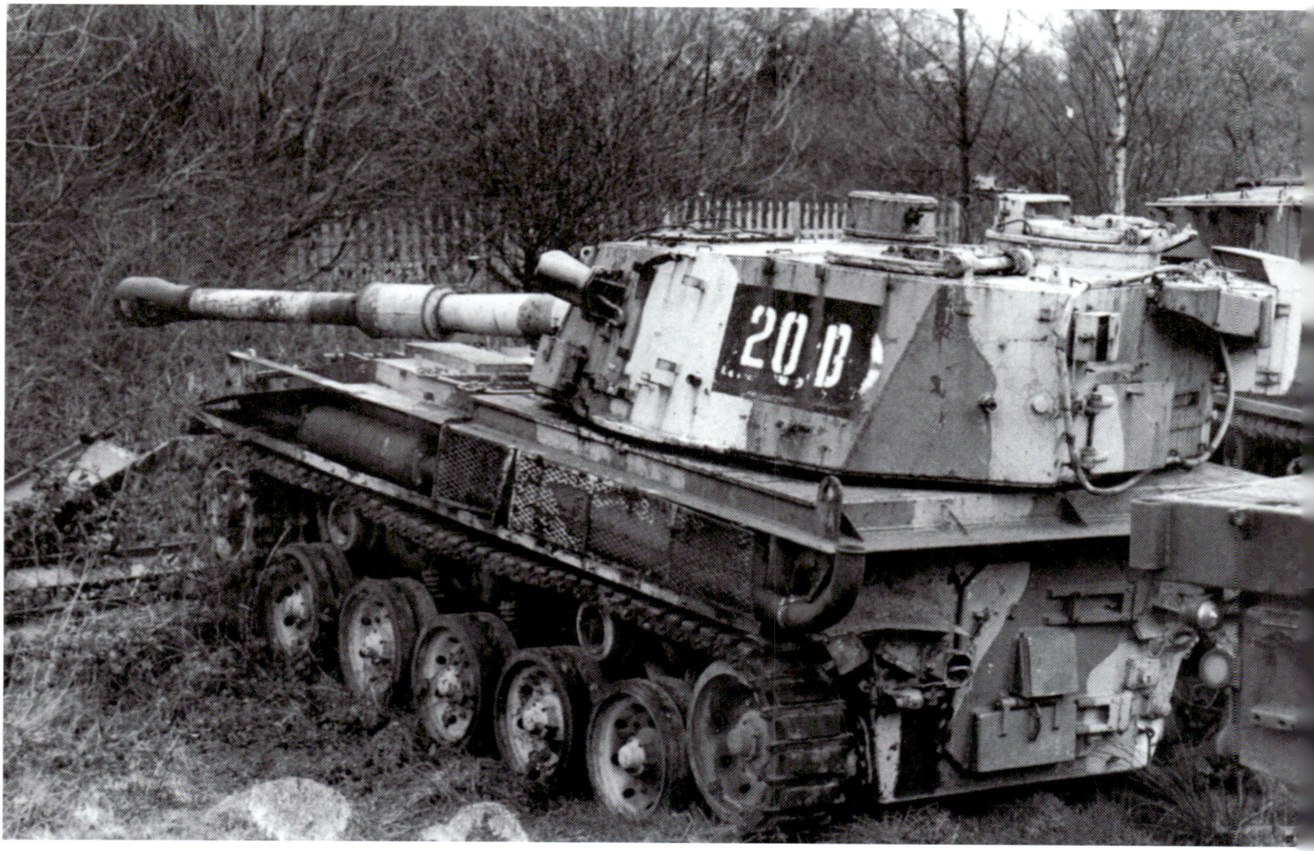
20 B

(**Opposite, above**) Some people have a car parked outside their house, others simply have an FV432. Perfectly road legal, this vehicle is kept in immaculate condition by its new owner. Note it is fitted with the Peak Engineering turret. (*Des Northover*)

(**Opposite, below**) Forlorn looking FV433 Abbot SPG. This one resided for a long time in R&R Motors scrap yard in 1995, so will have long gone to the tank park in the sky probably. (*R&R Motors*)

(**Above**) The other extreme is this Abbot enjoying a new life providing tracked driving experience for the public, and this bunch look as if they are having great fun. (*Author's Collection*)

This is how many old military vehicles ended their days, being used as hard targets on various ranges. The practice is not so widespread now due to the green protests and advanced computer programs to replicate it. *(Rob Griffin)*

This is another Abbot sat in a scrapyard c.1994. I understand that this was bought and restored, so another lease of life for it. *(Author's collection)*

For something totally different the corporate entertainment company Tanks a Lot have produced this. Why have a four-wheeled limo for the Proms, when you could have this? It is a combination of two APC hulls joined with the addition of a Fox turret and a lot more; needs to be seen to be believed. (*Courtesy Tanks a lot*)

When you own an FV432 and it needs a pack lift and you don't have an FV434 to hand, then this has to be the next best thing. It looks very precarious but I am told it worked well and was very stable. (*Rob Griffin*)

The lady looks very excited, but the rest seem apprehensive, could be they are worried about her driving skills! *(Rob Griffin)*

The fate of many vehicles once their time is up. The BR on the board stands for beyond repair. This is a licence for salvaging parts to make other vehicles fit for use again. *(Rob Griffin)*

For that quick journey when you just have to pop to the shops, an FV432 might not be the best vehicle, but it will certainly make short work of stowing your weekly shop, an eye catcher and perfectly road legal. *(Author's collection)*

Head on view of the ill-fated FV431 load carrier. It is rather a shame that no effort was made by any museum to preserve this vehicle before it reached this state. *(Plain Military)*

This steely-eyed member looks ready for anything. Judging from his outfit he appears to have 'done some service'. *(Rob Griffin)*

The FV430 series are popular among the military vehicle groups because of their availability and reasonable price compared to say a Chieftain tank. This one has been restored to its former glory, although collectors do sometimes use a bit of poetic licence, as can be seen here by the well wrapped up .5 Browning MG on the cupola. *(Rob Griffin)*

Another well preserved vehicle, this time an FV433 Abbot SPG. Providing the civil number plate is visible and is used when running on the road, the old military number can be displayed, and here we see 06 EB 79. *(Rob Griffin)*

One of the more unusual vehicles on the circuit is the Cymbeline FV432. Although the radar is mounted, a lot of its associated equipment in the vehicle has been removed. *(Rob Griffin)*

The well restored interior of the Cymbeline FV432. I suspect it was never this clean while on operations. *(Rob Griffin)*

A further view of the interior of the Cymbeline. The area where the bags have been stowed would have contained the screens and other associated equipment. *(Rob Griffin)*

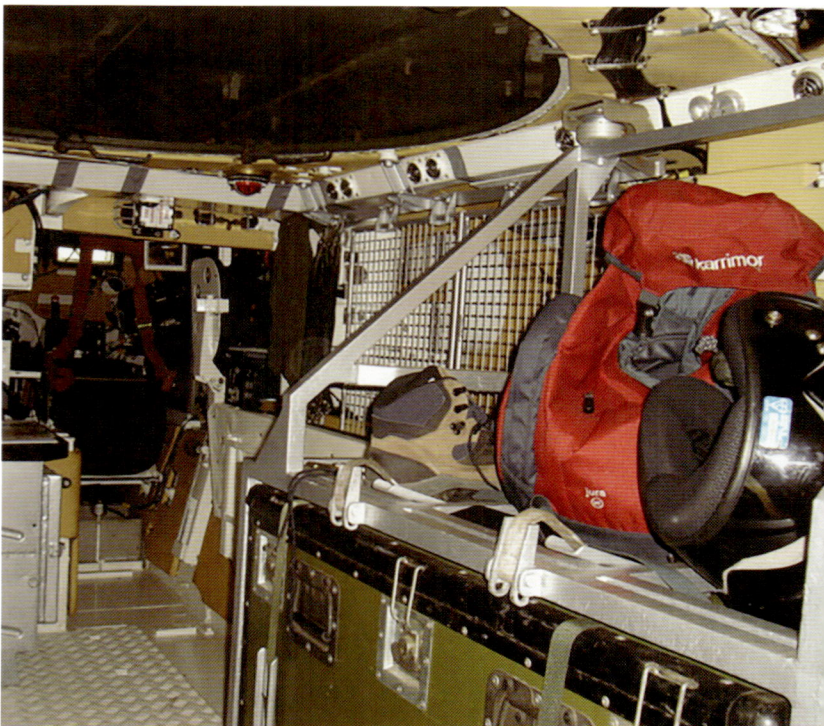

This MG equipped FV432 Mk 1 has just been delivered to its new owner and it can be seen it needs a lot doing to it, including removing the green growth, a result from being left outdoors with no attention. The rear view shows how much work is going to be needed to produce an almost brand new vehicle, but these restorers have great patience and the result will be stunning. (*David Giles*)

(**Above**) Work begins with all the old paint, which can actually be many layers thick, being removed so the hull is back to bare metal and the painters then have a good surface to work on. Notice the name of the last unit to use this vehicle painted just underneath the workman. (*David Giles*)

(**Opposite, above**) A great step forward, the red lead primer will help protect the vehicle till its final coats are applied; this shot gives a good idea of the layout of the exhaust system for an Mk 1 vehicle. (*David Giles*)

(**Opposite, below**) At last its final coat has been applied; the owner can now start to do all the cosmetic work to bring it back to life. (*David Giles*)

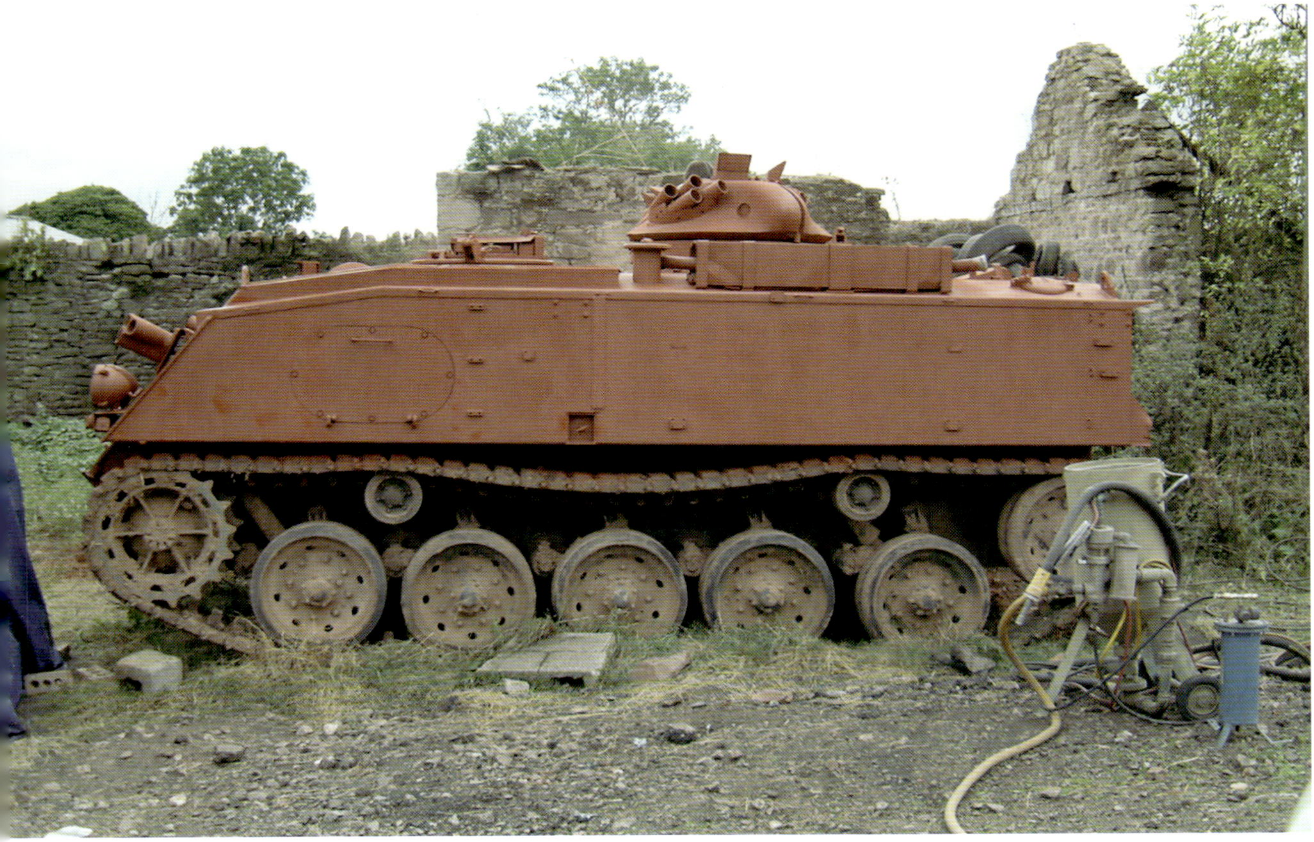

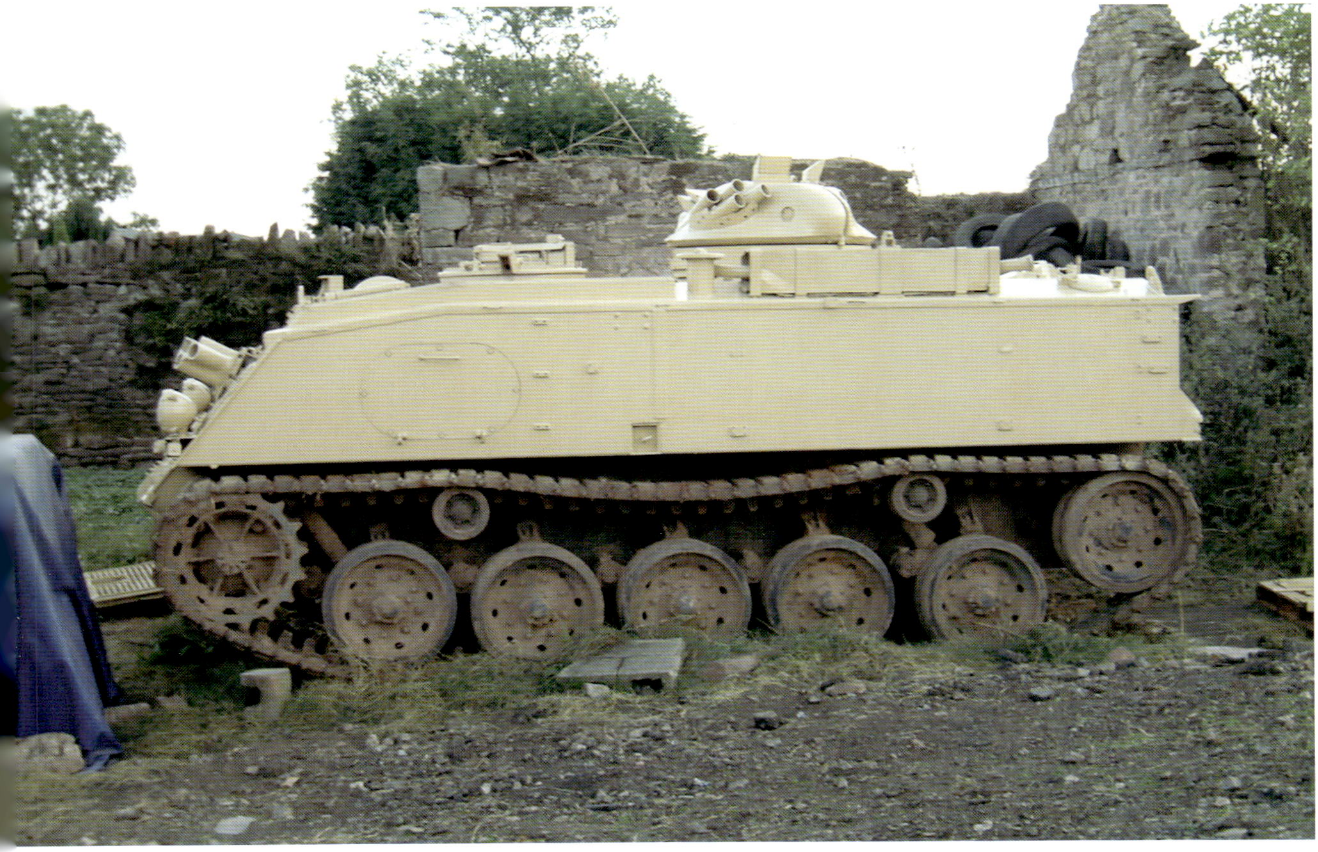

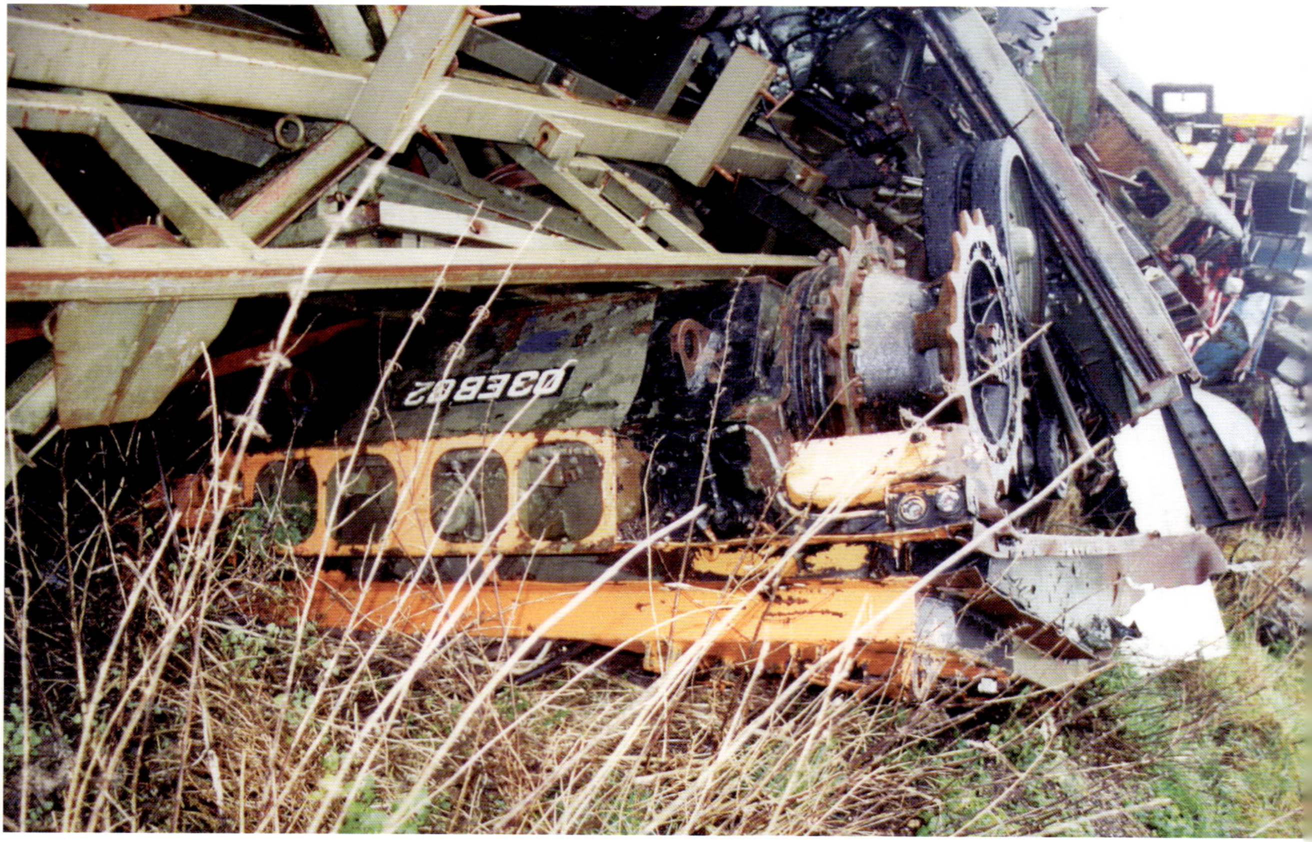

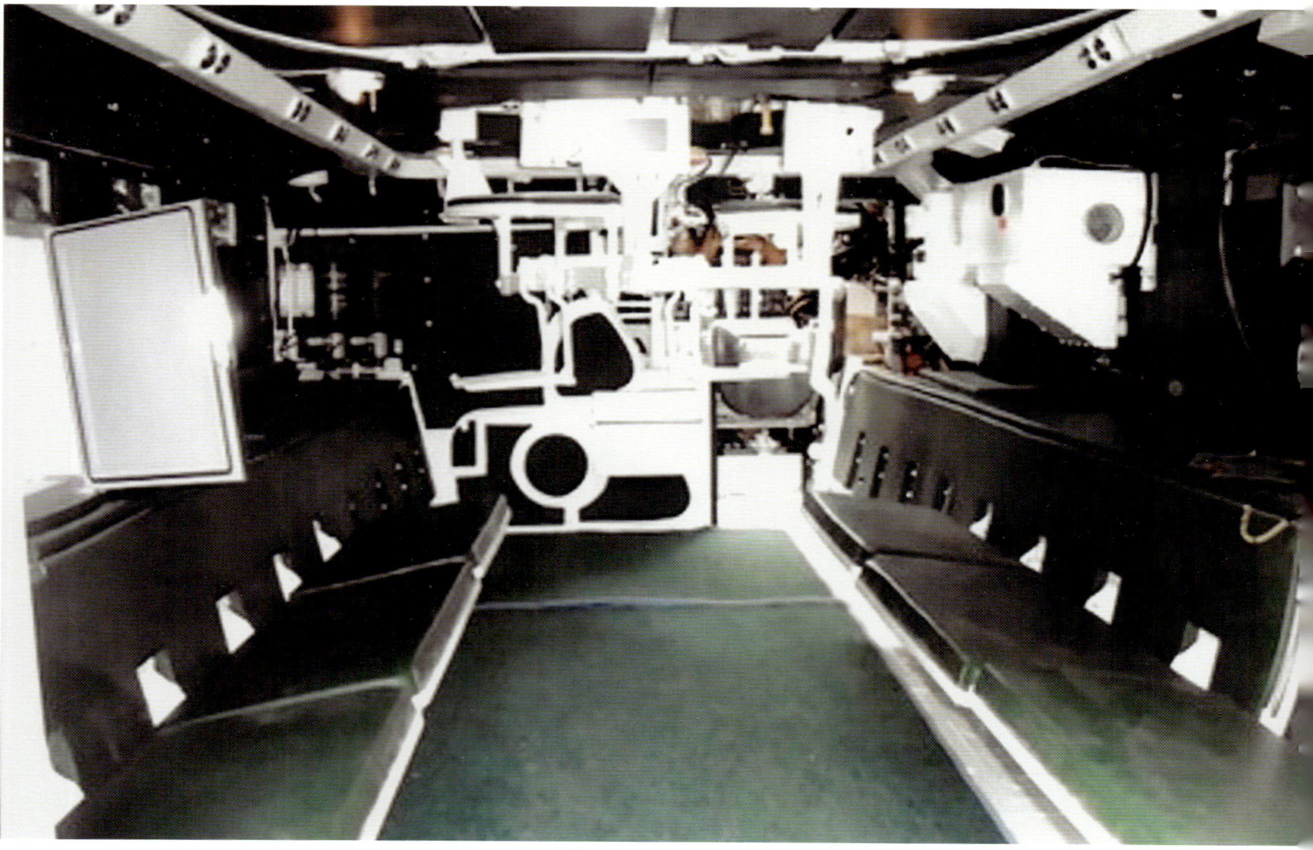

(**Opposite, above**) FV433 03 EB 02. This Abbot resided at the Bustard scrapyard located on Salisbury Plain. A rather sad end to it, but it was in good company for also there were the remains of Conqueror, Humber Pig and other assorted AFVs.

(**Opposite, below**) The inside view of the FV432 'limo' as produced by Tanks a Lot; this has to be the ultimate party vehicle. *(Courtesy Tanks a Lot)*

(**Above**) A typical example of how hard targets look after time on the ranges. It is not unknown for vehicles that may have not long been refurbished to be placed on the range, but they fare no better. *(Rob Griffin)*

Side view of the 432 limo. The extra length is readily visible as is the Fox turret. The sight of this and a group on a hen night does not bear thinking about. *(Courtesy of Tank a Lot)*

An unknown FV433 Abbot looking very derelict located on the RAF range in Northumberland. *(Steve Osfield)*

A rather gaudy but tatty FV433 appears to be wearing the remnants of a BATUS paint scheme. It was parked on the forecourt of Helston gunsmiths along with Chieftains and CVR(T), quite a sight when you drive past. (*Rob Griffin*)

Another Abbot left to die on the Ranges. The turret is painted red, allegedly so the RAF or artillery can see them. I suspect a bit of inter-service rivalry led to that. *(Rob Griffin)*

What every self-respecting stretched FV432 needs, champagne in the chiller cabinet. *(Courtesy Tanks a Lot)*

It could be imagined that this is part of an infantry company attacking in line, but it is in fact a selection of FV432s that were left on the training area at Catterick garrison, although the layout could be deliberate. *(Rob Griffin)*

10 EA 33 and ex-IFOR FV432 waiting to be towed onto the ranges at Otterburn. Notice that 10 EA 33 has had road wheels removed in a spares hunt. *(Steve Osfield)*

Another brightly painted range vehicle. FV433 Abbot located on the Otterburn ranges, just behind it can be seen yet another Abbot. *(Steve Osfield)*

10 EA 33 on the Otterburn ranges awaiting its final fate. Note it has lost its tracks already and other items of use will have been removed. *(Steve Osfield)*

A vehicle collectors dream yard, full of FV432s and FV433s plus Stalwart and even a Ferret Scout Car, all located at the hard standing on Otterburn Ranges. *(Steve Osfield)*

A rear view of one of the Catterick FV432s. Note how parts have been removed such as one of the rear bins and the light fittings below the bin location, this is quite normal before a vehicle goes onto the range. *(Rob Griffin)*

An entirely different idea of a wedding car, why not use your FV432? At least the couple look happy. *(Des Northover)*

With its gun in high elevation, this FV433 Abbot looks as if it is waiting for the last fire order. *(Rob Griffin)*

A well-presented FV433 Abbot at a military vehicle show. Note the use of the old style British Army deep bronze green, this always gives a lovely finish. *(Rob Griffin)*

It's amazing where FV432s will turn up for sale. This one was spotted a few years ago in a café carpark on the road to Evesham. No longer there so someone now has a new toy. *(Rob Griffin)*

FV432 at Duxford, the Imperial War Museum satellite. This is a good shot as it shows the hull top to great advantage and also how the mortar hatches fold back on themselves. *(Author's Collection)*

The sad life of a scrapped FV432. This along with others in the area now spend their lives being recovered by the REME and then once recovered they are pushed back into the water ready for the next time. *(Plain Military)*

It will not be long before this well battered hard target FV432 will collapse in on itself and become nothing more than a pile of scrap metal. *(Rob Griffin)*

This Abbot is located in the base area of BATUS in Canada, the large British Army training area there. Abbots spent a lot of their service in BATUS but finally their time has come. They will be towed out to the prairie and will become hard targets. *(Author's collection)*

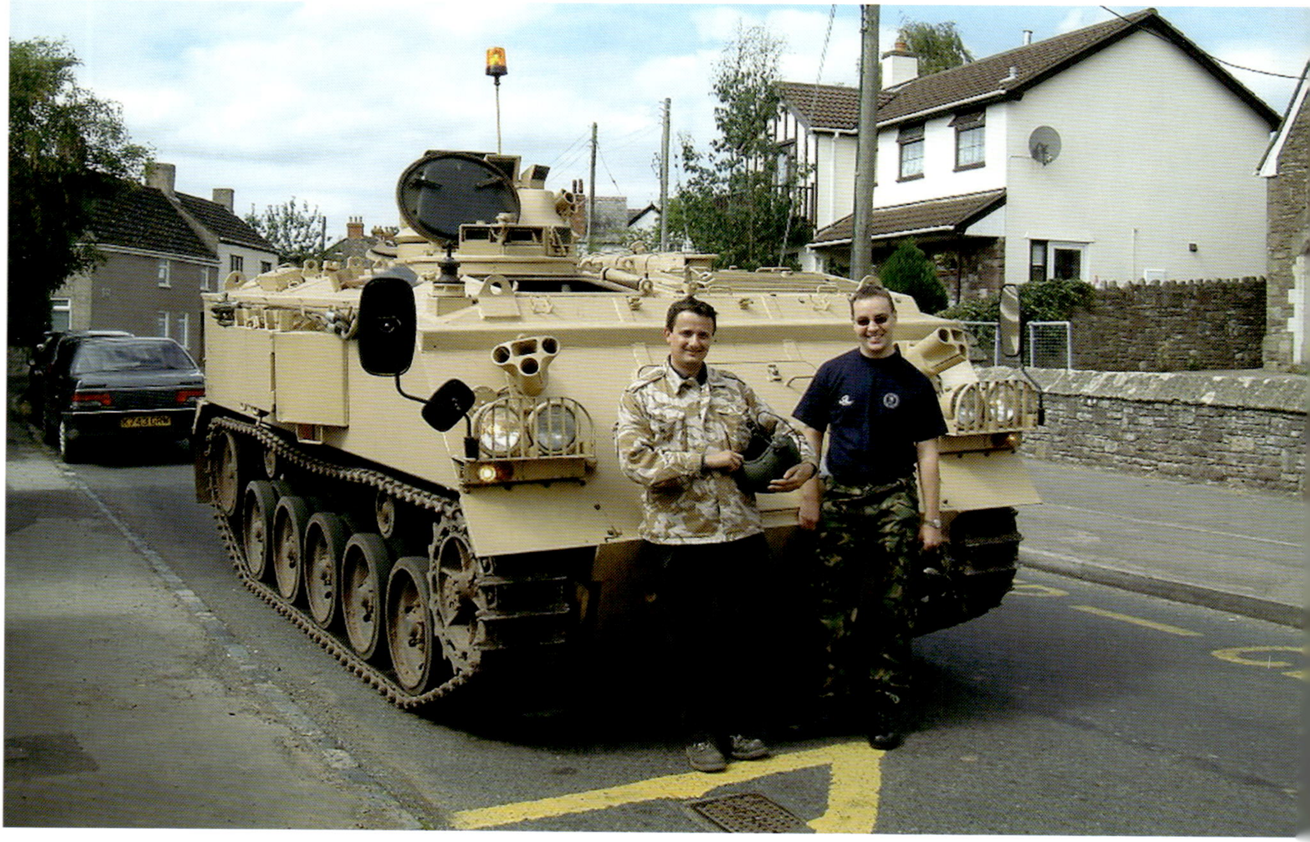

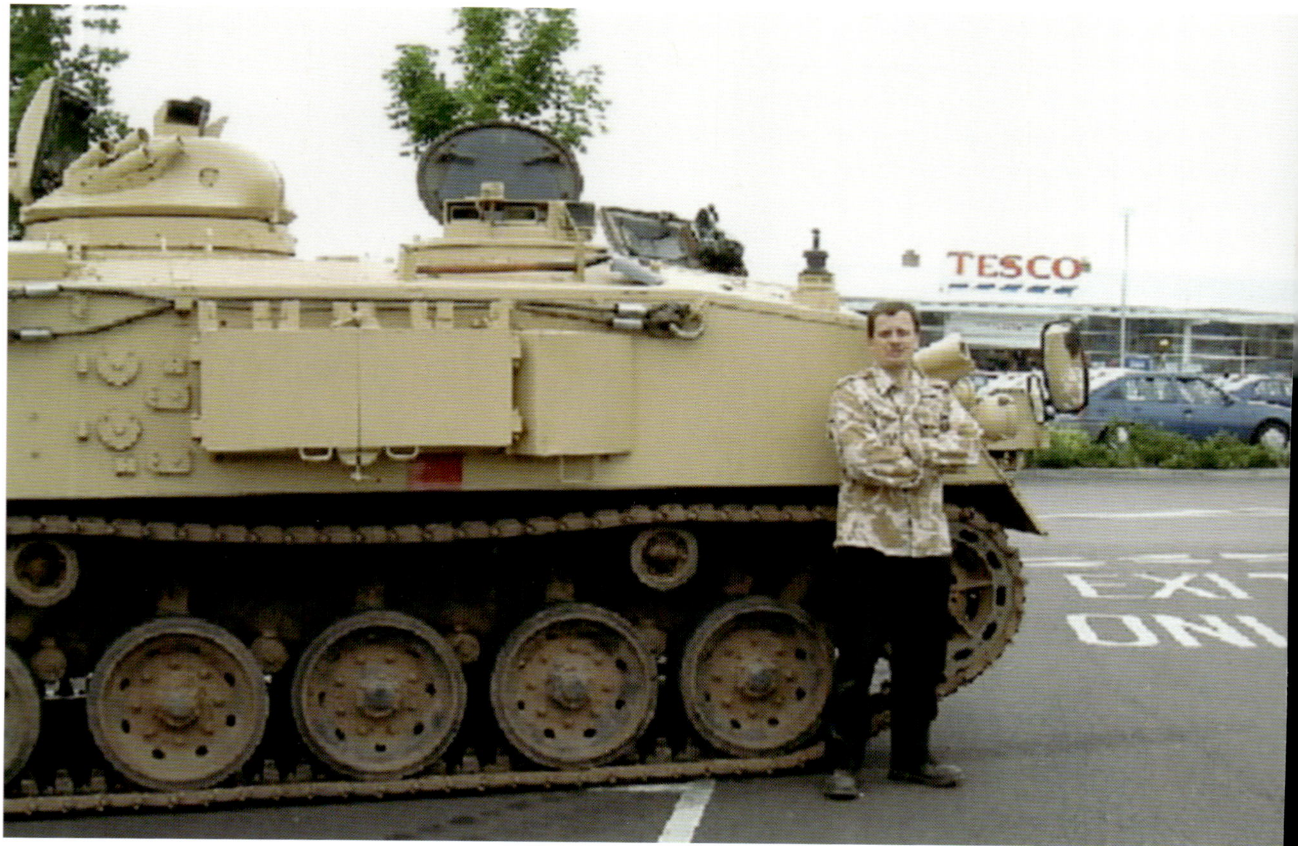
TESCO

(**Opposite, above**) One happy smiling face says that the person in the camouflage jacket has just obtained his H driving licence, entitling him to drive tracked vehicles on the public road. (*Author's collection*)

(**Opposite, below**) And having got your licence what better way to celebrate than a trip to Tesco! (*Author's collection*)

(**Above**) This evocative image of an FV434, could almost be called the sunset of the FV430. (*Plain Military*)

(**Above**) What to do when you have a spare FV432 that is nearly hidden in brambles, why not turn it into a tracked hearse? This is just what Tanks a Lot have done and although some may question its taste it seems popular. *(Tanks a Lot)*

(**Opposite, above**) This shows just how much had to be cut out to make the hearse viable. *(Tanks a Lot)*

(**Opposite, below**) Cut down like this would make a good instructional model for training. *(Tanks a Lot)*

TANKSI

Although it is on an AFV the basic shape is easily recognisable. (*Tanks a Lot*)

The original chequer plate floor can be seen here along with the new false floor above. (*Tanks a Lot*)

Its first outing and none seem the least bit surprised by its appearance. *(Tanks a Lot)*

Apart from its tracks, with the attendant next to it, it looks like any other hearse. *(Tanks a Lot)*

And finally it is doing what it was built for. I like it and that's how I am going. *(Tanks a Lot)*